MW01071143

The Fraternity

The Fraternity

Lawyers and Judges in Collusion

by John Fitzgerald Molloy

Paragon House
St. Paul, Minnesota

First Edition 2004

Published in the United States by
Paragon House
2285 University Avenue West
St. Paul, MN 55114

Library of Congress Cataloging-in-Publication Data

Molloy, John Fitzgerald, 1917-
 The fraternity : lawyers and judges in collusion / by John Fitzgerald Molloy.-- 1st ed.
  p. cm.
 Includes bibliographical references and index.
 ISBN 1-55778-841-3 (hardcover : alk. paper)
1. Molloy, John Fitzgerald, 1917- 2. Lawyers--Arizona--Tucson--Biography.
3. Judges--Arizona--Biography. 4. Practice of law--United States--History--
20th century. I. Title.

 KF373.M545A3 2004
 340'.092--dc22

                                                          2004009351

Manufactured in the United States of America

The paper used in this publication meets the minimum requirements of American National Standard for Information Sciences—Permanence of Paper for Printed Library Materials, ANSIZ39.48-1984.

10 9 8 7 6 5 4 3 2 1

For current information about all releases from Paragon House,
visit the web site at http://www.paragonhouse.com

CONTENTS

PROLOGUE

Opening of the Scripture

I commence this confessional diatribe in March of 1991. At this time I am the head of a successful law firm of forty-one lawyers, located in Tucson, Arizona. At seventy-four years of age, I am somewhat over the hill at my specialty—trial law.

My law firm had been growing steadily for over two decades—since September 1969, when I resigned as an appellate court judge to go back to my old law firm. When I came back after twelve years of serving as a trial and then an appellate judge, it was to practice law in a firm consisting of five (counting myself) partners and one associate (a newly admitted lawyer) in the very same offices where I had practiced a dozen years before. And from that, over the next two decades, there developed a firm of forty-one lawyers, plus a staff of some fifty secretaries, paralegals, and receptionists. And then that which was created disintegrated. The changes in our culture that caused this rise and this fall is the story told here.

To understand what happened, we must look at the practice of law as it existed in the small town of Yuma, Arizona, where my father had been a lawyer before me. In my childhood years, Yuma

1

County, one of Arizona's fourteen vast counties, had just one judge—a Judge Kelly, who stood six feet three inches in physical height and miles above that in the regard that the community had for him.

We all knew that Judge Kelly was different from the rest of us. He was the conscience of the community. He was there looking out for our interests and meting out punishment, in a fatherly but stern way, to those who transgressed. He was not a mere lawyer. He was a different breed entirely. If he were to have been defeated at any of the elections at which he was reelected every four years, always without opposition, we could not imagine his lowering himself to be a lawyer. Judge Kelly knew our community, and most of those living in it, and most of those living in it knew Judge Kelly and respected him for his office and his decisions.

I had never, in all my "growing up," expressed the desire to be a judge—even to myself. I was always going to be a lawyer—"like my Daddy." But, after a dozen years of law practice, when I was offered the appointment by Arizona's Governor McFarland, in whose election I had, coincidentally (?), served as his campaign manager, I realized that, deep down, I would like to be a Judge Kelly.

Twelve years later, after seven years as a trial judge and five more as an appellate judge, I knew I could never be a Judge Kelly. For one thing, my height of five foot ten and one-half inches (when I stand very erect and place the bump on the top of my head immediately under the measuring stick) is not sufficiently awe-inspiring to carry the role, but, even more so, there didn't seem to be much of an opportunity to better things, for all of us, as Judge Kelly had done.

Instead of molding the morals of the community as Judge Kelly had done, I found myself in the role of a referee in an endless series of ball games in which lawyers were the players. When I behaved as a good referee and called the balls and strikes according to the intricate rules established by lawyers for their games, I was praised by my fellow lawyers. When I stepped out of this role and attempted to stem the tide of lawsuits that kept augmenting by the year, I was coolly greeted by my fellow judge-lawyers, and, after I became an appellate judge, I sometimes found myself left with futile dissenting opinions.

When I tired of judging and came back to my old firm, it was to a different-spirited group than that which I had left.

Judge Hall, who had been the Judge Kelly of our county and the founder of that firm, had died in the prior year, and with him had gone qualities that had dignified our profession. We had been a proudly professional group that knew that our compensation had to come in good part not in dollars—because we, as lawyers, accepted the dismal fact that we could not compete in that regard with other more lucrative callings—but rather from enjoying the role of being a trusted adviser/savior to our clients. Making money was a goal—yes—but not the decision-maker of whether to take on each and every case.

When I was first promoted to "partner" in the Judge Hall firm—in 1947—we did not charge by the hour. "Charging by the hour is for plumbers," we had said proudly, "but we are pro-fessionals." And, we actually told potential recruits to our firm: "You'll never get rich practicing law." And my earnings as a newly admitted lawyer were comparable to what teachers and skilled craftsmen earned.

Of course, we did not hold ourselves out as doing free work, but we did adjust our fees to the pocketbooks of our clients. These adjustments would happen when we met, the three of us, almost every morning, in Judge Hall's office—"Judge" because our senior partner had served ten years as a trial judge and, very importantly, we sensed that the use of the title pleased him, and, more impor-tant perhaps, brought in clients.

At these morning conferences, if it was time to bill for work done, there would be discussion as to what the dollar amount should be. Time-to-bill was almost always when we had finished with a particular job. Then we would discuss what it was worth—in terms of: 1) what we had achieved for the client, 2) what the client was able to pay, and 3) what the client expected to pay. All of the above, as we will get to in good time, is a far cry from what occurs in the law offices of this country today.

Even before I had gone on the bench in 1957, billing by the hour had started to infiltrate the profession and, upon returning to practice twelve years later, I found that the metamorphosis had accelerated during my time of playing judge. My returned-to firm startled me, and, I must confess, pleasantly so, with its focus on moneymaking.

I was soon exposed to discussions among our lawyers that proclaimed that fees were now of the essence. Representing a client and not being fully paid at the augmented rates was something of a black mark for any of us who permitted this to happen. Charges to the client now started out as a mathematical multiple "by the hour"—which really meant by every six minutes (because every hour was divided up into tenths for entry on our time sheets). These recordings were multiplied by some ordained dollar figure, which dollar figure far surpassed the hourly rate of the most organized of plumbers . "Special" matters—by reason of the amount of property involved or the intricacy of the legal issues—received a "special billing"—appropriately increased.

So I became the "president"of this moneymaking entity; my "partners" became my "fellow shareholders." I wish that I could say that I was appalled at these changes. But, to the contrary, I was intrigued with this new approach to my father's profession. I sensed with enthusiasm that it would be more lucrative—and, it was—oh yes, yes, it was!

For my new "regular" clients—inherited from the member of this same firm who had been appointed as a trial judge at the same time that I had resigned—I accepted billing by the minute as the way of life. By this time, 1969, all top-rated lawyers were doing the same thing, and judges had come to endorse this "time-is-money" concept to the point of even requiring time records when the matter of fees was to be determined in a court hearing—something none of the trial judges of Judge Hall's day would have ever thought of doing.

So, our firm went about keeping track of every minute spent on a client's affair, including the time necessary to keep track of that time, and multiplying the accumulated time by dollar amounts that grew consistently over the years—leaving cost-of-living indices far behind.

And, of course, since our smallest entry on our time records was a tenth of an hour (after all, how far in the decimal system would you expect us to go?)—equivalent to six minutes—*and* as it was necessary to satisfy this new system that there be an entry for every phone call, no matter if it lasted only fifteen seconds (you wouldn't expect us to ignore it, would you?)—mathematics worked very nicely in our favor in computing bills.

At first this rewarding multiplication was done by hand. Then computers nicely came along, and what previously had been only a calculation that had a chance to be adjusted for other factors—such as, for instance, that, alas, we had lost the case for the client—now became the bare minimum of the "true" measure of the worth of what the lawyer had done. After all, if a computer itself has come up with an amount that is accepted by auditors, why isn't the recipient of this symbol of unquestioned accuracy obligated to pay that amount? Who dares to quarrel with a computer?

And, as this time-is-money concept became gospel, the time necessary to get things done extended wondrously—oh, yes!—wondrously!

It was not that records were falsified, but simply that when one knows that the longer he/she works on a matter, the more compensation there will be, the matter at hand simply *cries* for more work—one more hour of research, or one more legal motion, resulting in one more hearing, etc., etc.

Then, at about the same time computers became the accepted way of life, law firms began to use business managers, who were usually, but not always, lawyers, but who were always selected for their business acumen rather than their professionalism—which means getting the maximum dollars from the most prestigious clients that can be induced to patronize their firm.

In the courtroom, where my efforts were usually devoted, I noticed that procedures became more and more complicated, so that, not only did one need a "trial lawyer," but one needed a trial lawyer specializing in the particular kind of litigation at hand.

As priests of religion weave their webs with incense and ceremony—so that their parishioners will be impressed and puzzled—so have the lawyers of this country fashioned our legal structure. This complexity has been brought into being always with the assertion that it is to better "the system"—an argument made by lawyer-practitioners who may not realize the subliminal motivation to better "themselves."

But, of course, better themselves they do. The more complicated the procedure is, the less lay persons can do for themselves, and the more important lawyers, members of this legal Fraternity, become. The concept that a person could represent himself in our courts "pro per" (without a lawyer)—which had occurred from time to time in my early years of practice—has now become a bizarre event.

Thus has the practice of law changed during my time.

While in my prejudge years, in the Hall firm, we had all been generalists, ready to take on any legal problem that walked through our door, by the time I came off of the bench, the law had developed enough appendages and special crevices so that there were only a few "generalists" remaining, and they tended to receive the scorn of the rest of us.

Then, as the evolution continued and our little firm merged with a larger one, and subsequently picked up a couple of little firms, we, along with competing firms, developed "departments," such as "Commercial," "Probate and Trusts," "Tax," "Real Estate," and "Trial." I gravitated toward trial work and became head of our law firm's "Trial Department."

For the next two decades after leaving the bench, I was the recognized leader of a firm of ambitious lawyers, which grew from six practitioners to forty-one, with three floors on the top of Tucson's tallest building, across the street from the courthouse, and with several branch offices—one in downtown Phoenix (our state's capital).

In addition to growing by mergers, our firm had an aggressive recruiting program—going after the brightest law school graduates—an idea that seemed obviously correct when adopted but which proved to be my downfall—the story of which will unfold.

And so, as life's juices dry up and I exchange my briefcase for a tennis racket—I still enjoy this combative game that has some of the attributes of the litigation of my past—I write this book to try to explain why there has been such an evolution in my profession:

> Why are the energies of our people now devoted so much to litigation? Why are court trials so complicated and prolonged? Why are lawyers now needed so much more than when my father practiced? Why do lawyers charge so much that many of my friends do not consult with a lawyer when they should? Why have jury awards grown to astronomical amounts? Why are the results of litigation determined so completely by the respective skills of the lawyers?
>
> Who or what has brought about these pervasive changes? Legislators? The school system? Lawyers? Judges? All others? None of the above?

My life's experiences cause me to firmly point the finger of responsibility, for all of this, at my own profession—a Fraternity composed of lawyers and judges. I have been continuously impressed by changes in the law brought about by the decisions of judges—always urged on by lawyers. I have come to realize that the judicial innovations in our legal structure have an important common denominator—they make more work, and ever more income, for our lawyers and judges.

Yes, I combine these two professions when it comes to financial gain, because the salaries of judges are always increased by lawmakers after hearing arguments as to what lawyers are customarily making, and, of course, the argument goes, when we select a judge, we want to hire a *good* lawyer. Perhaps after reading this tome, if you can stand the course, you may have other ideas about how judges should be selected. But, we are getting ahead of our story. Let's return to the evolution in the legal profession.

When my father was practicing law (1906–22), there was much less for a lawyer to do. Then, there was one lawyer/judge for every 705 persons in the U.S. (108,000 lawyers and judges versus 76,094,000 people).[1] By 1992 there was one lawyer/judge for every 323 persons in our population (788,000 lawyers and judges for 255,162,000 people)[2] a change of something over twice as many lawyers per person as was the case before. Since then, the number of lawyers has continued to grow much faster than our population—by 2002 there were 966,000 lawyers and judges,[3] in a country with a population of 280,306,000,[4] meaning one lawyer for every 290 residents in this country.

And the growth continues, but probably not fast enough to take care of the new causes of action and legal complexities thrown into our legal systems by the Fraternity—at least it has not been noticeable that there is such a glut of lawyers as to see legal fees cut in the least.

The one preeminent reason for this ballooning of lawyer-work is that the law itself has been changing, at the insistence of lawyers, so that there are more things now that can happen that permit juries and judges to award damages, big damages, and our trials require more and more lawyers and judges to play the games that have been created, like Monopoly games, out of our state and federal Constitutions.

Accurate statistics to compare jury verdicts of my father's time to what we are now getting are difficult to come by. No

---

1. Historical Statistics of U.S.—Colonial Times To 1957, pp. 70–75, U.S. Census Dept.

2. Statistical Abstract of U.S. 2002, Bureau of Census, p. 381.

3. Statistical Abstract of U.S. 1999, Bureau of Census, p. 416.

4. Statistical Abstract of U.S. 2002, Chart # 3.

two injuries are exactly alike, and, of course, verdicts vary. But, all indications are that damage recoveries in our courts have ballooned—vastly and grossly in excess of cost-of-living inflation.

Here are some modern jury awards, translated into 2004 present values (PV04s):[5]

The average of the ten highest jury verdicts rendered in the U.S. in the year 1990 was (in PV04 dollars), $65,682,600. Five years later,[6] in calendar year 1995, the top ten verdicts totaled $1.3 billion, averaging (PV04) $165,978,530 each. In 1998, the ten largest verdicts totaled $2.8 billion dollars, averaging (PV04) $303,750,000 each![7] And, in 1999 the ten highest verdicts tripled in that one year, totaling $8.86 billion, averaging, in PV04 dollars, $961,153,100 each![8] And here is a late one, to make everyone realize that something is happening to the climate in our court rooms: A Los Angeles jury awards $28,000,000,000 (yes, 28 billion dollars!) in punitive damages against Phillip Morris for inducing a woman to smoke its product.[9]

Of course, the juries that are bringing in these awards are not the same juries of the past, because the rules have changed as to what a "jury" is. Over the years since Daddy's day, the qualifications to be a jury have been "democratized."

In keeping with this movement, the minimum age to serve as

---

5. These "PV04" figures for December 31, 2003, are based on the Consumer Price Index (www.bls.gov/cpi) released by the U.S. Bureau of Labor Statistics for 2003, projected by the inflation rates for 2004 from the Congressional Budget Office, and the purchasing power of the dollar formulae and factors developed by Valorie H. Rice, librarian at the Karl Eller Graduate School of Management, College of Business and Public Administration of the University of Arizona.

6. According to an AP release of January 14, 1996.

7. AP release from Boston, January 7, 1999, quoting *Lawyers Weekly USA*.

8. AP release from Boston, January 10, 2000, quoting *Lawyers Weekly USA*.

9. *New York Times,* October 5, 2002. This award, of course, is subject to a possible reduction in both the trial court and on appeal, but reductions of jury verdicts from the bench have tended to be much less vigorous as the years have passed.

a juror, which traditionally was 21 years, has been reduced to 18 years in all but four states.[10] Exemptions from jury duty, granted either outright by statutes or dispensed by judges, now permit most professionals, doctors, lawyers, etc. to escape jury service. And, to accommodate the tremendous increase in damage-seeking litigation, the number of persons necessary to constitute a jury has been decreased, so that the traditional twelve is not required in twenty-nine of our states nor in our federal courts—the reduction being from twelve to either eight or six jurors. In almost all state courts, in civil actions, a majority of either six out of eight or four out of six is now sufficient to render a verdict, regardless of the amount or the tenor of the action.[11]

Fifty years of exposure to our trial systems have convinced this author that the younger the jurors are, and the fewer jurors in the jury box, the greater will be the influence of the particular skills of the trial lawyers upon the outcome. This is so—as to the lesser number in the jury box—because the trial lawyers can concentrate their skills on fewer people—meaning, in part, research into individual backgrounds of those jurors, and more eye contact when the critical last arguments are given. As for youth in the jury box, this gives the skillful lawyer more opportunity to influence the result, because there are, in these younger ones, fewer pretrial, fixed conceptions of what is just and right—based on the experiences in living that older persons have had.

Besides persuading juries to bring in larger verdicts with their ever more clever arguments, the Fraternity has increased its "take" by devising multifarious new theories for suing someone. It used to be thought that changes in our law would be made by our elected legislatures, but that was before the Fraternity assumed power.

---

10. Nineteen years of age is required in Alabama and Nebraska, and the states of Mississippi and Missouri still cling to the twenty-first birthday. See "Juries: Frequently Asked Questions," Table 39, pp. 263–68, published by the National Center for State Courts. <http://www.ncsconline.org/wc/FAQs/KIS_juriesFAQ.pdf>

11. Id., Table 42, pp. 278–82.

Product liability suits—oh, how wonderful, for lawyers, that there are so many products out there that injure so many—are one of the more lucrative of these inventions of the Fraternity, but there have been many other creations, such as suits for "invasions of privacy," and for "battery" by surgeons who operate without making "full disclosure" to the patient, and a myriad of other lawsuits—all created whole-hat by the Fraternity in its judicial writings.

Another important escalating factor has been the "discovery" of damaging evidence against target defendants—a process in which our Fraternity excels. There are skeletons in every closet, and big corporations have many closets (because of a diversity of employees). Real jewels to induce juries to become incensed against a defendant can be "discovered" *if* one digs hard and deep with the legal tools—depositions etc., etc.—provided by our Fraternity to its members. No other legal system on this Earth has been so generous in bestowing this power to any one segment of its society.

One of the best-known uses of evidence discovered using these "tools" of trial lawyers is an engineering report, which became "Exhibit 125" at a jury trial, pertaining to the development of Ford Motor Company's Pinto model. This report is given credit for persuading a jury to award $125 million (PV04 $252.1 million) in punitive damages for Ford's failing to guard the gas tank of this model from bursting into flame on rear-end impact.[12]

Another of our modern lawyer-tools, beyond the competency of any litigant trying to represent himself, is the "motion to suppress evidence"—known in lawyer-trade as a "motion *in limine.*" These have increased geometrically during my time of observance of our legal scene. By such motions, lawyers require judges to "suppress" evidence that they do not want juries to know about. The court orders so obtained—ordering parties and their lawyers not to even mention to the jury, or even to hint at, the existence of

---

12. 174 Cal. Rptr. 348 (1981).

certain facts—are often more determinative of the outcome of a litigated case than the actual facts themselves, i.e., the defendant, charged with a house burglary, was found with the burglarized silverware in his home, but without a search warrant being used to find it. So, the jury determining guilt or innocence will never know about the defendant being caught red-handed with the silverware, if his lawyer makes the right motions.

These orders—putting blindfolds on juries—have populated our courts like uncontrolled breeding rats during the last half century. Most of such are predicated upon mandates from the Anointed Nine in Washington, DC, and we will from time to time in this work focus on these decisions that have changed the lives of all of us.

Citations to these legal decisions are given in this work to tease you into reading these life-altering orders that have impacted your life, and to permit you to appreciate the writing skills of the very best. Supreme Court decisions are always written in the very most inspiring language that the Anointed of the Fraternity—with the assiduous help of brilliant law clerks—can devise. You can read these literary masterpieces on the Internet, in several places, among them at <findlaw.com> and at <versuslaw.com>. There, by just typing in one of the citations given here, you may read some of the most beautiful prose ever written—prose that determines the legal and social system that controls your life.

A perverse reason for giving you citations is to refer, here and there, to opinions written by myself as an appellate judge. If my citation-dropping bothers you, either ignore it or stop reading now, because there will be more of the same as we go along.

These references to legal opinions, each and every one, are to events that have impacted my life, because of my profession. A good share of them have impacted your life also, and perhaps decisively, but, unless you are a lawyer/judge—a member of the Fraternity—they have done their pervasive work on your life pretty much without your knowledge.

Individually, each of these myriad of judicial decisions

sounds reasonable and virtuous. This is so because the judges who author these decisions and their talented law clerks are craftsmen with their word processors and reverently wrap their decisions in our Constitution, in words which condemn as sacrilegious any dissent from their particular construction of this "sacred" document.

Thus have our judges/lawyers become the priests of a new religion—the worship of our Constitution—and, over the years, there has been manifested an ever-increasing need for more priests. And, as the need for lawyers' services has gone up, so have lawyers' earnings.

Graduating law students now join large firms at salaries double or triple that of newly hired teachers in affluent school districts. The law firm they join will be run by a business manager, the most influential person in the firm, who has special skills to control what clients the firm accepts and to manage their billing, so that profits will be maximized and uncollected fees minimized. These managers shield their lawyers from suffering the embarrassment of having to turn away clients who need lawyers but who are unable to pay the obscene hourly charges set by the business managers. Most incoming clients are first interviewed by the manager or by an "intake paralegal" before they ever even see a lawyer.

Most of this drastic evolution in law practice comes about from the fact that all judges are, first and last, lawyers. Having operated from both sides of the bench, I know that judges receive little acclaim, or even cordiality, at the annual bar convention (of which organization they are, of course, honored members), after delivering a well-reasoned decision rejecting a new theory of liability. Conversely, when a plaintiff's verdict has been upheld on appeal—based on some new theory of liability—congratulatory slaps on the back come from the many plaintiff lawyers at the next bar luncheon.

Even defense lawyers, however, give deference to the judge responsible for a large plaintiff's judgment being affirmed—for the larger the verdicts come, the greater the threat to their clients, and therefore the more appropriate a substantial fee for their cleverness in defending future cases.

The unique symbiotic relationship between bench and bar has resulted in making a game of our trials, a game played by clever and expensive lawyers whose skills in technical rules and in salesmanship control the outcome. Today's judges do not interfere with the games lawyers play.

In my early contacts with our judicial system, I witnessed much more of an independent, truth-seeking attitude from trial judges—to the point of taking affirmative action, such as asking questions of a witness that an inept lawyer had failed to ask. This taking a part in the trial by the trial judge was particularly true when litigants without a lawyer came into court to represent themselves as happened much more often in yesteryear.

As the years have progressed, the judiciary has taken more and more of a passive role during the taking of evidence. Judges now almost never ask questions in trials because the Fraternity frowns upon such aggressiveness—judges are expected to be content in their function as umpires at contests of skill between lawyers.

And that which depends on these skills has grown to grotesque proportions through the massaging of our Constitution by the Fraternity. For the last two centuries now, the all-powerful tool used to increase the power of the Fraternity has been to *sanctify, through the writings of judges, the particular words chosen by those who wrote our Constitutions, and to give these words sanctimonious, and, above all else, expansive meanings.*

Let us see if we can prove this methodology by using the example of the constitutional guarantee of a jury trial, which is as close to the "sacred" as one can get in our new religious world. That which has now been sanctified by the Fraternity bears little resemblance to what a jury trial was in our judicial history.

Our jury system originated in England. It is very unique to the English-influenced world. The other judicial systems of the world make little use of laymen as fact finders.

The English system originally was a simple one, and, significantly, one in which lawyers did not participate. That system had two great virtues: it created the popular conception that justice, according to the common sense, was being administered, and, equally important, it *worked*.

These original English juries consisted of people from the "neighborhood" who "were men chosen as being likely to be already informed" as to the nature of the crime and the character of the accused.[13] They were encouraged to take the reputation of the litigants into account. For example, English law books chronicle the eighteenth-century case of a man named John Read who was charged with stealing a horse. This was not his first offense—the court report states: "Read [the defendant] could say little in his Defense, and being an old Horse Stealer, the Jury found him Guilty."[14]

These ancestral courts were not concerned with the "prejudice" of prior knowledge in the fact finder—in fact, previous knowledge in the jury of the defendant and his propensities was deemed useful in determining guilt. There were no lawyers in this ancestral scenario to profit from the age-sanctified industry of horse-stealing. Few guilty pleas were accepted nor were any plea bargains offered. These early courts frowned upon guilty pleas and actively urged defendants to take their trial so that the facts could be fully appraised and a just result reached.[15]

This spirit of honest inquiry is similar to that which once prevailed in the juvenile courts of the country—that I presided over in 1957–1960—before Justice Abe Fortas's decision of *In re Gault*[16]

---

13. J. B. Thayer, *Preliminary Treatise on Evidence at the Common Law* (Boston: Little, Brown, 1898), p. 90.

14. John H. Langbein, *The Criminal Trial before the Lawyers*, 45 University of Chicago Law Review 263, 303 (winter 1978), citing Old Bailey Session Papers (Dec. 1707) at 3.

15. Id. at 278.

16. 387 U.S. 1 (May 1967).

turned these children's courts over to lawyers' games. You will find more about this devastating decision as we go along.

An array of decisions of the Great Court, of which *Gault* is only one of many destructors, have systematically accomplished, during my lifetime, a complete redo of all the criminal courts of this country. Change has been consistent and inexorable—always moving the law in directions that make the lawyers more important.

And this explains the arrival on the modern scene of the pay-by-the-minute charges of lawyers. The born-too-soons, like my father, limited by their lesser influence on trial outcomes, simply didn't feel comfortable charging in this most magnificent—for the Fraternity—fashion.

Today, any attempt to try a John Read before a "knowledge-able" jury, as in our historical past, would be heatedly condemned by every lawyer/judge in the land—including myself—steeped as I am in lawyer religion.

Nevertheless, after working with our evolved system for a lifetime, I am convinced that the "neighborhood" trials came as close, or closer, to declaring the truth, and presented no more, and perhaps even *less, of a chance for an innocent person being convicted of a crime,* than the copping-of-plea system that has taken over our criminal courts. Let us see if I can document this terrible indictment as I review with you, in this tome, my life's immersion in our legal system.

As an introduction I first point out to you the suspect nature of the reasons given for the revolutionary judicial decisions that have, for many generations of lawyers, shifted our law—always in the direction of more legal work and the greater importance of lawyers.

The rationales always given—announced in prolix, sermon-like decisions by lawyers-turned-judges—are not predicated on what our society needs for its good. These momentous decisions, making it radically more difficult to convict the guilty of crime and creating more lucrative work for the Fraternity in civil actions, do not refer to real-life statistics—which might conceivably be out there—to justify the decisions being made—if, for instance, crime rates in our society were *d*own, or corruption in public office had proven to be less of a threat, or the products sold in this country were becoming more dangerous to use.

Instead of pragmatic facts, these decisions are almost routinely based on words that our Glorious Forefathers chose when they wrote our Constitution, and assertions that these words have preordained the innovation which is being then adopted into our law. The premise used to gain acceptance is that these "sacred" chosen words contain no flaw, when interpreted, that is, by these latter-day saints of this religion. The concerns of those who lived under, and wrote about the tyranny of monarchs are thus restructured to control the lives of those who live under democracy.

This is the way that cataclysmic changes in our way of life are mandated by my Brethren for reasons of worship of the past and with the invariable result of increasing the importance, and, sequentially, the earnings of the Brethren. This process, of course, is violative of the most fundamental concept that these Founders had in mind—the separation of powers between the three ordained branches of our government.

Judges were simply not intended by our Founders to have the power to *make* law. It is impossible for any rational person to read our nation's Constitution without finding a clearly expressed intent that the powers of government be apportioned between its three branches, the legislative, the executive, and the judiciary. The lawmaking power was crystal clear—not delegated to judges. But, as you read the history of my life, which inextricably is the history of the court systems of this country, you will see that the law that affects us the most directly is made—not by the legislators of our states, nor by the congressmen of our nation—but by judges—members of the Fraternity. And, as we turn this thing off, we will see how the Fraternity has taken upon itself the selection of the president of the United States—an awesome power indeed.

My conviction—that our judicial system has evolved to where

it serves the Fraternity too well and our culture too poorly—is a late-bloomer with me. I have lived most of my life with a profound respect, part worship, for the system in which my father distinguished himself and in which I have gleaned such good recompense. In this Fraternity I have lived well and prospered. So what I see now, so clearly, may be creeping senility—you must be the judge.

The damning fact you will learn about me is that I actually contributed to this sanctimonious takeover by the Fraternity—as a trial judge, as an appellate judge, and as a plaintiffs' lawyer.

And, it's nice communicating with you, and so we begin.

CHAPTER ONE

My Lawyer Father
1906–1923

In Daddy's time—and please try to excuse this childish reference to a father who died as I was attaining six years of age—a lawyer was prohibited from advertising—whether such be in a newspaper, in a telephone book, or wherever/whatever. Such a lawyer was subject to disbarment. The best that he could do was to have his name on his stationery, have a calling card, and have a modest sign out in front of his office.[17]

For his time and place, Daddy was considered well educated, but his total formal education was five years of elementary school in Ireland. And yet, in 1906, in the Territory of Arizona, he passed the bar examination to become one of Arizona's leading lawyers. The qualifications to be admitted to the bar of Arizona at that time were:

---

17. See American Bar Association Code of Ethics (1908), Canon 27.

...that he is possessed of a knowledge of legal principles and their application, of the rules of pleading
and practice, of the rules of evidence, of the rules of
construction, of the ethics of the profession of law; *is
possessed of at least a common school education*, of a reputation for truth, honor and moral character, has lived
in the Territory at least six months, intends to reside
permanently in the territory and practice the profession
of law therein.[18]

This statute did not define a "common school"—Daddy's
five grades in Ireland satisfied that requirement. With his limited education, Daddy would never have made it to argue to any
of today's juries. His wonderful ability to recite, by memory, the
First Canto of Sir Walter Scott's *Lady of the Lake* would mean
absolutely nothing to the bar examining boards of today. These
boards know that one of the ways to increase the earnings of lawyers is to make it difficult for anyone to become a lawyer, thus cut-
ting down on competition. The more difficult this can be made to
be, the fewer lawyers there are, and the more these Chosen Ones
may charge for their services.

Another way to increase these earnings is to change the law
to make it more complicated. During the years that Daddy practiced, the law did change, but almost imperceptibly compared to
the speed of my day. The lawyers and judges of Daddy's day pretty
much stayed with the "common law" as fashioned over the centuries by the judges and chancellors of England. But the Fraternity
saw a terrible defect in this law—it was not sufficiently lucrative
for lawyers.

In Daddy's day, *only* when a person had been wronged, without
fault on his own part, did he bother the courts with his problem because, under the law of that time, he had no case if he were partially
at fault. The boldest of plaintiffs' lawyers, and Daddy was one of

---

18. § 394 Revised Statutes of Arizona (1901).

them, would have ridiculed anyone arguing for today's "comparative negligence" doctrine—which today permits negligent plaintiffs to recover damages, the amount to depend on the degree of fault involved, and, in some states, even allows a plaintiff to partially recover when the plaintiff is more at fault than the defendant![19] Of course, under these delightful new standards, there is hardly any accident that cannot be a source of lawyer fees.

The terrible proclivity to make lawyers' services necessary had its insidious inception as far back as the time of Daddy's admission to the bar in 1906. By this time, of course, the "neighborhood" jury system was gone, and the system of an uninformed jury panel—achieved by lawyer/judge ministrations and strikings[20]—had been accepted, at least in theory, but there were still things to be achieved for the Fraternity's benefit, which were yet to come.

By 1906, lawyers had been able to establish the dogma that juries were supposed to be completely without any prior knowledge of the facts of the case upon which they are to sit. This, of course, provides jurors to whom the individual persuasive power of the lawyer becomes very, very important. Knowledgeable jurors are meticulously eliminated by lawyers' cross-examination and judicial orders. Lawyers now demand that judges excuse those who have any knowledge of the case, or even of any similar case, or upon the juror's showing of any "prejudice" (such as having,

---

19. For example, in *Alvis v. Ribar,* 421 N.E. 2d 886 (Ill. 1981), the Supreme Court of Illinois admirably traces the evolution in the law of contributory negligence as it legislates into the law of Illinois the "pure form" of comparative negligence. Under this "pure" doctrine, a plaintiff can, theoretically, recover 1/100th of his/her damages even when he/she has been guilty of 99% of the total negligence that caused the accident. This is the "pure" form of this doctrine, which became the law of Illinois in the Alvis decision. At the time of that decision, ten of our states were "pure" in this regard. 421 N.E. 2d 891 et seq.

20. We are referring to the procedure that permits trial lawyers to "strike" (i.e., disqualify) a certain number of potential jurors for no reason other than the lawyer's opinion that the particular juror might be likely to vote for the other side of the case.

perhaps—in a case of a prosecution for burglary of a home—a strong distaste for burglars—having had their own home previously burglarized).

More importantly for the Fraternity, lawyers had by my father's time achieved the right to eliminate a certain number of jurors from any proposed panel of jurors for no reason at all—usually with four to six of such "peremptory strikes" for each side in the litigation. A clever lawyer, by adroit questioning of the prospective jurors, can often come close to freeing his criminally charged client just in this very process—as it takes only one dissenting juror in a criminal case to block conviction. With such clever tools for lawyers to use, it is indeed foolish for anyone not to get the best trial lawyer available whenever one gets involved in litigation.

Peremptory striking has grown in importance over the years, with significant modifications, such as lawyers employing professional jury consultants, sometimes with degrees in human mental processes—if one has sufficient money, as O. J. Simpson did—to assist in the questioning and the elimination of prospective jurors.[21]

But, if we go back to Daddy's day, in a town the size of Yuma, with perhaps three thousand to four thousand inhabitants, jury trials were a close cousin to the English trial by a "neighborhood jury." In a jury of twelve persons there was apt to be at least one juror, after he got into the jury's deliberations, who would recall the reputation of a Johnny Read, the horse thief, charged again with the theft of a horse. Such a jury would pay less attention to the arguments of lawyers, no matter how eloquent they might be delivered, than the sanitized juries of today do.

Thus handicapped as Daddy was, no matter how persuasive he might have been in his jury arguments (which Mother told me were superb), there were those on the jury whose opinions he

---

21. A recent publication, *The Hidden Jury, and other secret tactics lawyers use to win,* by Paul M. Lisnek (Source Books, 2003) depicts the employment of jury selection experts as a necessary expense to win a case in our courts of today.

could not sway by his oratory. And, juries of that day had more knowledge to go on because of many fewer exclusionary rules of evidence, which we lawyers have since invented to keep facts from modern juries. To obtain more susceptible jurors, exclusionary rules of evidence have been created, one after another, by which juries are kept in ignorance of some of the most pertinent facts. Because of the creation of these wonderful rules, by the time I came along to try my skills at jury persuasion, I had the luxury of addressing juries exposed only to evidence that I had helped tailor with my carefully crafted objections. Much of this change in our law, from which I have benefited so much, happened after Daddy tried his last case.

Daddy's law denied recovery to any who were injured by a defective product that was not warranted to them by the seller. The bonanza of products liability law was yet to be conceived by the Brethren. There was an accepted adage of Daddy's law that said "buyer beware," and it controlled the drastically fewer legal complaints of the time.

There was even somewhat of a social stigma to suing someone in Daddy's day. The Canons of the American Bar Association (the premier association for members of the Fraternity to join) in his day contained a strong warning against being too quick to sue. Canon No. 8 used to read: "Whenever the controversy will admit of fair adjustment, the client should be advised to avoid, or to end, the litigation." Canon No. 28 stated: "It is disreputable...to breed litigation by seeking out those with claims for personal injuries or those having any other grounds of action in order to secure them as clients."

These professional admonitions from the 1908 Canons of the American Bar Association—recognizing the obvious—that litigation is nonproductive and depletive of social energy—remained essentially the same until 1967! Then, the Fraternity cast them disdainfully aside. By this time lawyers had come to the obvious conclusion that, for their own benefit, such a lucrative institution as litigation should be encouraged, and most certainly not condemned—"One should not bite the hand...." So, massive changes were implemented in the canons, and the above-quoted distasteful provisions were repealed by the Brethren so as to take all stigma away from litigation.

As for advertising, Daddy was at the edge of what was allowed for his time. In front of his office he had a half-barrel sign, about a foot-and-a-half in height, proclaiming his name and profession. Only a few personal injury clients responded—the inducement of large monetary recovery simply wasn't there.

When an injured client did show up, Tom Molloy would take the case on a contingency. Many years after his death, in rummaging through his papers, I came across his form contract for a contingency retainer agreement—it called for a fee of 25 percent of the recovery and meticulously specified that the client would pay filing fees in advance. We insist on better percentages today, and the advancing by the lawyer of the filing fees, plus the very massive costs of litigation, is the norm rather than the exception whenever a "good"—meaning really "bad" from an injury standpoint—case comes along. It's a much better day for plaintiffs who suffer horrendous injuries, and even better yet for their lawyers.

Daddy's jury verdicts were low, even after factoring for inflation. One of Daddy's "big" cases was against the Southern Pacific Railroad for wrongfully throwing a passenger off of a moving train. The passenger was a "coloured man" whom the conductor had called a "nigger" in the process of forcefully ejecting him from a moving train (quoting above from the decision of our Supreme Court).

The jury awarded the sum of $865 (PV04 $9,454) for this physical injury and indignity. The railroad appealed to the Arizona Supreme Court. There, the railroad's sole contention was that the award was clearly "excessive" and that the jury should never have been allowed by the trial judge to award such "punitive damages." Daddy won that appeal on February 7, 1924[22]—five months after he had bled to death in a Los Angeles hospital. One of Daddy's lawyer-friends had filed that last winning brief for

---

22. *Southern Pacific Co. v. Boyce*, 26 Ariz. 162, 223 Pac. 116 (1924).

him, as a donated courtesy to a deceased brethren and his grieving widow. I have not come upon similar courtesy from members of today's Fraternity.

Daddy's practice did profit, however, from a few of the magnificent "breakthroughs" that the Fraternity even then had made—to increase the take of lawyers' cash registers.

For instance, as early as 1822, an English court—the Fraternity was just getting its charter about this time—adopted the revolutionary concept that damages could be awarded for the pain and suffering of a person injured by another's negligence. Up until then there had been no reported case allowing damages for pain unless there was an *intentional* act of violence. But the Fraternity had been pounding on this obstinate door for a century, and in the case of *Pippin v. Sheppard*,[23] the door was opened for the award of damages for the *un*intentional infliction of pain. The Fraternity has been rushing through that door with bigger and bigger hauls ever since.

Every trial lawyer treasures the wonderful value of these pain and suffering damages, for, not only are they very lucrative, but, even more important as far as the Fraternity is concerned, this is an area where the skills of the trial lawyer are especially needed to achieve the result. If there is any one situation in which an individual cannot represent himself effectively—i.e., be his own lawyer—it is in arguing, in a jury-appealing way, how much he should receive for his own pain. Nobody likes a whiner. It takes a trained lawyer to handle the turning of this intangible into large sums of money.

Perhaps as important as *Pippin* for the Fraternity—and from which Daddy also derived benefit—is *Marbury v. Madison*[24]—acclaimed as a blockbuster in every law school in our land.

Marbury is a case over which lawyers drool. It established that

---

23. 25 Rev. Rep. 745 (Ex. 1822) and see O'Connel and Simon, *Payment for Pain and Suffering* (Champaign-Urbana, IL: Insurers Press, 1972), p. 93.

24. 5 U.S. 137 (1803).

judges can declare legislation, regularly adopted by Congress, void and of no effect. There are only a very few countries in this entire world in which judges have this much power. In the other countries with English common-law ancestry, there is very little of this "judicialization," as it has been called.[25] Only in very recent years have the courts of other countries assumed such an awesome power—up until now, only in those of France, Germany, Italy, and Sweden[26]—where lawyers have taken inspiration from the U.S. achievement.

The author of the wonderful (for the Fraternity) *Marbury* decision was Chief Justice John Marshall. He carefully chose his spot to be so daring. The problem that came before Marshall's court was whether Secretary of State James Madison could be forced to deliver over to a certain Mr. Marbury a commission of appointment as a justice of the peace of the District of Columbia. It looked as though Marbury might very well win this one, as, without any question whatsoever, Congress had expressly granted to the Supreme Court the authority to issue writs of mandamus such as the one sought by Mr. Marbury, and the facts of the case were in his favor.

So, Marbury had a hands-down case for winning. He was coming to the High Court in pursuance of a statute which had expressly granted to that Court the right to do exactly what Marbury was asking it to do. But, in a verbose decision approaching today's standards, Justice Marshall first pontificated that, sure enough, Marbury was entitled to his commission, but, pages later, we learn that—very unfortunately for Marbury—the *Supreme Court did not have the power to issue the writ which Congress had authorized it to issue, because Congress simply did not have the Con-*

---

25. See C. Neal Tate and Torbjörn Vallinder, *The Global Expansion of Judicial Power*, (New York and London: New York University Press, 1995), p. 72 (hereinafter Tate & Vallinder). It is interesting and a bit surprising to note that the assemblage of legal specialists from around the world whose studies are published in this work were uniform in condemning this gradual assumption of power by our judiciary. See pp. 526–528.

26. Tate & Vallinder, at pp. 210–211, 272, 358.

stitutional authority to bestow that power upon the Court!

What a clever way to assert a monumental power—that of declaring an act of Congress *void*—*because the act gave the Court too much power!* If one branch of government was to slip into a superiority over another, a dedicated "equal" branch of that same government, without provoking a contest, this was the way to do it!

Marbury started things in the right direction for the Fraternity. But, it had a long way to go to achieve what it has today. Though Daddy had the benefit of this bold declaration of the supremacy of the court, he also had to live with the historic fact that after *Marbury,* the case of *Worcester v. Georgia*[27] came along—in 1832.

It seems there was a President Andrew Jackson who didn't think lawyers were so much—perhaps he hadn't seen many of them at the Battle of New Orleans. So when Justice Marshall followed up the *Marbury* decision with one holding that the Cherokee nation had certain rights in land in the state of Georgia, Jackson scoffingly announced: "John Marshall has made his decision, now let him enforce it."

The Cherokees did not get what John Marshall said they were entitled to, but instead went on a presidentially mandated march to Oklahoma, where the ones who survived were amalgamated into the population. The Fraternity has had to live with this demonstration of its inadequacy in its infancy, but, it has grown stronger and stronger and has prevailed, oh yes, it has prevailed!

One way to make lawyers more important is to create complicated rules of evidence that only lawyers can manipulate, in order to keep evidence from juries. One early move in this direction of lawyer supremacy was the High Court's pronouncements in the case of *U.S. v. Boyd,*[28] giving the criminal trial lawyers of this country a means to keep trial juries from knowing the most incriminating of facts. *Boyd* was a shocker—up until this time it had been naively thought that juries were entitled to learn about the

---

27. 31 U.S. (6 Pet.) 515 (1832).

28. 116 U.S. 616 (1886).

crucial facts of cases before them. This great-for-the-Fraternity decision was written by Joseph Bradley, appointed to the Highest Court by President Ulysses Grant because of his being—not an experienced judge—but a highly paid lawyer for railroad companies. This Bradley-authored decision holds that an invoice for the purchase of fine glassware can*not* be subpoenaed from the defendant to prove fraud of customs laws, provided, of course, that an astute lawyer makes the right objection.

Another big step forward—for the Brethren—occurred in the 1914 decision of *Weeks v. U.S.*[29]—rendered when Daddy was in the middle of his law practice. Here, the Great Court promulgated an all-encompassing exclusionary rule in order to blindfold jurors in federal courts. Remarkably, Justice William R. Day, the author of this revolutionary opinion, had only a few years before authoring it written *Adams v. People*.[30]

The *Adams* decision was concerned with the seizure by law enforcement of private papers of the defendant—which papers established that the handwriting upon certain "policy slips" (illegal gambling paraphernalia) was that of the defendant. The seizure of these private papers was *not* authorized by the wording of the particular search warrant by which these papers were discovered.

In this *Adams* opinion, Day had adopted an approach that the Fraternity absolutely detests: "…the weight of authority as well as reason limits the inquiry to the competency of the proffered testimony, and the *courts do not stop to inquire as to the means by which the evidence was obtained.*"

What an uncomplicated way this was—to find out what has happened! And, if the police overstep and burst into property where there is no crime, then let the imposed-upon get jury retribution in a civil action. But, the Fraternity detests decisions such as *Weeks* because civil actions for guilty defendants are a hard jury-sell. And there are millions upon millions of criminal actions

---

29. 232 U.S. 383 (1914).

30. 192 U.S. 585 (1904).

in which a clever lawyer can display skill to keep evidence from juries. So the Fraternity was to have its way with Justice Day. After all, as he looked around him on the Highest Court, he saw that experience as a trial judge was unimportant. None of his colleagues had so served, and the last chief justice who had served as a trial judge was ex-president William Howard Taft, who obviously had been appointed for some reason other than his lowly trial-judging experience.

So in *Weeks*, this very same Justice Day, who had once thought it best to let juries know the true facts, promulgated the pernicious exclusionary rule that keeps evidence from jurors. Ten years of associating with selected members of the Fraternity had changed his perspective.

Weeks holds that lottery tickets seized without a search warrant by federal officers cannot be used to convict a person of using the mails to conduct a lottery—cannot, that is, when the proper motions/objections are made. In writing this one, Justice Day, who had previously used the pragmatic language of *Adams*, now used pulpit-like language such as "sacred right" and "established by years of endeavor and suffering" to justify this new law. Thus became enshrined as religious doctrine that which makes the Fraternity so powerful—for the Fraternity is to know facts of a case that are to be kept from jurors, providing, of course, that the right objection is made at the right time by some skilled member of the Fraternity.

Justice Day's opinion expressly concedes that the law being proclaimed was diametrically the opposite of decisions of state appellate judges throughout our nation. These state judges—who had seen many, many more juries in action than this justice could conceive of—had been faced with the same problem many, many fold and had come to a conclusion more conducive to declaring the truth, but much less needful of the services of lawyers.

In refusing to follow the wisdom of these trial-experienced judges, Justice Day's opinion falls into the pattern of other revolutionary decisions of this Great Court. These decisions uniformly make no reference to any social studies or any other source of information suggesting that any problems in our society or in our law enforcement recommend the change that is being imposed upon our people.

Rather, Justice Day relies in this opinion upon semi-historical, semireligious verbiage to block the pursuit of truth, in order perhaps to prevent Cromwell from coming back with his troops to search our homes. The public good of solving and punishing murders and other crimes is never mentioned in the religious spinnings found in decisions such as *Weeks*.

The *Weeks* decision came at a time when the Holy Nine had not as yet dared to determine what evidence our state judges could submit to their juries. The sovereignty of states was still recognized to a degree. So this decision, the same as its other "exclusionary rule" decisions—as they came to be called—obfuscated the truth only in the federal courts. State courts continued to follow their own perception of justice in these areas—letting juries know facts. But the Fraternity would continue to gnaw away at these ancient laws of our states and in a couple of generations would have its way with them, *all of them*, too.

So in Daddy's day, and for forty years thereafter, in our state courts the pursuit of the truth continued to be regarded as important enough that punishment for illegally obtaining evidence was something that was to be handled in some other proceeding—in a civil action for damages or in a criminal trespass prosecution—but certainly *other than* in the proceeding where the evidence was critically needed to expose either guilt or innocense.

The leading state decision,[31] staying with the established practice of letting the truth come out, was rendered in January 1926—not long after Daddy died. New York's eminent Justice Benjamin Cardozo wrote that opinion in which he scornfully described the federal courts' then relatively new exclusionary rule in these words:

---

31. *People v. Defore*, 242 N.Y. 13, 150 N.E. 585, 588 (1926).

...the criminal is to go free because the constable has blundered...the pettiest peace officer would have it in his power [if this rule had been adopted in New York] through overzeal or indiscretion to confer immunity upon an offender for crimes the most flagitious.

This Cardozo view of letting the truth be told in our courts persisted in our state courts even during my tenure as a trial judge. And, at least from my perspective, no one seemed to consider that Cromwell-like police were riding roughshod over peoples' rights as a result. But the Fraternity was to do much, much better for itself than this as the years passed.

Weeks appealed to the Fraternity so much that it champed at the bit to make it universal. After all, if a lawyer can make the right objection at the right time, and magically free a guilty client, this is power! Too bad Daddy didn't live long enough to enjoy it.

CHAPTER TWO

My Grand Juror Grandfather
1923–1945

I grew up in Yuma, a sleepy town with a half-Mexican, half-mixed "white"population situated where Arizona, California, and Mexico come together. One of my early memories is of heading home from grammar school to visit my grandpa's cabinet-making shop. His one-room, board-constructed shop was immediately across the street from the towering[32] county courthouse, which Grandpa himself had built a couple of decades before. Grandpa had been Yuma's principal building contractor for many years, but now, as he was bending over with the advent of old age, he confined his activities to making tables, chairs, and cabinets to the order of his customers.

Grandpa was always glad to have a visit from one of his grandchildren—he had only five at this point (with only one more to come). His shop was on the way home from school, and I spent hours watching Grandpa make furniture such as a table

---

32. It sat on a hill, overlooking the little town of Yuma, three stories high with a dome. It was "towering" for this town of maybe thirty-five hundred persons.

or a cabinet. It was particularly fascinating to see how wood was shaped on his lathe with a razor-sharp chisel as he churned away with a foot treadle. And while doing so, he told me of one of his proudest moments—when he served on a grand jury of the Yuma County Superior Court.

Under the law of that time, not everyone was allowed to serve on a jury. Grandpa had been selected as one of a group of citizens by the Board of Supervisors of the county as a person "sober and intelligent, of sound mind, and good moral character, over twenty-one years of age," to be a juror when called by the court.[33]

From that selected list, a grand jury of twenty-five had been summoned by our local Superior Court judge, and Grandpa's name had been drawn to serve on this panel.

But this type of honor was far too undemocratic and nonegalitarian to survive in our evolving culture. Not long after Grandpa had so served, a major "improvement" upon the jury system was authored by the Fraternity—in 1925—three years after Daddy tried his last case. Then the decision of *Lawrence v. State*[34] was written by our Supreme Court's Justice Lockwood.

There had been a murder conviction and a death penalty imposed for the killing of a police officer. The defendant had challenged the jury panel for the reason that the Board of Supervisors had selected only one-third of the registered voters to be on the jury list.

A death sentence had been imposed after an extended trial, and, on appeal, it was decided that, indeed, the jury panel selection method that had been in place for decades was defective. In his written opinion, to outlaw forever that historic jury selection system, Justice Lockwood relied upon the statutory qualifications for *voters*, which were somewhat similar to, but strikingly different from, the qualifications for jurors. Jurors, by Arizona's statutes, were required to be "…sober and intelligent, of sound mind

---

33. §§ 3516 & 3522, RS Arizona (1913).

34. 29 Ariz. 247, 240 P. 863 (1925).

and good moral character…and shall understand the English language; …," while a voter was required only to be "able to read the Constitution of the United States in the English language…and to write his name."[35] A legislative intent to make some difference between these two different functions fairly screams at the reader, with substantially more required to qualify as a juror.

But, Justice Lockwood was not at all impressed with the old adage—if the thing is not broken, don't fix it. He did *not* leave alone the system that had been working so well since Arizona had been created as a separate territory in 1863. And, to reach his result, the court had to violate a fundamental rule of statutory construction: *If there is a difference in statutory wordings, courts have since the beginning of our jurisprudence expressed the doctrine that they are supposed to give some meaning to the difference.* After all, this is just a fundamental courtesy to another of the three branches of our government, which branch the Founding Fathers clearly intended to have the prerogative of passing our laws.

But the equality between branches of our government is something that the Fraternity moves around at its discretion. Justice Lockwood was also a lawyer and undoubtedly sensed the massively increased influence his Brethren would have if the average intelligence in the jury box were lowered. He, as a lawyer, had to know that the less knowledgeable the jury, the more influence the skills of trial lawyers will have.

So, Justice Lockwood's decision changed the course of jury selection in our state's courts, and that automatically changed the method of selection in the federal trial courts in this state, for, prior to 1948, federal courts used the jury rules of the law of the state in which they were located.[36]

Subsequently, Congress yielded to the preaching of the Fraternity and passed legislation establishing that jurors are to be drawn "by lot" from a "cross section of the community."[37] So, we

---

35 Compare § 2879 with § 3516, both in Civil Code, RS Arizona (1913).

36. 28 U.S.C., 1940 ed., §§ 411–15.

now live in a society that no longer trusts public officials to select people like Grandpa to be our jurors.

But this does not stop the Fraternity from referring to the "ancient" right of a jury trial, which, in fact, is no longer the jury trial of our history. Now any Arizona resident who has a driver's license *or* is registered to vote is a qualified juror in both state and federal courts. My experience leads me to believe that a higher quality of juror is achieved by the drivers' license criterion, for such a person must at least pass some sort of test in order to qualify.

And, before we leave Grandpa's days, let's take a quick look at the stage of evolution of our court systems. Judges in those very same days were more reluctant to grant new trials than today, as illustrated by the *Lawrence* decision. After all, retrials cost tax money, what with judges' and clerks' salaries, lawyer fees, and such. So, despite his condemnation of the jury selection system, Justice Lockwood refused to let Mr. Lawrence avoid the hangman's noose, explaining: "...since the record fails to show any prejudice to the defendant, we will not reverse."

Courts of today, with more aggressive lawyers to urge them on, and with more Scripture now written by the Fraternity, are much quicker to find "prejudice" from such as happened to Mr. Lawrence. Today an appellate court would easily come to the conclusion that Mr. Lawrence did not receive a proper trial, pointing out the "inescapable"—that limiting the *Lawrence* jury to those of "good moral character," rather than permitting any person who had registered to vote to sit in judgment made it a bit more likely that he would hang—which he did.

It was in Grandpa's days, in 1924, that the Fraternity made a really great breakthrough to increase its powers—this time by an extension of the "sacred" Fifth Amendment. The Brethren chose the case of *McCarthy v. Arndstein*[38]—decided two years

---

37. 28 U.S.C. §1861.

38. 254 U.S. 71 (1920), on rehearing 262 U.S. 355 (1923), and on rehearing 266 U.S. 34 (1924).

after Daddy had tried his last case—to proclaim that this country had never understood that portion of the Fifth Amendment that specifies that "no person shall be compelled in any criminal case to be a witness against himself."

There are more civil cases in which to earn fees than criminal cases, so why not, the Fraternity asked itself, extend this preclusion to civil cases, giving trial lawyers another ace to play in trial?

So, with *McCarthy*, the simply worded constitutional restraint applicable "in any criminal case" became sacred doctrine in *all* cases, criminal and civil. This result was reached despite a congressional act[39] that mandated that no testimony required to be given by a person in the civil proceeding could be used against the person in a criminal proceeding. This solution—which would have made the ascertainment of truth in our civil courts much, much easier—did not suit the Fraternity. It prefers less direct approaches that can be manipulated by the Brethren while fees are being collected.

McCarthy's specific holding was that it was illegal for a court to require, in a bankruptcy hearing, a bankrupt to disclose whether he had concealed his assets. This decision now controls *all* civil litigation (bankruptcy or whatever) and specifically cripples the efforts of bankruptcy trustees seeking to assemble the assets of a bankrupt when the petitioning bankrupt is a bit of a scoundrel.

The power conferred on the self-incrimination clause by *McCarthy* would have made more sense in historic times. Early English common law had held that all felonies were punishable by death.[40] But the convoluted reasoning to justify McCarthy's result did not come into being until some two hundred years later, when

---

39. Bankruptcy Act § 7.

40. In W. Blackstone, *Commentaries on the Law of England*, (1897), vol. 4 pp. 97–98, 216, we find this quote: "The idea of felony is, indeed, so generally connected with that of capital punishment that we find it hard to separate them; and to this usage the interpretations of the law do now conform." See also F. Pollock and F. W. Maitland, *The History of English Law before the Time of Edward I*, 2 vols., 2d ed. (Cambridge: Cambridge University Press, 1968).

the death penalty had become something of a curiosity.

Even in Grandpa's day the Great Court was enhancing its image, to give it the aura needed to dominate the other two branches of government. For reasons embedded deep in the human psyche, it is difficult for those who hand down religious doctrine to do so without mausoleums and temples.

So, it was in these days that our Great Court found itself in need of a temple—to provide an Olympian-like atmosphere for it to exercise its godlike powers. Up until 1935 it had occupied offices that had originally been built to house the Congress itself. Since 1860 it had sat in the Old Senate Chambers, adequate in every sense as far as space was concerned, but inadequate to give a sense of walking into the sacrosanct.

The Court's new quarters were completed in 1935 at a cost of $9,649,000 (PV04 $125,296,990). Over $3 million (PV04 $38,957,620) was spent just for the marble in these halls to give the proper deified atmosphere.[41] These expenditures were lobbied through Congress with the argument that, since the judiciary was a "coequal" branch of government, it needed quarters that equaled what the entire Congress had. No heed was paid in this argument to the fact that there were hundreds of legislators compared to nine justices. Numbers of personnel had nothing to do with the enhancement of the image of the Great Court, for within this mausoleum were to be the Nine who were to exercise the power of nullifying legislation that the Congress might pass, of changing the shape of the Constitution, and, eventually, of even determining who would sit in the White House.

We have been pointing out the Great Court's awe-inspiring growth in power. We should note that there was one era in the history of this country when the High Court did not do so. This was during the presidency of all-powerful Franklin Delano Roosevelt.

"FDR," as he was labeled in the press, had been frustrated by

---

41. See *Booklet* prepared by the staff of the U.S. Supreme Court and published by the Supreme Court Historical Society.

the Holy Nine in his attempts to take the country out of a persistent economic depression. One of his attempts had been the Agriculture Adjustment Act, which a compliant Congress had passed at his instigation. This act had sought to bolster the depressed price of farm products.

The High Court thereupon, in its *Butler* decision of January 1936,[42] declared such legislation to be beyond the powers of Congress. Thereupon, FDR set about to "pack the court"—as the press labeled his endeavors. Our frustrated president proposed enlarging the membership of the Holy Court to fifteen, so that he could appoint enough to reverse some of the "obstinacy." As the measure to reform the court was working its way through Congress, the Nine looked down from their exalted heights to see what was happening below, and then began to uphold Roosevelt's New Deal measures.

FDR's dramatic landslide victory in the 1936 election was part of what the Nine saw.

On March 29, 1937, the Great Court announced its decision in *West Coast Hotel Co. v. Parrish*,[43] where it upheld, by a squeaking five-to-four majority, minimum wage laws for the country. *Parrish* was the beginning of the "Roosevelt Court." Justice Roberts voted with this New Deal bloc, formed with Justices Hughes, Stone, Brandeis, and Cardozo. And thus did the venerable Constitution take on a different meaning.

Subsequent decisions of this Roosevelt Court included upholding the Wagner Labor Act and the Social Security Act. In June 1937, Justice Van Devanter retired and FDR replaced him with a senator who would be much more supportive of his programs—Hugo Black, the U.S. senator from Alabama. Justice Black proceeded to be, particularly during the first half of his lengthy judicial career, the most liberal of the liberals in finding new meanings in our Constitution.

---

42. *U.S. v. Butler*, 297 U.S. 1 (1936).

43. 300 U.S. 379 (1937).

Justice Black, of course, fits the pattern—he had never sat on a trial bench before his anointment. But he was not a run-of-the mill appointment, by any means. He had been a member of the Ku Klux Klan in his home state of Alabama.[44] He had also been a laboring man's and a plaintiff's lawyer, and these are the roles—not that of a Ku Klux Klansman—that he took when he jumped up to the highest bench in the world—without judicial experience. And there he proclaimed the law, for more than a third of a century. Only William O. Douglas, a contemporary non-judge, served for a longer term—thirty-six years.

There are no term limits for priests.

It is little wonder that, with these two prolific and persuasive writers sitting on the High Court, the law of this land moved very far from where trial judges would have determined it to be.[45]

So, FDR, perhaps our most popular president ever, blunted his spear in attempting to put his appointees in the Temple, but nevertheless coerced them into doing his will. And, FDR is the last president to have the courage to face up to the Almighty Nine. *No subsequent president would be this powerful, for the shifting of power to the Fraternity has continued inexorably.*

When I was in law college, coming close to getting a law degree, war inconveniently interrupted my plans to practice Daddy's profession. For the next four and a half years I was integrated into our military, and there I encountered a legal system in which the Fraternity was not involved. The legal system that I had so intensely studied was simply not in that picture. The "precious" rights that the Nine Gods in Washington have glorified with their decisions were close to nonexistent in these years of my life. Lawyers were simply not present, as lawyers, in the war in which I fought. And the remarkable thing is that we didn't miss them at all!

---

44. See *The American Court and American Politics* (Harvard University Press, 2000), p. 5.

45. For a diagnosis of their pervasive influence, see Dennis Hutchinson, *Lives in the Law,* 93 Michigan Law Review 1885 at p. 1888 (May 1995).

But all that, of course, has changed. From such a dismal beginning, the Fraternity has rallied magnificently.

After WWII, a lawyer-authored article in a leading law journal announced that there had been an "uproar"after World War II in "veterans organizations" to extend the "civil rights" of those in the army.[46] In this period I was active in both the American Legion and the Veterans of Foreign Wars, our two principal veterans' organizations.[47] I failed to observe any such "uproar." Nevertheless, the postulated "uproar" culminated in the Uniform Code of Military Justice of 1950, which now, with amendments to make lawyers more important, has brought the Fraternity into every phase of military justice.

This means lawyers everyplace, and this has put me, very nicely, in a profession that is steadily increasing its importance. And it has become steadily more difficult to join its ranks.

I took the bar examination mid-February 1946, and on February 26 the results were out. Applicants of today wait for the results of bar examinations much, much longer. Those who grade bar examination papers appear not to be eager to admit new members to the Fraternity. It now takes three months to get the results in our state, and the pass rate has *lowered*, though the law school standards are *higher*. The Fraternity sees obvious reasons to make their status exclusive.

Grandpa died on April 13, 1946, just as I was starting as a minimally paid apprentice lawyer. If only he could have been present for my first jury trial—well, on second thought, let's make it the second trial. That first one was a fiasco. At my second trial, as an ex–grand juror, he would have been proud.

---

46. See *American Military Law in the Light of the First Military Act's Tricentennial,* 126 Military Law Rev. p. 1 (1989).

47. Yours truly has been a member of these two organizations in Tucson, Arizona, the largest veterans' organizations in that city. He served as commander of the Legion post in 1949–50.

CHAPTER THREE

Lawyer Internship
1945–1952

In the Law Offices of William G. Hall and Associates, in Tucson, Arizona, is where I received my apprenticeship in the practice of Daddy's profession. The "law offices" started out as the office of one ex-judge—"Judge" Hall as we called him—and two World War II veterans, Hamilton R. Catlin and myself. Ham had been in tanks in Italy and had gotten shot up, so as to return ten months before yours truly. Ham and I were the "associates" in this firm's title.

My initial salary was $250 per month (PV04 $2,418). Beginning lawyers of the day considered this excellent compensation; today's graduates demand considerably more. A year after this wage began, Judge Hall, with no forewarning, announced that our "association" had become a "partnership." According to Hall, as he explained it to us, a partnership was like a "marriage"—it lasted indefinitely and included a duty of complete loyalty. After being so "married," Ham and I received a "draw"—the total of which, every six months, was determined by an allotted percentage of the "take" of the firm. It was Judge Hall who determined, from time to time, without consultation with anyone, what that percentage would be, i.e. 18 percent to Ham and 16 percent to me that first year of our being "partners." Ham and I were left to understand that a "marriage" had to have a head of the family to make it work—to wit, in our case, Judge Hall. During those first years the Judge brought in the clients, and Ham and yours truly serviced them at his direction.

I shall always remember one afternoon, when the Judge assigned me my very first solo jury case. The conversation went like this:

> *Hall:* "I've got a case for you to try, John."
> *Molloy:* "Oh—[with the involuntary nervous system going into high gear]—what kind is it?"
> *Hall:* "Well, it's a drunk driving case. Shouldn't take too long."
> *Molloy:* "Who is the client?"
> *Hall:* "His name is Ryerson; he's right outside in the waiting room. I'll introduce you to him."
> *Molloy:* "Oh!—When is the case going to trial?"
> *Hall:* "Tomorrow morning."
> *Molloy:* [Long pause.]
> [End of drama.]

To appreciate this "drama," one must have some glimmer of knowledge as to the flow of litigation in our modern courts. Nothing, absolutely nothing, happens very soon. The Ryerson case was a jury trial. It is the one that I would *not* want Grandpa to have observed. It came about in this way. When, in preparation for this test of fire, I had asked my new client, in my office, "exactly" how many drinks he had imbibed before his arrest, he announced emphatically: "Only two—just two."

As he said it, he shook his head in a disgusted way, to indicate how unreasonable the arresting police had been. The next day, when I got my client on the stand to rebut the very distasteful testimony from two police officers, I asked him the very same question. His answer came in a slightly different form: "Just two, just two—[long pause]—*that I can remember.*"

The jury was out thirty minutes. I lost my first jury case.

Defeat is a powerful motivator. Only a trial lawyer can appreciate the tension of awaiting a jury verdict. One's gut always quivers. The Ryerson case was merciful in that regard, in its short delay, though its tenor hurt like a kick in the stomach. No matter if this guy deserved what he got; lawyers never want to lose. Thereafter, I did a better job of preparing my clients for their critical adventure on the witness stand. I went over their story three and four times with them, cross-examined them, and there were no more that-I-can-remembers, that is, *that I can remember.*

Our law firm conferenced often; it was standard procedure for the two "associate-partners" to meet with our leader every morning in his office. It was at these morning conferences that we came to conclusions as to what fees to charge our clients.

One needs to understand that underlying this conferencing activity was the accepted axiom of that era that lawyers did not get rich in their profession—this we even articulated, in a sad but proud way. It was not that we didn't want to get rich, but just that all of us recognized that lawyering was just not the type of endeavor that could accomplish this.

We had no time sheets to affect our judgments. We simply did not keep track of our hours. As far as I know, none of our fellow lawyers did, either. Nor was there any bookkeeping as to what fees any individual lawyer brought into our firm.

More important, both Catlin and I knew, from what our leader said, that it would be a breach of etiquette to keep track of what we, as individuals, brought into the firm. After a few years, when I thought I was doing pretty well in this regard, I cheated on this understanding by keeping a list of the fees I had personally brought in, but I guarded its existence and would have been ashamed if either Hall or Catlin had discovered what I was doing.

In these fee discussions, to determine what a client should

pay, the time needed to dispose of a particular matter might be mentioned, as an estimate only, in passing, but the hours spent on a client's affairs was only one of several factors in determining what to bill to the client.

To fortify the dogma that lawyers are not plumbers to charge by the hour—and to make it sound more lucrative—Judge Hall told us the story of a mechanical engineer called into a factory that had stopped working:

> The owner of the factory had tried everything to get it started, to no avail. An engineer was summoned and when he came, he carefully inspected the machinery, and then asked for a ball-peen hammer. With the hammer he hit a particular machine in a particular place, and the factory machinery immediately started to hum again. For his services, he sent the owner a bill for $1,000. The owner protested and asked for a break-down of the charge. The accommodating engineer sent an itemized bill:

Hitting machinery with ball-peen hammer:	$100
Knowing *where* to hit machinery with ball-peen hammer:	$900
TOTAL:	$1,000

According to Hall's apocryphal story, the client paid the bill cheerfully.

This thousand-dollar story was about an engineer, because we accepted the fact that engineers earned more than lawyers. Unfortunately, no Ball-peen Hammer Case came along during my law practice. The cases that I got involved with all seemed to take up considerably more effort, though the skill to make the right objection, and/or to file the right motion, provided they were made at the right time, as in the ball-peen hammer situation, was always at a premium.

That HCM (Hall-Catlin-Molloy) charging system, now fossilized by the new charging methods of the Fraternity, was, first off, a valuing of the success or failure of what we had done for the client. Sometimes this was very evident, as when, on the very, very rare occasions—as my memory tells me—we had lost a case. Fees got drastically diminished when this happened. More often my helpful memory tells me we had great victories. What the client could afford, and would expect to pay, then became very much a part of this delicate balancing. There was a great virtue in this system—it did not encourage a lawyer to take time to get things done.

We of the Fraternity in this stage of its development were intensely motivated to dispose of a matter as soon as reasonably possible, so as to collect a fee based on what we had accomplished. Other lawyers were operating under similar motivations, and judges did not expect voluminous, meticulously kept time sheets to collect fees in court.

Retainer fees up front were seldom demanded in the HCM type of setting. Subconsciously, I suppose, we knew that the location of our office, in the only high-rise in town, where the best law firms were ensconced, would keep nonpaying clients away. We had only a few corporate clients; but we had many small business owners, home buyers, divorce seekers, car accident victims, heirs to small estates, and occasionally larger ones, attracted by the fact that they were coming to the office of an ex-judge, who had been the only judge in our county.

Years later I was to learn of the much more efficient and profitable billing system—that of billing by the hour/minute. Such would have been rejected out of hand at the Hall, Catlin, Molloy stage of the philosophical development of our particular branch of the Fraternity.

In these early post–World War II days, the competition to acquire clients was very keen; the Fraternity had not yet realized its potential. These years were dismally lacking in the many wonderfully lucrative causes of action which have since been invented by the Fraternity—such as product liability cases, sexual harassment suits, unfair competition, invasion of privacy complaints, etc.

Contingency contracts were common for plaintiffs' cases, but they were much more favorable to the client than today's. When there was substantial risk involved in recovering, our firm took them for "25% if we settle out-of-court, 33 ⅓% if we try the case." For less risky cases the percentages dropped according to the lessening of the risk. These percentage contracts at that time meant that the costs of the action (court reporters' fees, expert witness fees, etc.) came out of whatever amount was recovered before we took our agreed percentage. Many of the contingency contracts of today have more favorable formulae for the lawyer.[48]

I was often called to Judge Hall's office to receive assignments of work. His name was known by everyone who was anyone in our county, and clients came steadily—clients with all kinds of problems. Whatever the problem, we had no hesitancy in assuring the client that we could handle it. Ham and I had passed the state bar examination, so, "What is your problem? We've got the answer," was our unspoken motto. And, amazingly, the system worked, because the system was in its comparative infancy insofar as lawyer-generated intricacies were concerned.

But the Fraternity intuitively knows that the more complex the system, the more necessary its services become. So progressively, over the next half century, and more, I have witnessed a continuous change toward the more complex and abstruse, and have gleaned my share of compensation from coping with it.

Somehow, as if by predestination, I drifted into trial work, and Ham became more active preparing contracts, probating estates, and politicking. The cases that I came to try, as was true of most trial lawyers of this era, were as varied as the merchandise in a

---

48. If you should sign a contingency contract with a lawyer today, read it carefully on this subject. You may very well find, as expressed in the fine print, that your lawyer's percentage, perhaps 40 percent of the recovery, comes out of the gross, while your share pays the out-of-pocket costs, such as travel expenses of your lawyer to attend out-of-state depositions, the fees of expert witnesses, the cost of deposition transcripts, etc..

modern mega-department store. Most were just run-of-the-mill, such as defending a drunk driving case or fighting over the devolution of a decedent's estate.

It was during these times that the Fraternity was jousting to extend the federal courts' exclusionary rule to *all state courts, so that state juries would also be kept in ignorance of evidence obtained without proper protocol. This resulted in a last stand in* the all-powerful Court against imposing the exclusionary rule upon all the state courts of this country.

This last stand was *Wolf v. Colorado* (1949),[49] written by Justice Felix Frankfurter, in scholarly fashion, taking pains to recite the roll of the highest state courts as to their acceptance or rejection of the reasoning of *Weeks*—that blockbuster decision of the Infallible Nine that had imposed the exclusionary rule on our federal courts. During the thirty-five years since *Weeks* had been rendered, the tabulation was that, of the 47 states that had considered the problem, 30 had rejected the *Weeks* reasoning as unsound and not in the public interest. Seventeen of these state decisions had bent to the wishes of the Fraternity, acceding to the view of the Infallible Nine that juries should be kept in ignorance of all evidence obtained without the proper formalities being observed—providing, of course, that there is a timely and proper objection or an appropriate motion filed. These provisos are, of course, for the Fraternity to handle, and get paid for doing.

The *Wolf* opinion noted that of ten jurisdictions within the United Kingdom and the British Commonwealth of Nations that had considered the question, none had held that evidence obtained by a search without a search warrant should be kept from the judicial fact finder. Justice Frankfurter also called attention to the fact that the state jurisdictions that had rejected the *Weeks* doctrine had not left this matter of police overreaching without a more appropriate means of redress:

---

49. 338 U.S. 25 (June 27, 1949).

Indeed, the exclusion of evidence is a remedy which directly serves only to protect those upon whose person or premises something incriminating has been found. We cannot, therefore, regard it as a departure from basic standards to remand such persons, together with those who emerge scatheless from a search, to the remedies of private action and such protection as the internal discipline of the police, under the eyes of an alert public opinion, may afford."

Wolf did not please the Brethren, because the importance of their skills was minimized by it. Consequently, the decision proved to be but a reprieve, which lasted for only a dozen years, before the Fraternity had its way.

CHAPTER FOUR

Politics Competes with Trial Practice
1953–1957

We have come to the time when President Truman was declining to run again for his hectic job because of the electorate's dissatisfaction with his ordering of General MacArthur to pull back in Korea.

It was during this epoch that I joined the American Trial Lawyers Association (ATLA), an association of plaintiffs' trial lawyers—with a just a few of the Brethren specializing in defense coaxed into membership to show that the organization was not entirely made up of plaintiffs' lawyers. In our ATLA conventions, we were educated by experienced/successful plaintiffs' lawyers on how to enlarge the verdicts we were obtaining. We learned that there are several better ways to "sell pain and suffering" so as to convince juries to bring in verdicts that are "more adequate."

By this time, pain and suffering damages, the innovation that an imaginative English barrister had sold to the Court of Kings Bench back in 1822 (remember *Pippin*—that marvelous breakthrough case for the Fraternity), had blossomed into a gold mine for the plaintiffs' bar in this country. So I was eager to hone my skills in this area. At an ATLA seminar in Phoenix, I was gratified to be instructed in new variations in the enhancement of verdicts:

First, before ever getting on the witness stand, the client must be coached as to how to describe their agonies to a jury so as to *not* seem like a "whiner." Basically, the trial lawyer must "drag out" the facts—in their ugliest light—from a witness seemingly reluctant to impose their suffering upon others.

Then, for jury argument, I was given various suggestions of how to go about "selling" pain and suffering. We practiced our approach in "mock trials" to sharpen our skills before mock juries—bringing in housewives, secretaries, waiters, whomever was available.

I give you in the following something of the nature of what I learned to do—combining the *"per diem"* and the "job offer" arguments—placed together here for your perusal in too close a proximity and brevity to achieve the best persuasive effect.

For this illustration we will use a hypothetical case of a Bob Smith, who lost an arm in an automobile accident. (Bob was smoking a cigarette with his arm resting on the top of an open window of his car when he was broadsided.) When we come to this part of the closing argument, if one has had to use notes in the previous part of the argument—not recommended except in very complex cases—one puts them aside when delivering this finale, for it is time to "get into the jury box."

And, one needs to instruct one's clients on how to sit, act and look during jury argument—the client, and whatever family this person has, must look soulfully and very sadly at the jurors at all times. The lawyer during this oration must look the jurors intensely in their eyes, focusing on each one by one, individually (and the fewer jurors there are, the more "focusing" we can do) while a message such as this is being "poured into" their minds:

> Let me read to you the instruction that His Honor will
> be giving you in a few minutes:

[Then I read to the jury, looking up into their eyes with every other word, a stock instruction—the wording of which has been tailored by a committee of trial lawyers, which presented their recommendations to our Supreme Court for adoption. The chosen words cover, in poignant language, every aspect of injuries and damages that my client with the smashed arm has suffered. Then, I lay my script down, and really go to work on loss upon loss, on pain upon pain, on suffering upon suffering, and, always, on my eye contact. Then, as I am nearing the end:]

So, you are jurors, whether you like it or not—and I know you didn't ask for this job—it has fallen to your lot as citizens of our community, to give a value to Bob Smith's agony and disfigurement. I know that this is a difficult task. It's not pleasant to have to dwell upon the suffering of anyone—all of us reflexively turn away from it. We simply do not want to think about pain and mental agony. But, unfortunately for you, it is your duty, as a citizen of this country of ours, to do just exactly that, and I know that you will live up to your responsibilities courageously.

The suffering that my client is enduring, and has endured now for three whole y-e-a-r-s [with today's crowded calendars you are lucky to get a trial date this soon], is an e-v-e-r-y day—nay—an e-v-e-r-y minute thing. What would *you* [looking into as many jurors' eyes as possible] take to endure this type of suffering? Supposing someone would offer you the job to endure what Bob Smith is going through, and will be going through, until he dies? For there is no putting that arm back. What would you want to be paid? ["Job offer" argument.] Would you do it for one dollar a minute? How about a hundred dollars a day? [*"Per diem"* argument.] I don't think you would take the job at that price. But that's the job that Bob Smith has had imposed upon him by this accident.

Dr. Learned, the professor of economics from our University of Arizona [or from Harvard, perhaps, though it would cost more] has come here to tell you that my client has a life expectancy of 30.2 years. At just a mere hundred dollars a day, that comes out to $1,182,600. That may sound like a lot of money to some of you, especially when you add it to the fair sums that you must award for the past pain and suffering, and the medical bills and the lost wages and lost income, past and future, that my client is sure to endure. But, the important thing is not how much it may seem to you, as an individual, but what is just and right under the law that the court is giving you and that you are duty bound, *by your oath,* to follow.

And that is all my client, his family, and I are asking you to do—no more—no less—they are just asking you to do your sworn duty.

After you have rendered your verdict, and as you are leaving this courtroom, I want you to be able to look this Smith family in their eyes, and know that you have given them justice under the law and have rendered your verdict in accordance with the judge's instructions. You want to have a clean conscience, knowing that you have done your duty without fear or favor.

For there is no coming back. This is Bob Smith's one and only chance for justice, and you are the only dispensers of justice that he will ever have for this wrong. For, no matter how unfortunate his course of life may be because of this injury, the only recovery he will ever have for this injury will be what *you* here determine it to be.

I leave this matter in your capable, and *courageous* hands.

A *Pippin* (pun intended) of an argument such as the above, but much more eloquent, is delivered in trial courts all over this country, from other students of seminars similar to the ones that I have attended, with much more persuasive skills than yours truly, and with new and better arguments devised from time to time by ingenious members of the Fraternity who have tried them out on actual juries. These eye-contact arguments are one-sided, especially if your case is against a defendant such as General Motors, in which case there is no way for the jury to have eye contact with the defendant. Such arguments, better delivered, have produced magnificent results for the Fraternity, which year by year has improved its skills and year by year has gloriously added to jury verdicts until they are now many times what they were when I had my turn at bat.

And, of course, such arguments are not ones that a Bob Smith can make for himself—for how could he be so unmanly? And, when such eloquence is left ringing in jurors' ears, as they retire to the jury room to deliberate, without the defense having any opportunity to respond, it is effective, to say the least. A persuasive lawyer thus becomes an absolute necessity to obtain the kind of "justice" that plaintiffs desire, and that the Fraternity savors. Thus, lawyers have created a system in which their services are preeminently indispensable.

The Fraternity cherishes the "right"—a right devised by fellow members of the Fraternity—that gives plaintiffs' lawyers both the *first* and the *last* closing argument in all jury trials. Defense counsel are sandwiched in between these renditions. Defense counsel accept this terrible disadvantage as absolute dogma—because subconsciously they know that the larger the verdicts, the more necessary their services (and hence the higher their hourly fees).

Of course, experienced defense counsel have their standard ways to cope, which would be much, much more effective—if they had the last word, which the Fraternity will never give them.

In a criminal case, when the prosecution has the duty to convince jurors, who are sworn to bring in a "not guilty" verdict unless there has been proof presented to them that the defendant is guilty "beyond a reasonable doubt," and where unanimous verdicts are required, there is justification for this first-and-last-argument dogma. But in civil actions, in which the jury is told that all the plaintiff has to do is to convince them that the plaintiff's case is "more probably true than not" and where unanimous verdicts are generally not required, this advantage results in a warping of justice.

During my term of exposure to this system I have seen the "burden" (to prove by the "preponderance of the evidence") watered down to practically nothing. Plaintiffs' lawyers stand before juries and make the "scales of justice" argument, which goes something like this:

> Ladies and Gentlemen: There is no greater honor and at the same time no greater burden, than being called upon to be the judge of one of your fellow citizens. Today you will be exercising that power, and carrying that burden for my client, Bob Smith, who sits before you in confidence that you will treat him fairly, and that is *all* that he asks—that you follow the law of this land that his Honor will give to you, without fear and without favor.
>
> One of the first things you must decide is whether my client is entitled to anything at all.
>
> His honor will tell you that, as the plaintiff in this action, my client has the burden of proof to establish that the defendant was responsible for this accident. So we come to the question of what is this burden and what does it take to carry it?
>
> Let's see if I can help you with an analogy. I like to think of a delicate scales of justice, which at the beginning of this case was empty, and there it stood, perfectly balanced. Then there came elements of proof, from both sides, seeking to cause the scales to tilt one way or the other in their favor. And now, as I stand before you, that loading of the scales is completed, and you

must look to see which way the scales are tilting. And if the scales are tilted one way, or the other, even if only slightly, then that side is entitled to your verdict and you are bound, by your solemn oaths, to render your decision in that person's favor. [Here would follow a recitation of evidence, ending with the conclusion that the scales are clearly tilted appropriately.]

This protocol (first and last argument by specialist members of the Fraternity) does not mean, of course, that plaintiffs always win, because we plaintiffs' lawyers can come up with some ridiculous cases and against some very clever defense lawyers. Moreover, there are some underlying, strong feelings that can upend the most capable of advocates. Malpractice cases against medical doctors, for instance, are notoriously difficult for plaintiffs to win because the medical profession has its aura of respect. A majority of such cases that are tried result in defense verdicts.[50] And, of course in those states that have adopted the law of comparative negligence, then there are practically no negligence cases to be lost.

As important as trial eloquence is the skill of the lawyer in discovering everything that your opponent has, or knows, that may help you win. The importance of this was in its infancy when I started practice. Our leader, Judge Hall, was not intrigued with the deposition-taking madness that was just starting to dominate trial practice. He was very prone to file his plaintiffs' cases, and then pay as little attention to them as possible until shortly before their trial date. Then he would start negotiating intensely to try to reach a settlement. But he was always ready to go into court and skillfully pick a jury, and his opponents knew it. His clients generally received fair and adequate settlements, or, if the other side was obstinate, favorable jury verdicts. Judge Hall would have been

---

50. Though the average of the amount of a plaintiff's verdict appears to be higher than in other cases. See *Law and Contemporary Problems, Juries and Justice: Are malpractice and other personal injuries treated equal?*, 54 Law & Contemporary Problems. p. 5 (Winter 1991).

severely handicapped if he had to comply with modern-day practice, which requires disclosure of *all* pertinent evidence to one's opponent well in advance of trial, and settlement conferences in front of judges trying to coerce settlement before one ever gets a firm court date. Just a waste of court time and tax money Judge Hall would say. But, this is no longer Judge Hall's day—not by a long shot!

And, as I was becoming used to arguing before juries, I was appointed to the Examining Committee of the state bar, to serve with four other actively practicing lawyers. We administered a system for the admission of applicants much more difficult to pass than when Daddy went before a committee of three to be admitted. Desire to make lawyers' services more expensive, of course, was never expressed by anyone within our committee as being a factor, but the days of admitting an immigrant with a fifth-grade education were gone—a long, long ways gone.

Very few members of the Fraternity ever want to do anything except raise the barriers to becoming a lawyer—bit by bit, as we go along. For each of the three years our committee met to discuss the papers that we were grading, the opinion invariably was expressed by at least one of our members that the quality of the applying law graduates seemed to be "going down." The speaker of such an opinion, of course, would follow up with the suggestion that the percentage of those *not* passing should be raised a bit.

When I was on the committee, I was no knight in shining armor to advocate that we pass as many as 90 percent (which in retrospect seems the least that would be reasonable, considering the high standards established for even *taking* the examination),[51] but I did muster enough courage to speak up on two or three occasions to argue against raising the threshold for admittance, and in the process confessed my inability to conclude, as my astute

---

51. Having a bar examination is somewhat unusual in most of the world. In many countries, graduating from an approved law school is considered sufficient. Here, such graduation is the minimum requirement for taking the examination.

brethren had, that this year's "crop" was worse than last year's.

It was about this time that I became involved in politics.

When Joseph Judge, local chairman of the Democratic Party, resigned in April 1952 to be state chairman of Daddy's adopted party, a committee of a dozen or so Democrats came to my office to offer me the job of county chairman of the Democratic Party. The committee contained several legionnaires of our Legion post, where I had presided as its "commander" over meetings, slot machines, and funerals. The committee included John Greenway, a young lawyer whose mother, Isabella Greenway, had been the only female ever to represent Arizona in the U.S. Congress. Part of the Greenway property was the nicest resort hotel in town, the Arizona Inn.

Not finding it within myself to quarrel with the opinion of the committee that they had chosen a most worthy leader, I accepted forthwith and found that my first official assignment was to preside at a Democratic dinner to be held at the Arizona Inn. The principal speaker had already been selected, none other than the ambassador to the Court of St. James (England), Lewis Douglas, a descendant of a pioneer Arizona family. This was the time when Democratic hopes of electing a president had centered on Adlai Stevenson, the governor of Illinois, to run against the war hero, Gen. Dwight Eisenhower.

I had barely enough sense when I learned of the ambassador's selection to be our speaker to ask the committee: "Is Ambassador Douglas going to support the party ticket?" John Greenway, the spokesman for the group, responded with these epic words: "Ambassador Douglas owes too much to the Democratic Party not to know what to say at a Jefferson-Jackson Day dinner."

I was carried away with the logic and swing of those words. I was ready to preside!

The evening started out portentously. All of the local party leaders were there. After a sumptuous dinner, about five hundred avid Democrats, plus Ambassador Douglas and Senator MacFarland (who was then majority leader of the U.S. Senate), filed out to an outdoor patio where a platform had been set up, upon which were an assortment of chairs for the many VIPs, and on which had been installed a podium. Placed on the front of the podium were dozens of microphones. All of the national radio hookups were participating—this was before national TV coverage.

I opened the meeting graciously, I thought, and introduced Senator MacFarland. He in turn introduced the ambassador with flowery language. Whereupon the good ambassador proceeded to make a speech that sickened my mind as it fought its way into my reluctant consciousness. The ambassador's speech made these headlines throughout the country: AMBASSADOR DOUGLAS: "MY COUNTRY COMES BEFORE MY PARTY—VOTE FOR EISENHOWER."

When this person, who didn't seem to think he owed any-thing to the Democratic Party, was finished, protocol demanded that I close the meeting. My numbed brain told me that I had to say something about what had happened. After all, I had pre-sided at and presumably had scheduled this nationally witnessed act of hara-kiri.

I stepped up to the many microphones. I heard myself taking issue with what had just been said. There are two sides to every coin, I solemnly reminded my audience, and even great statesmen can make political misjudgments, particularly when they have been out of the country for as long as Ambassador Douglas had—in England.

Several times in this spontaneous recitation of platitudes I was interrupted with the applause from my prejudiced audience. The ambassador had not done nearly as well—I began to feel a sense of exaltation. Then, as I was winding down, I heard myself telling a joke that I had heard that morning, which I had thought was hilarious. It was about a Catholic father who had gone to Rome to visit the pope. As the good father was leaving, there was this conversation:

> *The Pope:* "Son, I am very impressed with you. I have a cardinalship which is about to open up in the United

States and I am thinking about appointing you."

The Father: "Ah!" [Overwhelmed.]

The Pope: "But, there is one qualification, you must never have taken the name of the Lord in vain."

The Father: [Hesitating.] "I am sorry, your Holiness, but I did on *one* occasion."

The Pope: "Tell me about it, my son. There may be some extenuating circumstances, and I may be able to forgive you."

The Father: "Well, I was playing quarterback for Notre Dame. It was in the last game of the season, and we were against Northwestern. The score was tied—six to six. There were only thirty seconds left to play. We were on Northwestern's three yard line. I called for the quarter-back sneak. They opened up a hole in the line for me; and I dashed through it. The crowd was going mad! And then I looked down at my hands and said 'My God, where is the ball?' "

Thereupon, the pope leaned forward and exclaimed: "Jesus Christ, where *was* it?!?"

My audience loved it! There was uproarious laughter. After all, anything was better than what they had heard from the ambassador. So I decided it was time to close the meeting.

"We will now have the benediction," I solemnly pronounced and then I looked down at the program. A Catholic, Father Carscallen, had given the invocation, so surely there would be a Jew or a Protestant of some kind to give the closing prayer. But, abomination! There I saw that Father Carscallen was scheduled for the benediction, too! And, and why was he not coming forth to do his duty? As seconds ticked on to a minute, a heart sickening sensation began to engulf me. I looked around frantically. No one was coming forward. I looked again; cold fear was saturating my entire being.

I called out: "Father Carscallen…Has anyone seen Father Carscallen?"

From the audience, the voice of State Sen. Tom Collins, a good Democrat and also a good Catholic, boomed out: "He left when you told that joke." The impact of his message sank in—sickeningly. I could see microphones all around me. I couldn't think of one word to say as I looked out on my stunned and waiting audience, then out came: "We are adjourned."

I went home to a night of groaning and punching my pillow, and when it came time to elect precinct committeemen for the Great Party that September, I didn't get enough votes to qualify. So that was, presumably, the embarrassing end to my political career.

But it didn't happen so.

After Ernest W. McFarland was defeated in his run for re-election to be Arizona's senior senator—by Barry Goldwater in 1952—McFarland became a candidate for governor of our state and, for some strange and undisclosed reason asked me to be his campaign manager in the southern part of our state. I accepted, and McFarland carried my territory, and the state, by a landslide.

Not long after this victory, when wife Josephine had just delivered a fifth child into our family—that was Tommy, now an eminent heart surgeon (please forgive my taking this opportunity to boast of my fifth-born)—Governor McFarland called me to a private breakfast at that very same Arizona Inn where I had made a fool of myself, to inform me that he wanted to appoint me to a vacancy on the Supreme Court of our State.

This was shockingly unexpected. The offer of the appointment came at a time when I had a burgeoning family of five children and a wife. I went home to discuss the matter with her and learned that she thought it would be a good idea, even though it meant a cut in income. I expressed to her the belief—which had been germinating for years—that no lawyer should be appointed to the appellate bench until that person had served a stint on a trial court. By this time, I was beginning to realize that blockbuster decisions, changing the law of the land in pervasive ways, were coming down from appellate judges who had never observed as a trial judge what those decisions were doing in the courtrooms of the country.

Josephine agreed with my take on the situation—I suspect that her desire to stay in Tucson to raise her family was much more important to her decision than whether or not appellate judges should serve a stint on a trial court.

I called the governor and informed him that I could not accept the appointment to the high court and expressed my view that appellate judges should be experienced trial judges. I suggested that if he would appoint a senior judge of our local trial bench to the Supreme Court, I would accept an appointment to the vacancy thus created. And this is what happened.

On September 1, 1957, I was installed as the judge of Division One of the local trial bench, replacing Judge J. Mercer Johnson, who was appointed to our Supreme Court. My law partners were openly disappointed by my decision to leave, but, nevertheless, Judge Hall, as the principal speaker at my installation, gave me words of praise that I shall never forget—even though they were not as flamboyant as I had hoped. Egos can be disgusting.

And, before we depart this era, we need to take a quick look at what the Holy Nine was doing to change the law of this country. The fact is, real blockbuster decisions were not coming down during these dozen years of my law practice with HCM. As in the war years, they were leaving the changing of the law pretty much to the legislators of our country, but we were soon to learn that during these times, they were tooling up for the really cataclysmic changes to come.

So, on September 3, 1957, with judicial discretion not tremendously different from that given to Judge Kelly in my home town of Yuma, I was installed as a trial judge. During the next twelve years, while I served in black robes, I was to see that same discretion of trial judges drastically reduced by decisions of the All-Knowing Nine, always granting more power to those fee-taking members of the Fraternity who had carefully read and digested their decisions.

It was during these coming years that the Most High Court was to become known as the Warren Court and the most magnificent things were to occur—for the Fraternity, that is—and the most devastating for our people.

CHAPTER FIVE

Two Diverse Judicial Systems in America
1957–1960

My installation was in Tucson's venerable Division One courtroom, where I had tried dozens of cases as a lawyer and which had now become *my* courtroom. It was the largest and oldest of Pima County's courtrooms, with an impressive mahogany bench and walls decorated with Greek pillars of mahogany. The bench was at an elevation that permitted me to look down on everyone in that impressive room.

One has to experience such wondrous looking-down to appreciate it—to have the glorious feeling of being a little closer to the Divine than anyone else in the room. Having everyone stand up when I stalked onto the bench from my special door, with my black robes flowing, enhanced the exalted feelings.

I've known very few judges who, after sitting on the bench for ten years, didn't think they were sitting at the right hand of the Divine One. This is particularly true of judges who are selected for life, such as the Nine Priests in Washington and their subordinates, the Federal judges, both trial and appellate. It is less true of judges, such as Judge Hall, and yours truly, who had to run for election periodically.

Judge Hall told us that after he had been the only judge in Pima County for ten years, he felt godliness coming on, so he decided it was time to get back to law practice. Maybe coming from the backwater country of the Ozarks helped him make that decision. Some among you may crassly attribute his decision to wanting to make more money—which he proceeded to do.

As part of the ceremony of my being anointed as a judge, I ascended to the bench and was presented with a gavel that I forthwith used to "pound the court to order." This was the first and last time I used the gavel, because menial tasks such as this are for bailiffs to do—not for those of us on the Higher Level. Immediately after my anointment ceremony, I went back to my chambers through the special door in back of the bench.

Chambers are sanctuaries for judges. There you retire to ponder your decisions. And there you have your own private toilet room, so that you will not be seen by mere mortals doing something as mundane as relieving oneself of bodily debris.

On this special occasion—when I had just been anointed as one of the Chosen Ones—I met in my chambers with my three fellow judges to conduct our first "judges' meeting." There was no "presiding judge" [this was to come in later years]; we were an assemblage of equals, though I felt a strong sense of inferiority in the presence of these dignitaries, whom I had been calling "Your Honor" for so many years.

"Justice" [new title] Johnson, who was graduating to even higher celestial levels—the Arizona Supreme Court—joined us for a short time, wished us well, and then departed. Then I had my first conjugal meeting with the Anointed. As I listened to my new fellows, it seemed that, now that Judge Johnson was gone, we needed a new juvenile court judge for our county, and (what was going on here?), my three colleagues had agreed that it was to be me! My response was an immediate "Why me?"

The answers they gave centered around the fact that I had more children than the other three put together. A modicum of research establishes that I had had more children than any juvenile judge in the recorded history of our county—and I wasn't through yet—our youngest, Craig William (named after Judge Hall and an unknown Nordic ancestor) was born four and a half years later.

I knew that our county's juvenile judge was always getting his name in the paper. Judge Johnson had served in this capacity for ten years. One of the talks of the town was that his son, occasionally, had made the headlines as a juvenile. I had one teenager at home and four more maturing and could easily see the downside of this unexpected proposal.

But, my ever-hungry ego overcame. After all, if *they* thought I was the best qualified to run the juvenile court, with a forty-plus member staff, who was I to argue?

So, on September 8, 1957, I found myself conferring with the Pima County Juvenile Court staff. Nervously, I found that I was learning about an entirely different kind of court than the one in which I had been playing lawyer games—one destined to be destroyed by the Fraternity for the very reason that it did not cater to those games.

As I listened to my new employees, who had decades of experience dealing with juvenile problems, I realized that I was being presented with an amazingly new idea. These people were not dealing with games to be won or lost in the courtroom. They were only interested in developing the truth, as effectively as possible, to determine what had occurred, and to eliminate and/or ameliorate as expeditiously as possible the problems of those referred to them. The games lawyers play were not a part of what was happening.

The purpose was not to punish, but to correct and prevent. The juvenile's record was routinely destroyed when the child reached the age of eighteen, and these records could *not* be used—in criminal prosecutions or whatever, to tarnish the juvenile's adult life. Whenever the juvenile judge, after a hearing, determined that punishment was more appropriate than social treatment, the juvenile was "remanded" to the adult court for criminal prosecution, but the procedure (testimony, etc.) that had occurred in the juvenile court could *not* be used against the remanded juvenile in the adult court.

The building in which our juvenile court was housed was relatively new and had separate, spanking-clean quarters for boys and girls, an immaculate kitchen, and a "courtroom" up front—a far cry in its accoutrements from the splendor of the Division One courtroom. The "bench" was nothing more than a desk. This "courtroom" was full of chairs, like a classroom, with about thirty seats.

I soon came to realize that I was expected to be the commander of a task force of forty or so professionals—dedicated to combating delinquency. That caused me to feel as awkward as when I first started directing, for the Third Fleet, the combat air patrol off of Tokyo in June 1945.

Juveniles coming before me very seldom had lawyers, and they, at this time—before the Great Court changed things—had no right to claim the Fifth Amendment against self-incrimination, because what we were doing was not considered "incrimination,"[52] though we were usually involved in determining what had occurred, which, *if* an adult were involved, would be a crime.

This lack of the good old Fifth Amendment to block the finding of the truth gave civil libertarians, mostly the lawyers in that group, more and more anguish as the years went by, but during my watch on this court (1957–1960), it was *the* law, despite the gnashing of teeth by some of the Brethren over the "high-handedness" of these courts.[53] And without it, the ascertainment of truth was infinitely easier.

The juvenile court over which I presided was similar to those in the rest of our nation. In this system, "juveniles"—or "children," as this law referred to them—were all those under a certain

---

52. See *In re Holmes*, 379 Pa. 599, 109 A.2d 523 (1954); and Annot., 43 A.L.R. 2d 1128, 1133–38 (1955).

53. See "Civil Liberties Record of the Great Philadelphia Branch," ACLU, February 1956.

statutory age. In Arizona that age was eighteen years—there were no states with a higher age limit—and there were a good many states with a sixteenth birthday cutoff and a few with the fourteenth birthday as the dividing line between these two disparate legal systems.

Arrested "children" became "delinquents" only after the juvenile court formally adjudged them to be such, after a "juvenile hearing," at which everyone could tell their story. Lawyers were permitted to attend hearings with their juvenile clients, could insist on witnesses being called, could ask questions of witnesses and could make arguments. But not as much attention was paid to what these lawyers said as was paid to what the parents and the child were saying. With such slighting, very few lawyers showed up in juvenile courts.

The most significant differences that I found in this strange, new court was that the facts of what had happened were always crystal clear, and there was tremendous discretion placed in the judge as to what to do about those facts. There was no statutory standard set to determine which children to "remand" to be prosecuted as adults, or which to treat as children—we judges were expected to exercise common sense in these things.

The safeguard against autocracy was that our Supreme Court could set aside any order entered by a juvenile court judge as being "arbitrary or capricious," *and*—perhaps even more significant—we judges all had to run for office and be elected. My first electoral comeuppance occurred at the very next election, one year after my appointment, and then my job was up for grabs before the electorate every four years. And, for the most part, our electoral district was small enough so that only one or at most two trial judges came up for election at the same time, so the electorate had an excellent opportunity of knowing whom they were voting for, or against.

In addition to delinquents, we juvenile judges had responsibility for "neglected" and "dependent" children. Once a child was adjudged "neglected" or "dependent" (because of parental neglect or lack of support), the court had the power to place the child in someone else's custody, and even to sever—permanently—all parental rights and place the child for adoption. These awesome responsibilities were to be exercised in my jurisdiction by nervous me, and during a time when I was also learning how to act as a trial judge in a court of general jurisdiction.

There was much less work in adjudicating the problems of our youth in this day as compared to now. While I was the only juvenile judge in our burgeoning county, I was at the very same time a trial judge in the adult court—sitting there almost as often as my three fellow judges. In my county, Monday was the only day of the week set aside for juvenile court—so for the most part I was available as a trial judge in the "adult" court four and a half days a week instead of the regular five and half days. In those days, Saturday mornings were included—that was the Spartan—by today's standards—work schedule which had been in place for as far back as anyone could remember for all judges in our part of the world.

Though the population of Pima County was approximately 230,000,[54] this one day a week, plus a day or so now and then for special juvenile hearings, was all it took of judging time to handle our juvenile problems.

There were many ways in which that juvenile court of yesteryear differed from the adult criminal courts of this nation. Foremost was that the juvenile court was professedly, and dedicatedly, nonpunitive. In this way we avoided encouraging miscreant behavior in those *seeking* punishment. My experienced staff explained to me that there are twisted minds in our populace that actually do things seeking punishment.

Our court was not trying to control by threats and fear. Rather, juvenile offenders were exposed to a lot of persuasion, coming from our probation officers, and from the "bench"—i.e. from yours truly during my tenure. Very little threatening was involved.

---

54. From *Arizona State Review,* 14th Annual Edition, October 1958.

Persuasion often went along the lines of extolling the fabulous opportunities available to all who happened to be so lucky as to be citizens of this marvelous country and to point out the skills and potentialities of the particular juvenile before the court—potentialities that were being wasted by juvenile behavior.

We had only a few of the "copycat" crimes that tend to plague our society. My staff explained that for some perverse, pathological reason, crimes that hit the front pages of papers, especially if accompanied with photographs, seem to prompt similar crimes to follow. Perhaps a sick desire to see one's picture on the front page has something to do with this. For this, and truth-seeking reasons, the records of our juvenile court were closed to the press and all others except staff. News stories came from the police, not from our court. The press was banned from all juvenile hearings, and our records were absolutely closed to reporters.

The press, of course, innately despises being shut out from anything that will sell newspapers, so perhaps the demise of this wonderful court system, which I will chronicle for you, could have been avoided if newspaper reporters had been permitted to sit in on its hearings and, with the headlines so generated, increase their circulations.

I was mightily impressed with the efficiency of what I found myself heading. When a juvenile was taken into custody for an offense, he/she was brought to "Mother Higgins," and an "intake officer"—an experienced probation officer selected for investigative skills and judgment—took over. These intake officers as well as all of our probation officers had college degrees in social work or public administration, with an emphasis on juvenile court work. Approximately 50 percent of all referrals to the juvenile court were "adjusted" by an intake officer after a consultation with the parent(s) and the child. But, this staff was totally subject to my control; there was no civil service protection in their jobs. During my tenure, I never felt called upon to discharge any one of them; they all functioned so well.

But these "adjustments" by the staff could not adjudicate a

child "delinquent"—a legal status essential for official supervision ("probation") and/or commitment to a juvenile institution. To be placed in any such status, there had to be a hearing, which required us to send notices to the interested parties (parents, victims, etc.) of the time and place of the court hearing before the juvenile judge. It took an adjudication of "delinquency" or "dependency" to give the court "jurisdiction" to make orders determining the custody of a child.

I came to regard myself as a member of a team, striving to cut down on delinquency and its near-relatives, child neglect and abuse. We were not officiating at games of wits, as I was having to do in the adult court. In this pre-lawyer era of our juvenile courts, each Monday there would be two or three of these "intake officers," and several probation officers, with the probation violators, to present cases to me in "hearings" for decision. Each of our officers would have three or so cases to present. My intake officers were well educated and experienced in this work and included Myra Koplin (who later became dean of UCLA's School of Social Work) and Christine de Cook, a graduate from child welfare work with over a decade of experience at handling juvenile court cases. Joel Valdez, who later became financial vice president of the University of Arizona, was one of my lead probation officers.

If it was a case of a child "on probation" who had been picked up by the police for some violation, then the probation officer assigned to that particular child would assist in the "workup" of the case and attend the hearing. When a child-probationer "fouled up," as with such a subsequent violation, the probation officer who had been assigned to that juvenile took it as a personal defeat.

On a first referral of a juvenile to the court, usually, but not invariably (depending upon the seriousness of what had happened), the delinquent was formally adjudicated to be a "delinquent" and placed "on probation" for an indefinite period, under the supervision of a probation officer, either male or female, always of the same sex as the delinquent. The child could be taken off of probation—restored to ordinary child status by court order—at the recommendation of a probation officer.

The time involved in determining a law violation that had brought the juvenile before the court invariably took very little time compared to that devoted to the determining of what underlying problems had caused the violation, and in counseling on how to deal with such. An average complete hearing on facts that would merit a burglary "conviction" in an adult court—we never used the word "conviction" in the juvenile court—would almost invariably be over in less than thirty minutes, and then we would move on to a more important problem—what to do about it?

Today, now that the Fraternity has "improved" our law, it takes close to that much time for a judge to go through the procedure mandated by the All-Powerful Nine before merely accepting a guilty plea from a juvenile charged with a crime.

There was no right of bail recognized by this juvenile court of old. Whether a child would be held in detention pending a hearing before the court was strictly a matter under the control of the juvenile judge. As to this, there were disgruntled rumblings from the Brethren. Well-reasoned judicial decisions of the 1945 vintage declared there was no right to bail, but the Fraternity was lining up to take this prerogative away from juvenile court judges—in its decades-long project of destroying a system that paid too little homage to the Fraternity.

My position, sitting as a newcomer on both of these contrasting courts, forced me to compare them—the adult versus the juvenile court. In the juvenile court only sporadically were witnesses called to testify, because there were practically no "who-done-its?" coming before the court. On a typical Monday, I would hear twenty cases (shades of the "neighborhood" courts of eighteenth-century England), which, if they had been in the adult court, would have kept at least forty lawyers busy for months.

I sensed an intellectual freshness in the air after a session in the adult court as I shifted my duties to "Mother Higgins" (the name given to our juvenile court quarters—named after the first *chargé d'affaires* of the juvenile detention quarters of our County).

The most significant factor was the absence of lawyers and their influence. There was no coaching of witnesses—a major part of the activity of the modern trial lawyer—varying, of course, in great measure on how much the defendant can pay in lawyers' fees. Readers of today, indoctrinated into the "sacred" legalities that now afflict all our juvenile courts, will wonder how any judicial system as autocratic as my 1950s-vintage court could possibly satisfy the mandates of our Constitution, which had the same pertinent provisions as today. But significantly, my tenure on this bench came before the Fraternity had extended its realm to this court. Most of my Brethren had no idea of what "monstrous" things were going on in the juvenile courts—because they never got there.[55]

But in the years 1957–1960 (my watch in the juvenile court), only the extreme civil libertarians were complaining that there was a lack of "due process" for juveniles. Many years later I was to learn that our now-displaced juvenile court system was very similar—in permitting judges to affirmatively seek the truth without having to be led there by lawyers—to the courts created under the Napoleonic Code of France—the essentials of which still prevail in Western Europe and Latin America.[56]

And then, just as I was getting used to my dual role as a juvenile court judge and a trial judge in the adult court, the juvenile court game went "tilt." The Boy Killer Case came along.

I was stretched out on the floor of our newly constructed home in Tucson, Arizona, watching television at about 10:30

---

55. Realizing their need to know, in case they ever came into juvenile court, I wrote a law review article for our university's bar journal. See Molloy, *Juvenile Court—A Labyrinth of Confusion for the Lawyer,* 4 Arizona Law Review 1 (1962).

56. See Danner and Benal, *Introduction to Foreign Legal Systems* (Oceana Publications, 1994), chapter 3, authored by George A. Zaphiriou. Under this system, judges direct fact-finding endeavors and control litigation to a much greater extent than in this country. See *Lessons from Abroad: Complexity and Convergence,* 46 Villanova Law Review 1 (2001), and the citations given therein, expecially at fn's 41 and 42.

P.M. on October 12, 1957, when a news flash came on. The news announcer was talking excitedly. It seemed that two young boys, who were fifteen years of age, had killed an air force captain.

These two had been trying to rob a Captain Westin, as he was leaving his duty at the army's radar site on top of Mount Lemmon, twenty miles north of Tucson. After the killing, the two fifteen-year-olds had hidden themselves under a bush next to the scene of their bloody crime, and there they cowered until they were apprehended. The TV broadcast that had startled me out of my lethargy had a picture of the two "killers" after they had been pulled out from under the bush by sheriff's deputies. Their eyes looked like those of two scared rabbits. Then, as I was relaxedly viewing the next TV news story, with those scared eyes fading in memory, my mind jolted back to them.

Was this bizarre happening something that I was going to have to become involved in as the newly appointed juvenile court judge—far-fetched as that might seem? But, who else? No one came to mind!

I pondered the problem a little and then went to bed, still wondering how I would be involved in the case of the two "boy killers," as they were referred to in the broadcasts and in the morning press. The scared rabbit picture accompanied banner headlines on the front pages of both daily newspapers. The press, TV, and radio had their lead stories for the next eleven days—regaling the populace as to the evolving situation as to the "boy killers."

Those eleven days were some of the most intense of my life—to figure out what to do with these two, who had never been arrested before and whose families were ordinary citizens of Tucson. The press—meaning both newspapers and radio and TV media—was relentless in pursuing an answer from me, the juvenile judge, as to what was to happen. The press had been well-educated in the now-displaced law that gave a blanket of protection to juveniles insofar as criminal prosecution was concerned and was bitterly resentful at the "throttling" of newspaper coverage, which was an adjunct to the then-existing juvenile court system.

My investigating probation officers reported that both families included a natural mother and father. One family was faithful, churchgoing—the other totally nonextraordinary—both typical Tucson families with no warning of what was to happen to them. It developed that these "killers" were both of almost the exact same age—fifteen years and three months, born within one day of each other. As many other teenagers, they had watched many holdups on TV.

There was never any question as to what had occurred to result in the demise of Captain Westin. The boys separately told the same story to our intake personnel, after absolutely nobody had warned them that they had the right to remain silent and not incriminate themselves. They recited what had happened in a guileless way, and their stories were consistent with the facts—the bloody facts.

Both of these young men were held in Mother Higgins' detention as I tried to figure out what to do with them. I ordered that both boys be examined by child psychiatrists at the recently created Child Guidance Clinic—staffed by two volunteer psychiatrists. In the press headlines these doctors were dignified by being referred to as "alienists," though this was the first and possibly the last time they played such a role—if this is proper nomenclature for the task they performed.

These psychiatrists reported back that these were normal families which had produced these "boy killers," and that what had occurred on October 12 was an anomaly in the lives of these two—there was no discernable threat of such occurring again. They had been inspired by a western on TV about two boys who had run away from "mean" parents and had grown up living off of the land, shooting rabbits, and cooking them over a campfire. Neither of these two fifteen-year-olds had distinguished himself in any way—in scholarship, in athletics, in misbehaving, or otherwise.

Both of these psychiatrists postulated that there is in some children a perverse drive to be recognized—to be singled out for attention—and this was what we were encountering in these two.

Both of these specialists recommended that, for the benefit of other juveniles in the community that might be similarly driven, it would be best to keep the publicity of this event to a minimum.

Feeling the pressure of a whole community watching what I was doing, I proceeded to do some research about the law of juvenile crime. I learned that every organized civilization has an age at which a child is regarded as incapable of committing a "crime"—meaning that below this age, organized society imposes no formal punishment, leaving the discipline to parents and the displeasure and scorn of society as the only sanctions. In English common law it was seven years. And then there is an age at which it is "presumed" that the child is incapable of committing a "crime." In England that age was fourteen.

I talked to a rabbi as to the Jewish age of responsibility, who thought that generally the age of adult responsibility was thirteen. I learned that under France's Napoleonic Code, the age of responsibility was sixteen. I reviewed the origin of juvenile courts and found that the first juvenile court was formed in Chicago in 1899, to protect juveniles from the harshness of adult courts, and that the presumption of nonresponsibility was held for any child under eighteen years of age.

I had a vague notion that children in our culture mature less quickly than those who were raised in our historic past, when they were faced at earlier ages with more primitive dangers coupled with demands to contribute to the family welfare. I ended up thoroughly confused as to what I should do with these two just-turned-fifteen-year-olds.

So I proceeded to conduct separate juvenile court hearings, at which the families came in—one with its family lawyer, who took very little part in what occurred in the court. There were two almost identical reports by the investigating probation officers. There was a dialogue between me and each of the boys and their families.

I noted with disappointment that neither of the probation officer reports contained a recommendation for an order of disposition. Such a recommendation had been a significant part of all reports submitted to me by staff as a prelude to all previous hearings that I had conducted.

So I found myself squarely "on the hook" as to what to do.

Under unambiguous Arizona law, I had the responsibility of determining whether to "remand" these boys for prosecution as adults or to treat them as children. It may help to understand my dilemma to know that any killing of a human while in pursuit of a robbery is, by definition, first degree murder, and that first degree murder in Arizona carried a possible death penalty.

Both the morning and the evening daily Tucson newspapers favored me with a lead editorial advising me on what had to be done. The morning *Star's* editorial was entitled "Easygoing Justice in Pima County," and I was enlightened therein with these words as a final admonition:

> Much will depend upon what happens before weak judges, spineless juries and easy-going prosecutors. This time it cannot be blamed on the peace officers. They have done their duty; they have apprehended the killers. The time has come for juries, judges and prosecutors to administer justice in Pima County in such a just, firm, certain and speedy manner that it will serve as a deterrent.

The evening newspaper was also there to help with its editorial, entitled "Crime and Punishment," and quoted in its passionate context no less than Quisot of France [whose identity passed me by—perhaps the more learned of you will recognize the name] to the following effect:

> They [the welfare and social workers] forget constantly in this debate what is the aim of all punishment, of all penal legislation. It is not only to punish and repress the guilty, but to prevent the repetition of similar crimes.

This editorial ended with a categorical statement that this was *not* the time for a lenient juvenile commitment, but for prosecution as an adult so that the punishment could "fit the crime."

With all this help, I should have come to the right answer. And, I was trying—but perhaps confused. At the end of each of the two separate juvenile hearings, I ran for cover as far as the media were concerned. I took the decisions "under advisement"—a procedure often used in the adult court, but quite unfamiliar in the juvenile court.

Juvenile judges of the time just didn't take matters under advisement, for, after all, there were no lawyer-created legal conundrums to be solved; juvenile judges almost always ruled "from the bench" at the conclusion of a hearing. For the next two days I tossed various decisions around in my mind and discussed them with my bailiff—swearing him to secrecy as to my even consulting with him.

What should I do?

Remand both of these young men to the adult court for a murder prosecution (and thus satisfy the press)?

Or, remand the leader of the two (the brightest, who was the one who had come up with the ideas that got them in trouble) for adult prosecution for murder, and put the other boy on probation, or send this follower-killer to Fort Grant (the detention/training center for delinquents), or send them both to Fort Grant? Nothing seemed any better than any other.

Finally I came down with a written opinion—the longest that I ever wrote while acting as a juvenile judge, which, as quoted verbatim on the front page of both of our daily newspapers, read as follows: [with a few facts added in brackets and in italics, for your understanding of this cross fire situation in which I found myself]:

> The law provides than no child under the age of 18 years shall be charged with or convicted of a crime in any court, except where the juvenile court refuses to suspend prosecution. *[This was the law throughout the land at this time, except for variances in the cutoff age for juvenile offenders.]* There is no exception made in the

code as to the crime of murder. The proceedings before the juvenile court are in no sense criminal proceedings. The law provides that no adjudication by the juvenile court shall be deemed a conviction of crime *[and this also was the law of the land.]* Neither of these children to this date has been given a trial on any criminal charge.

The Court *[the "Court" was, of course, just me but this was no time to use the first tense when I suspected that this decision was going to be scurrilously attacked by the press]* is of the opinion that these boys determined on October 10, 1957, to run away from home together, intending to camp either in the Catalina Mountains or in the San Pedro Valley on the other side of the Catalina Mountains *[to get to the San Pedro Valley, these boys would have had to hike some forty miles over rough terrain—with nine-thousand-plus-feet-high-peaks to be circumvented]*, to live off of the land until they were of the age which would permit them to "join the Marines." Their plans for so doing were poorly conceived and showed poor judgment throughout. By the middle of the second day, they had run out of money and food *[these two "boy killers" had spent most of their cache of money on the first day renting horses at stables on the edge of town]*, and came to the conclusion they should stage a "hold up." The Court is of the belief that, though the two contemplated a robbery, no thought whatsoever was given as to what either should do in the event of resistance.

Both boys have consistently maintained that the rifle which killed Captain Westin was accidentally discharged when Captain Westin grabbed the gun and pulled it toward himself. The gun is a .22 caliber, English manufactured, bolt-action rifle. In placing a shell in the chamber, the gun is automatically cocked and cannot be relieved from this condition without firing the rifle, or removing the shell from the firing chamber. The gun will discharge when dropped to the floor from the height of 2 inches. *[This I knew from experimentation with the rifle in open court without a shell in the chamber. My attempted justification for what followed went on for another one hundred words, or so, but you get the idea.]*

* * *

Now, therefore, because the Court is not satisfied that the conduct of these two juveniles is beyond the scope of detention and correction as contemplated under the juvenile code,

IT IS ORDERED:

That juvenile _____[57] is hereby declared to be a delinquent child and is committed to the State Industrial School, until he reaches the age of 21 years, unless sooner discharged by the Board of Directors of State Institutions for Juveniles. The Court recommends that he be detained until his 21st birthday.

An identical order was entered for the other boy.

For several days the media excoriated my decision and me. There were several vituperative editorials and thirty or so letters to the editor by outraged citizens. It was pointed out that though my order required detention until the twenty-first birthday, *all* juveniles had historically been released by the controlling state board on their eighteenth birthday—*if* held that long. In fact, these two were subsequently released soon after their eighteenth birthdays without any further supervision imposed.

I did not attempt to defend myself with a futile letter to the editor in response.

Within a week the media let up and the Boy Killer Case was

---

57. I withhold the name here, in juvenile court tradition, because this "juvenile" is somewhere in our society, and I am hoping that this book will be published—very widely (as so all hopeful authors hope).

heard of no more. Though none of my juvenile staff had advised me to do what I did, by their respectful conduct, I sensed that they thought I had done the right thing. I recognized that this silent vote should be discounted, as the staff was notorious for its sympathies for our young ones.

To this day I am not sure that I did the right thing, but I have no regrets. And—whether it was keeping publicity down to a minimum, or whatever—during my next three years of tenure as a juvenile court judge we had nothing similar happen.

Looking back at the procedure employed, as far as the Fraternity is concerned, most clearly I did not do right, because I violated its sacred "due process" axiom—the most heinous of sins—as so declared in subsequent decisions of the Nine Priests. As I handled this case, these two had their sacred constitutional rights invaded because they were not told they had the right to remain silent when interrogated, and several lawyers were deprived of months, and probably years, of work in representing these two. My egregious sin was made apparent just ten years later, when the Nine Priests came down with *Application of Gault*.[58] More about this monstrous decision later.

Now, some forty years later and in the mood of looking back at the past, I talked with the mother of one of these boys as to how her son had fared. She informed me that he had never had another serious scrape with the law and that he had provided her with three fine grandchildren. Without a criminal record, he had honorably served a stint in our armed forces. She did not know what had happened to the other boy involved in this tragedy. His name was and is not listed in Tucson directories.

My retrospective evaluation is that the *Gault*-destroyed juvenile courts of old—while they did not succeed in keeping all offending youngsters from being perpetually out of the clutches of the police—succeeded in making a change for the better many-fold more often than the lawyer-dominated "adult" courts of to-

---

58. 387 U.S. 1 (May 1967).

day. That now-outlawed, "nonpunitive," but powerfully interfering system of the pre-*Gault* juvenile courts worked splendidly, as much for its basic philosophy as for its short response time. And, we should note that short response times are nonexistent in the lawyer-dominated courts of today.

Perhaps I should give you another example of how the old system worked, which stands out in my memory, but which in itself proves absolutely nothing.

This is the case of a tall brunette—a very attractive prostitute to whom I had just declared that I was giving custody of her two small children to their father. I was sitting at my desk/bench when I made this announcement.

In response, an enraged mother rose up from her front-row, classroomlike seat and glowered down at me from an awesome height. She leaned forward and, as she did so, placed both hands with long artificial nails, painted bloodred, on her abdomen, and screamed: "You can't take them away from me. You can't take them away from me. I had them, I HAD them, right HERE!" as she tapped her claws on her belly. Then, as she lunged at me to use those bloody-red fangs on my face, a probation officer grabbed her and I proceeded promptly out of the room by the nearest exit.

A few days later I received a call at my home at about ten o'clock at night. It was a muffled female voice that said: "I'm going to kill you." That is the only threat I ever received while acting as judge; I did not report it to the police. Nor did I have to dodge any bullets, neither then nor at any other time during these seven years when I was passing out what I considered to be trial-court justice to various disturbed individuals. And there were no police at the entrances to our courthouse, as is the situation today, with all carried-packages put through an x-ray machine. I can only surmise that there have been actual attacks on some judges, about which I have no cognizance, or perhaps it is just that the judges of today have acquired infinitely more value to the public to merit such expense.

But, back to the time when I was serving as the autocrat over Pima County juveniles. At the same time that I was learning how to be a juvenile court judge, I also acted as a trial judge in the kinds of trials I had participated in as a lawyer and was comparing the two systems. I found that I had much less responsibility in the "adult" court, and that it was much more relaxing—approaching fun—sitting up high on my bench, calling the balls and strikes as my fellow lawyers played their games below me.

When I presided at a jury trial, I seldom had to be concerned with finding out what the truth really was—I just had to sit there, pay attention to what legal problems the lawyers presented, and then rule. It did require listening, carefully, as to whether the proper objection was made—"improper" objections don't count— this is the rule in the courts of this land. And, of course, this makes it extremely important that, when you select your lawyer for your next contested court case, you get yourself a lawyer with very good hearing, an in-depth education as to what the proper objection is—among the infinite number of objections—and, above all else, a lawyer with a fast reaction time, because if your lawyer doesn't object before the next question is asked, with the proper objection, well, too bad.

Eight months after becoming a judge, in June of the next year, I had to learn how I felt about capital punishment—something I had never thought very much about.

We four Pima County trial judges alternated in administering the court system. Every six months, one of us was the "assignment judge." Whoever had this duty took all of the court work except the actual presiding at trials. This meant that, while the other three were trying contested cases, this judge heard and ruled upon civil and criminal motions in all cases, sat as the probate judge, entered temporary restraining orders, conducted mental health hearings, entered default judgments, accepted guilty pleas in criminal cases, imposed sentences on those who pled guilty and, generally, handled whatever came up in the way of judicial work, except the actual contested trials themselves.

It was a very efficient system for handling a busy trial calendar. With this system, we avoided empty courtrooms when cases settled at the last hour—as they very often do. When this happened, we routinely had another case waiting to be tried to keep that judge occupied. And, as mentioned, courts were open for business Monday through Friday and a half day on Saturday.

You will not find that courtrooms of today are occupied as much. Perhaps the judges of today, being more intelligent and more capable, don't need to take so long to get the job done—perhaps.

The most awesome duty of the "assignment judge" was to impose sentences upon defendants who pleaded guilty to criminal charges—"throwing themselves on the mercy of the court," as the saying goes. So, with this venerable system in place, in June 1958, I had my first stint as assignment judge, and it was then that I had to decide what to do with a cold-blooded murderer.

A first-degree murder charge had been filed against a Robert Fenton—a young (twenty-five-year-old) Caucasian male. At his arraignment before my predecessor assignment judge, Fenton had professed not to have enough funds to employ a lawyer, and two of our leading lawyers had been appointed to defend him—one was Robert Lesher, a trial lawyer well-recognized for his talents who had served a stint on the Supreme Court of our state, and the other was Alan Hanshaw, an experienced trial lawyer at the peak of his career. The county attorney was seeking the death penalty.

Two days before Robert Fenton's trial was set to commence before a jury, his lawyers informed me that he was electing to enter a guilty plea to the charge of first-degree murder. This meant that I, as the assignment judge on duty, had the responsibility of imposing an appropriate sentence. That the case would be assigned to me for this duty was, of course, well-known to the defense team.

The presentence report prepared by the court's probation officers revealed that, on being arrested, Fenton had given a complete confession. He had put eight bullet holes in the head and body of Mrs. Opal Coward, a lady who, with her husband, had taken him into their home when he appeared homeless at their door. A month or so after enjoying this hospitality, Fenton, with gun in hand, demanded of Mrs. Coward that she give him $200 as a "loan." Opal only had $40 on hand and offered it to Fenton which he accepted, and thereupon killed her. He took the $40 and headed south in the Coward family car. He was apprehended by police halfway to Mexico.

If Fenton had killed just eight years later, no knowledgeable criminal lawyer would have allowed him to plead guilty to murder, for the decision of *Miranda v. Arizona*[59] was then to be rendered by the Nine Priests, to make the solution of crime in this country infinitely more difficult. Miranda had been convicted of the kidnapping and forceful rape of an eighteen-year-old woman, and the conviction was overturned because an impressive litany of defendant's rights—*devised by Justice Warren in this very opinion*—had not been read to Miranda before he had confessed.

Both in *Miranda* and in my *Fenton* case, there had been no "reading of rights" because *they simply didn't exist* until Chief Justice Warren and his colleagues thus invented them.

When Fenton came before me pre-*Miranda*, with both of his counsel present plus a full courtroom of press, he entered a plea of guilty to first-degree murder. Whereupon, I ordered that the time for sentencing would be in two weeks. As he then stood before me with an armed sheriff's deputy close by, Fenton appeared to be a handsome, blond, blue-eyed, six-foot tall, slim and athletic young man. His only apparent unusual feature was his smile, which was there during most of the time he stood to make his guilty plea—it was a twisted, quirky smile, definitely not congenial.

Under the law, I had the choice of imposing either imprisonment, up to "life," or the death penalty. There were no guidelines in our law, nor in our practice, as to when a death sentence should

---

59. 384 U.S. 436 (June 13, 1966).

60. The law has evolved and convulsed since Fenton came before me. Subsequent Revelations from on High have made the imposition of the death sentence a legal quagmire. See *Ring v. Arizona*, 122 S. Ct. 2428, (June 24, 2002) with its four concurring, and one dissenting, opinions. The one dissent is by Justice O'Connor—among the very few of these semigods who ever sat on a trial bench.

be imposed.[60] "Life"—the alternative sentence—did not mean, historically, incarceration for the actual life of the defendant. Because of the functioning of the parole board, the average residence in prison for a "lifer" at that time in our state was about seven and one-half years.

I appointed two of our best local psychiatrists to evaluate Fenton—Dr. Charles Neumann and Dr. J. K. Bennett. Then I sought refuge by consulting with each of my three fellow judges.

I learned that none of the three would impose a death sentence. Their reasons for making this hypothetical decision ranged from total opposition to the death penalty—in the case of one of my fellow judges—to the fact that Fenton had pled guilty and had thus saved the state the expense of a trial, as to my other two brethren.

The probation report—the report from the probation officer assigned the duty of interviewing the defendant and reporting to the sentencing judge the facts of the crime—was lengthy, but, dismally, for my peace of mind, contained nothing in the way of recommendation as to a life or a death sentence. This report concurred with the evaluations rendered by the two court-appointed psychiatrists: Fenton was a psychopath, a person without a conscience, and would probably remain so for the rest of his life.

The night before sentencing, well into a sleep-poor night, I felt a deep-down emotion. The firm conviction came over me: those who kill, in the cold-blooded fashion such as this man had done, should die, damn them. I could feel anger welling up within me. The next morning I heard myself pronouncing these words in open court:

> He has injured the people who have been kind to him....
> He is dangerous. I have talked to Dr. Bennett who also
> examined this man and his opinion is the same as Dr.
> Neumann's, that he is a psychopath—a sociopath; he is
> amoral and has no conscience whatsoever and, that, at
> the present time, there is no cure for him; ...for the rea-
> sons I have stated I am choosing the death penalty.

I then directed the sheriff's deputy to bring the prisoner immediately in front of the bench. I looked Bobby Fenton full in the eye and said:

> Robert Fenton, I hereby commit you to the custody of the Warden of the State Prison and order that on August 15, 1958, you be put to death in the manner prescribed by law.

The above quotes are from the *Arizona Daily Star* of June 21, 1958. According to our local newspaper, my voice trembled, "choked with emotion." As I was laboring emotionally, Fenton had a cynical smile on his face. He said absolutely nothing.

Dismally, I was so nervous that I goofed as to the timing of the date of the execution. After adjourning court, my bailiff, Teddy Heyl, a retired lawyer, excitedly came to me with a statute book in hand: "Judge, you've set execution too soon! The statute says you've got to allow sixty days for an appeal between a death sentence and an execution."

I proceeded to read it, for the fourth time. He was right! I groaned. "Bring him back in." Fenton was brought back from the jail by the deputy sheriff. His shackles were again removed so that he could stand before the bench without them. The cynical smile was still there. I repeated the magic words that were to take this man's life, but with an August 22nd instead of August 15th date. The press reported that Fenton still appeared in good humor and quoted him as saying after the adjournment of court, " 'I thought they were bringing me back to give me another pill,' he quipped, referring to the cyanide pellets used in Arizona's gas chamber at Florence."

Fenton's lawyers appealed this sentence to the Arizona Supreme Court, which, after granting a delay in execution, found no error.[61] I am glad that I never had to make this decision again.

In the mail on the day after cyanide pellets terminated

---

61. 86 Ariz. 111, 341 P.2d 237 (1959).

Fenton's life, I received two letters—one was a handwritten letter from Fenton, from his death row cell, in which he complimented me for my fairness, and said he would have done the same had he been in my place. I was pleased to get his missive, but then came the distasteful thought—that Fenton, the psychopath, would have "done the same" might be considered less than a compliment.

The other letter was from Mr. Roy Coward:

> Opal and I have been very close. Life will be dismal without her. Your sentence will restore none of what we had, it will not bring her back, but it cures the terrible hate I would have if Fenton were to live in a prison, at public expense, with me contributing part of the taxes to keep him, and maybe run into him on the street seven or eight years from now. I thank you from the bottom of my heart.

We have already looked at how Fenton would have been so much better off—most probably escaping even a murder conviction under *Miranda*'s rule, if he had waited just eight years to do his work. And, if he had waited fourteen years to do his killing, he *certainly* would have escaped the death penalty, for, despite the fact that the colonies, and thereafter most of the states, had for these several centuries vested a discretionary power in trial judges to impose the death sentence in first-degree murder cases, the Nine Priests discovered in 1972, in *Furman v. Georgia*,[62] that the Founding Fathers had prohibited any law that would allow a judge, in his discretion, as I had done, to impose a death penalty.

Any law permitting this is, according to Justice Douglas, "pregnant with discrimination."[63] Another of the Ordained Nine, concurring in the Douglas opinion, thought the death

---

62. *Furman v. Georgia*, 408 U. S. 238 (1972).

63. 408 U.S. at 257.

penalty itself should be completely outlawed as "cruel and unusual punishment."

What the law might be today, after *Furman*, is still unclear, even after its 232 pages of judicial philosophizing—with five separate opinions needed to constitute the one majority ruling—each opinion disagreeing from the others as to why what they were doing was required by our Constitution. The four dissenting opinions only contribute to the lack of clarity as to the why, but not as to the certainty, that the Arizona law was unconstitutional. *Furman's* four cogent dissents, pointing out the fundamental law that would permit judicial discretion in the imposing of a death sentence, are never referred to again by the Powerful Ones in their later majority opinions. Such expressions as given by these dissenters have become mere wailings in the winds generated by the Holy Court.

The bottom line is, if this *Furman* decision had been on the books when Fenton came up in my court for sentence, I would have been saved some soul-searching, and he would either be caged up like an animal at government expense, or, much more likely, would long since have been out in some community practicing his ways, whatever they might be.

Since *Furman* there have been a multitude of death-sentence appeals to the Nine Priests, and for every death sentence imposed, there is much lawyer-work in attempting to get an appellate court to set the sentence aside because it does not meet the nebulous standards of *Furman*, and years—yes, years upon years—go by in the process,[64] with the accused penned up like an animal while lawyers draw their fees. And this very delay, and the lawyers'

---

64. H. Mitchell, *The death penalty: An overview* (Greenhaven Press, 2001); at p. 36 (hereafter "Mitchell") we find the following: "Between 1973 and 1992, a total of 4,704 convicted murderers were sentenced to death, but only 188 of them, or 4 percent, were executed.... The average time between sentencing and execution was 114 months, or nine and a half years." A law review article of the 2001 vintage states that the average time between sentence and execution, if any actually occurs, has risen to twelve years. 67 *Brooklyn Law Rev.* 411, 422 (Winter 2001).

fees paid, are used by revisionists to argue that the death penalty should never be imposed.[65]

Fenton was executed in the gas chamber on July 25, 1959, for a murder committed eighteen months before, a delay well beyond the necessary time between killing and punishment—there were no abstruse factual or legal questions to be solved. But, in the arena which the Fraternity has created, the legalistic gyrations before a death penalty can be imposed are now invariably much, much more protracted.

As I write this, death penalties, which had been abjured by our nation's courts for decades, have come back into vogue just a bit, but the time between sentence and execution is always in excess of five years and often exceeds ten years, during which time judges are "agonizing" and lawyers are arguing, charging by the minute, with the bill usually paid by tax money.

I have not lost sleep over my *Fenton* decision—perhaps I was/am cruel and depraved. I recite it to you here, not to convince you of either my depravity or righteousness, but to point out the tremendous difference in governmental costs, mostly going to members of the Fraternity, now imposed by the extensive pontificating on the death penalty coming down from the Marbled Halls in Washington.

On a less morbid plane, looking back on my judging in the adult court, I think of the case of *Esquivel v. Southern Pacific,* which we will refer to as the Goose Pimples Case. There, I demonstrated how a dedicated plaintiffs' lawyer can turn against his Brethren after becoming a judge.

Esquivel was a railroad employee who, when passenger trains came into the Tucson depot, had the job of crawling under the cars and checking the brakes ("hot boxes") of the train cars for

---

65. See Mitchell, at p. 2: "Even the cost of trying and executing a single person is enormous. In Florida, the average cost is $3.2 million." See also Stuart Banner, *The Death Penalty: An American History* (Harvard University Press, 2002); and Lifton and Mitchell, *Who owns death? Capital punishment, the American conscience, and the end of execution* (William Morrow, 2000).

overheating. One day while he was doing this duty, the engineer mistakenly started the train!

When this happened, Esquivel hung on to a rod under the train, and was dragged about seventy yards before the train stopped. If he had *not* held on, he would have been mangled by various equipment hanging down under the cars. When the train stopped, Esquivel crawled out from under the car, stood up, and then proceeded to faint—out cold on the sidewalk.

Thereafter, whenever he came near a passenger railroad car, he was intensely afraid and got goose pimples. The same—goose pimples—occurred occasionally when he took a shower in his own bathroom. Esquivel absolutely refused to go back to work and never worked again.

The firm of Magaña and Olney, a Los Angeles firm, with a reputation of many successes in this area of personal injury liability, garnered Esquivel's case. This firm had several excellent expert witnesses in its arsenal. One was a female psychiatrist who had testified for the plaintiff's lawyer, Dan Olney, in previous trials. At this jury trial, with me presiding, they demonstrated magnificent teamwork to collect money for fainting spells and goose pimples:

> *Olney:* "Did you say, Doctor, that this is a problem with the autonomic nervous system?"
> *Doctor:* "Yes. It is the system that controls all of your nerve functions that are not voluntary. We are talking about sweating, hiccoughing, goose pimples, breathing while asleep, the heart beating, and so on."
> *Olney:* "Could this be likened to a thermostat in a heating/cooling system in your home?" [With a look of speculative inquiry.]
> *Doctor:* "That is an excellent analogy—a thermostat— yes, YES." [Nodding of head in surprised agreement.]
> *Olney:* And what has happened to Mr. Esquivel's thermostat? [With a look of being afraid of what he is

about to hear.]

Doctor: It has been destroyed. [In a doomsday voice.]

Olney: "Destroyed?" [Showing puzzlement/amazement.]

Doctor: "Yes, DESTROYED."

Olney: "Is there any way to replace it?"

Doctor: "Absolutely none." [With a sad shake of her head.]

Olney: "So, Mr. Esquivel must live the rest of his life with these problems that prevent him from working and enjoying life." [Perplexed and agitated.]

Doctor: Precisely. [Cold and professional.]

As he testified at trial, Esquivel had less than full motivation to work. He had seniority enough to have a full pension for life from his employer, Southern Pacific Company; his accident had brought him no medical expenses because his employer had provided, and was still providing, medical care with its medical staff and its hospitals.

Esquivel's record of his medical treatment was sufficiently extensive so that it was five to six inches thick. Lawyer Olney had the entire record in the courtroom, which he dramatically picked up and laid down feverishly, for the jury's benefit during his impassioned final argument.

Defense counsel was Richard Evans, an excellent trial lawyer, having fought his way up to be *the* trial lawyer for the largest defense firm in town, but he was no match for Olney on this occasion. The jury came in with a verdict of $68,800 (PV04 $425,595), which, according to the morning paper, was "the largest damage award of 1957 for local courts." Now such a modest award would hardly make the press.

The Southern Pacific filed a motion for new trial, contending among other things that the verdict was excessive, whereupon yours truly—the plaintiffs' counsel turned judge—mercilessly granted a remittitur (a reduction) of $20,000 (PV04: $123,685), leaving plaintiff with a judgment of $48,800 (PV04: $301,790).

The constitutional right to a jury trial requires that such an order must be in the alternative—either the plaintiff had to accept this reduction, or my order advised Olney, plaintiff's counsel, that there would be a new trial granted. Olney grabbed the lesser amount, and this was the end of the Goose Pimples Case.

Trial judges of today have this same power to reduce verdicts, but they very, very seldom do so. After all, would they like it if they had worked hard as a lawyer to convince a jury to bring in such a nice verdict, and then have a fellow member of the Fraternity take it away? If judges are mere umpires at a game—and, of course, that is what judges of today are expected to be—they should not play the game of deciding what is right in the way of damage verdicts.

I received no accolades from my Brethren for my order in the Goose Pimples Case, and perhaps none from you, my readers. But again, I have not lost sleep over deciding as I did. The feeling that I may have slowed down just a mite the ominous ballooning of the litigation industry, at least in my part of the world, soothes my conscience.

During the first three and a half years of my tenure on the bench, I continued to serve as the juvenile judge and found that duty to be engrossing, but sleep-depriving. Despite the fact that the adult system was proving that it had no solution to the problem of growing crime and that juvenile courts were doing an effective job, the juvenile court system would very soon be taken into oblivion with the religious dogma of the Fraternity. The problems constantly coming into focus were the unwanted pregnancies, which never seemed to stop—always to produce offspring giving social problems—larceny, rape, and worse. It was not the duty that I could deal with permanently. So in January 1961, I turned the court over to my newly elected fellow judge, Raul Castro, a twelfth child of the Castro family of Agua Prieta, Mexico—a former professional boxer and a person I felt certain would understand family and delinquency problems.

The very nature of the work of juvenile judge meant that

Judge Castro would receive more than his share of front-page/ news-hour coverage, and this he got, and that contributed to his later illustrious political career. Raul H. Castro was to serve as the governor of our state and as U.S. ambassador, successively, to Ecuador, San Salvador, and Argentina.

During these years of being a juvenile judge, things were quiescent on the big scene being painted by the All-Powerful Nine. But big debris was about to hit the fan. We are coming to the Egregious Eight years of metamorphosis in the legal system of this country, to be mandated by the Nine, ruling from above.

This awful period started as I was serving as a trial judge—not that I thought it was awful as it was happening. To the contrary, as a loyal member of the Fraternity, I took it as Gospel coming from above and was appreciative of the wonderful things it was doing for my profession. Some of it surprised me, yes, but rebel against it—of course not! Subordinate priests do not question explanations of religion coming from High Priests, especially when what they say is making us, of the Fraternity, much more important and much, much wealthier.

CHAPTER SIX

Trial Bench—Serving as the Umpire
1961–1964

After separating myself from the emotional problems of children and families that saturated the juvenile court scene, I concentrated on calling balls and strikes in the adult court as the lawyers played their games. It was exceedingly more relaxing. And, during my tour on the trial bench, the duties were extremely less complicated than those which are now imposed upon the trial judges of this land by the subsequent revelations of Gospel from the Nine Gods in Washington.

It was routine in our trial court of yesteryear, on "law and motion day"—almost invariably on Monday morning starting at 8:30 and usually terminating before the noon recess—to "take" somewhere around six "guilty" pleas to felony charges, to set trial dates for another six or so criminal defendants who had pled "not guilty" to various felony charges, to sentence to prison, or whatever, the six or so who had pled guilty the week before, and to hear, and usually decide from the bench, arguments on motions for "more definite statement" of criminal charges and the like. Then there was usually time left over at these Monday sessions to complete a calendar of motions in civil cases.

Efficient? Fair? Everyone seemed to think so, even the most ardent of our defense bar. But this was not to last. Really big things were about to happen to our legal system to make vast amounts of more lawyering absolutely necessary.

The first blockbuster in the "Egregious Eight years" came to clobber up trial court calendars in the form of the Nine All-Seeing Ones' decision of *Mapp v. Ohio*.[66] It was rendered on June 19, 1961. As this decision permeated the courts of this land, the pursuit of truth in all of our criminal courts became increasingly more technical and complex, and a clever lawyer's services more important.

The *Mapp* decision injected into the fundamental law of every state the mandate that all evidence not properly acquired—properly acquired as determined by the High Court—regardless of its verity, must be ignored in determining who has committed a crime. Until then, it had been considered by the vast majority of our state courts (the federal courts had been taken over with this inanity decades before by the *Weeks* decision) to be more important to expose and punish criminal acts, and to discipline over-zealous policemen by other means—as by permitting damages to be recovered against such.

Previous to *Mapp*, the highest courts of our states had overwhelmingly rejected the federal rule of exclusion—adopted in Daddy's day only for the federal courts by the *Weeks* decision.[67] The states' view rejecting this approach was, as you will remember, articulated by Judge Benjamin Cardozo when he sat on New York's highest court, in this scornful language: "The criminal is to go free because the constable has blundered."[68]

However, Cardozo's attitude had little support within the Fraternity. The Brethren hungered to take power from police officers and bestow it on themselves. After all, one can develop a

---

66. 367 U.S. 643 (1961).

67. *Weeks v. U.S.*, 232 U.S. 383 (1914).

68. *People v. Defore*, 150 N.E. 585 (1926), Justice Cardozo.

real dislike for police officers after one has been pulled over and ticketed a time or two. And what can give one a sense of importance any more than blocking a murder conviction by a neatly stated objection?

After *Mapp*, all of our state trial judges had to do what common sense told them was not in the public interest—turn criminals loose because of policemen's errors. We can speculate that Cardozo might have diverted this inane decision if he had still been on the High Court at the time, for he was a great persuader. But this great judge—trial and appellate—had died suddenly in 1938, and Felix Frankfurter, another lawyer who had never been on a trial bench, had taken his place on the Infallible Court.

And, while all this was going on at this highest of levels, I had to retain my judging job at the voting booths. This time I was challenged by a well-liked, experienced trial attorney. I put a one-day, quarter page ad in the local papers, extolling my virtues, with a carefully selected photograph to go with it. My challenging opponent did more, and leaned a bit on my "foolish" decision in the Boy Killer Case, but, nevertheless, virtue prevailed, as I like to regard it, and I was reelected.

So, I focused on presiding at trials, both civil and criminal, and came to miss the relative simplicity of the juvenile court system. In adult court, it just took so much more time and effort, on the part of lawyers and court staff, to accomplish anything.

These were the days when our criminal court system was moving steadily away from the jury-trying of cases to the process of plea bargaining almost all cases. But such bargaining as was going on, at least through December 1964—when I left the trial bench to write appellate opinions—was limited to the negotiations between the prosecuting and defense lawyers. Our trial judges did not participate in that bargaining. At least in my part of the country, it was not considered ethical to induce a plea of guilt with a promise of a lenient sentence, and certainly not to induce one person to testify against another by promises of a light sentence or an acquittal, coupled with threats of a long prison term if the person refused to testify against an accomplice. Such, in the courts that I presided over, would have been considered disgustingly perverse to an honest pursuit of the truth.

But, alas, these are the practices that prevail in the criminal trial courts of this country today. Since these incepting days of plea bargaining, the practice has grown until it controls that which occurs in our criminal courts. Today, over 90 percent of criminal charges brought are settled by the prosecutor "overcharging" the defendant, and then letting the coerced defendant "cop" a plea.[69]

My own life in these fecund days, when I was not the "assignment judge," was that of presiding over one contested trial after another. In this process, I came to the clear realization that it was the *skill of the trial lawyer* that, almost always, determined the outcome of a case. As an illustration, I give you two personal injury cases tried in my court, just months apart, one tried by a sterling defense attorney and the other by an outstanding plaintiff's lawyer. Both cases involved accident-paralyzed plaintiffs.

The first crippled plaintiff was the victim of an "office party" at Kingsley's Ranch, a restaurant/bar located halfway to the Mexican border from Tucson, Arizona. There was a swimming pool and copious amounts of beer were provided—for a price—by the host restaurant. Riley was a young man of about thirty-five years, a supervisor in a small business, who came to this restaurant/pool as an invited guest—a part of this annual office party.

The swimming pool was the centerpiece of this convivial gathering. It had been "home-designed" and built by the owner, without benefit of an architect or any past experience on the owner's part in pool-building.

Next to where the party was centered, arising out of the water, was a cement fountain, about five feet in diameter. It was only a

---

69. The U.S. Bureau of Justice Statistics, Criminal Case Processing Statistics, reports that in the year 2000, 95 percent of all criminal convictions in the U.S. that occurred within one year of filing were by a guilty plea. These figures are found on the internet at <http://www.ojp.usdoj.gov/bjs/cases.htm>; and see P*lea Bargaining's Triumph*, 109 Yale Law Journal 857 (March 2000).

foot or so above the water, and from it the pool was replenished with water. This structure had absolutely no lights—as a matter of fact, there were no underwater lights of any kind in the waters of the entire pool. Lights around the pool overhead were dimmed, so that the swimmer-drinkers could enjoy the party.

Sooner or later—with office parties going on night after night around this pool, with liquor being served—someone would do what Riley did. He dived in and collided head-on with the structure. He was forthwith paralyzed from the neck down—C-4 and C-5 fractured. His spinal cord was mangled to the extent that he would never again move a muscle below his shoulders.

The plaintiff's counsel, Pete Somers, an experienced and competent plaintiff's counsel—but not at an inspirational level for this case—presented evidence by experts that this pool, as it was built, was dangerous, without lights, and without proper planning.

Charles McCarty, a colleague of my college days, was defending. In years before, he and I had been on opposite sides of many arguments—first in philosophy classes, then in law school, and then in the courtroom. Charlie was small in stature, wiry, and an inexhaustible dynamo of energy. When he was "on," Charles was superb, and he was very definitely "on" for this Riley case.

Charlie started out when the jury was being qualified *(voir dired)* by asking penetrating questions of each prospective juror. He cleverly managed to get a commitment from each to follow a jury instruction that he was assuming that I, as the judge, would give to the jury at the conclusion of the evidence—a "stock" instruction of that time. Charlie, during the course of his questioning of the prospective jurors, asked each of them if they would accept and apply:

> If you find that the plaintiff's conduct fell below the standard of care of an ordinarily prudent person, and that this conduct was *one* of the proximate causes of plaintiff's injury, then the plaintiff is *not* entitled to recover and it is your *duty* to find for the defendants and against the plaintiff in this action.

There was no objection from Somers (the instruction was given in all such cases in our part of the world at that time) and each juror responded to Charlie's question that, "yes", they would. In his closing argument, after all of the evidence was in, Charlie harkened back to the *voir dire* examination, reminding the jurors of their oaths. His eye contacts were like multiple radar beams, penetrating into the conscience of each juror. Charlie did not address the subjects of the horrible human suffering caused by this misdesigned pool, nor the very substantial medical bills caused to the crippled man at the plaintiff's table, nor this family's loss of its wage-earner, about which his opponent had just waxed eloquent. Rather, such considerations were totally scorned as being unworthy of comment.

Instead, Charlie talked about the one instruction on contributory negligence and demanded, yes, demanded of this jury that it render a defense verdict, and this he got. The jury was out thirty minutes.

The other paralyzed plaintiff had for his lawyer the great persuader Morris K. Udall, who would later come close to being elected the president of the United States.[70] The case involved a young man named Godare, who had crashed his motorcycle and broken his back. He had gone to Nogales, Mexico, where he could buy brandy for less than in Tucson.

Going to Nogales, Godare had taken a dirt road going south out of Tucson, which street signs said it was Alvernon Way. A mile to the north of where this accident occurred, Alvernon was a major section-line street. But in the area where Godare rode, it was not a public street but a road on private land—private land purchased recently by Hughes Tool Company, the then-largest employer in this part of the world.

This dirt road, which continued on from where the dedicated public street left off, had been used for so many years as a road by the public that county personnel had mistakenly put up street signs to show this as Alvernon Way—the same name as the

---

70. He was beaten out in a close contest for the Democratic nomination by Georgia's Jimmy Carter.

legitimate public road to the north to which it connected.

At the time of Godare's brandy-purchasing trip, this road had been eroded by storm runoff from the east, coming through culverts recently built under a newly constructed north-south traffic artery—Palo Verde Boulevard. Erosion had caused sloughing off of the packed dirt of spurious "Alvernon" into gullies that were as much as four and a half feet in depth. None of these gullies had as yet gone clear across the road, so that when cycling *to* Nogales, Godare steered around these gullies without trouble.

Coming back with his brandy at dusk, Godare had considerable trouble with one of these washouts. Though there was still plenty of room to ride on packed dirt to the side, he rode his cycle into the deepest gully and then lay at the bottom of it with a broken back involving a severed spinal cord, and a broken bottle of fine brandy.

At the time of trial Godare was in a wheelchair, a paraplegic with no sensation or motor control below the waist and using urine and feces sacks. He was a good-looking, adventuresome young man who had all but destroyed himself.

Mo Udall, as Godare's lawyer, had sued everyone in sight— meaning Hughes Tool Company (owner of the washed-out road), San Xavier Rock and Sand (the contractor that built the new Palo Verde Boulevard, with its culverts for rainwater), and Pima County (which had placed the Alvernon Way signs on this private road without culverts).

In the middle of the trial of this case, Udall, without warning, called to the witness stand, from his seat at the defendants' table, Edward Earl, president of the building contractor that was constructing new Palo Verde. Only an extremely adept and confident trial lawyer would have the nerve to call an adverse witness as obviously intelligent and sophisticated as this president of a leading construction company without any prior knowledge of what that witness might say.[71]

---

71. No deposition of this witness had been taken in advance of trial—pretrial depositions were fairly common at this time, but not as all-encompassing as in today's practice.

Udall then proceeded to cross-examine him before the jury in this fashion:

> *Udall:* "Now, Mr. Earl, you knew, did you not, that the road you were constructing would gather the sheet flow from the desert to the east and channel it into these new culverts that you constructed."
>
> *Mr. Earl:* "I suppose so." [*Mistake! As far as jury-appeal is concerned, if you have to admit something, be very careful as to what that something might be, but, when admitting, be open and frank about it.*]
>
> *Udall:* "And you knew that Alvernon to the west was only a dirt road that had no proper bed for the road?"
>
> *Earl:* "I suppose so."
>
> *Udall:* "And you knew, without any doubt, that sooner or later it would rain?"
>
> *Earl:* "Rain?—I suppose so."
>
> *Udall:* "And you knew, without any doubt, that when it rained, this road which you built, with its culverts, would direct this rainwater into arroyos [*an "arroyo" is southwestern Spanish for a waterway that is normally dry, but which can be a raging torrent when it rains*] which were pointed directly at old Alvernon Way?"
>
> *Earl:* "I suppose so."
>
> *Udall:* "Well, you knew very well that it *would* didn't you?"
>
> *Earl:* "We-e-ll,—I suppose so."
>
> *Udall:* "And, from the natural flow of water, and the manner of the construction of Alvernon Way, it was inevitable that there would be dropoffs in the road such as the one that Godare fell into. *Right?*"
>
> *Earl:* "Inevitable??"
>
> *Udall:* "Yes, *in-evitable.*"
>
> *Earl:* "Well..., I suppose so."
>
> *Udall:* "And wasn't it also *inevitable* that sooner or later

someone would be coming down that road at dusk, or
at night, and fail to notice the dropoff?"
Earl: "Inevitable?"
Udall: "Yes, sooner or later an unmarked, unlighted
dropoff like this one would not be noticed by a traveler."
Earl: "Well, I think that most *every*one would see it."
Udall: "Yes, but *sooner or later,* on a traveled road like
this, at dusk, *someone* would *not* notice it, *right?*"
Earl: "Maybe, may-be so."
Udall: "Thank you, Mr. Earl.I have no further ques-
tions of this witness."

Closing arguments pitted Richard Briney, a very competent defense lawyer hired regularly by the most knowledgeable of insurance
companies, against the magnificent persuader, Morris Udall.

Briney got the very same contributory negligence instruction
as McCarty had received in the *Ryan* case. Udall had first and last
arguments, and this was the undoing of Briney, together with the
inimitable persuasive skills of Udall.

Obviously glorying in his opportunity to have the last words
with this jury, Udall cleverly used another burden of proof jury
instruction given by me—always given in cases such as this when
there is any possibility that the plaintiff was negligent. The instruction was: "The burden of proof as to contributory negligence of the
plaintiff is upon the defendant." Udall built his closing argument
on liability, after Briney had sat down, around this one instruction.

Udall held up to the jury a photo of himself, taken after the
accident, standing in the gully into which Godare had plunged, to
demonstrate the depth of the dropoff—only the above-belt-line
part of the gawkingly tall Udall was visible. As he talked, Udall
was "in" the jury box (figuratively) and catching the eyes of one
juror after another:

> This whole law of negligence—what is it all about?
> Isn't it to protect people from injury? Weren't we try-

ing to protect young fellows like Godare here [pointing to his client who sat stoic in his wheelchair] when this law was crafted? Of course, if we were passing out grades, from a "1" to a "5" on those whom we want to protect from injury, we wouldn't give Godare a "1," but wouldn't we give this young man at least a "3"? What young man worth his salt doesn't do some adventuresome thing such as he did on this evening? Sooner or later, someone like Godare was going to go into that hole. *Are we going to give license to the crippling of all the "3s" and "4s" in our country?* [Long pause]

Mr. Earl knew that sooner or later, yes, sooner or later—you heard him say it—someone would do what Godare did. You heard Mr. Earl on the stand. Just think how easy it would have been for him to fill in those gullies. Would it have taken one of his "blades" as much as an hour? To fill in those traps to the travelers he knew, sooner or later, were going to use that road at dusk? …the most dangerous time?

And, where is the evidence that Godare had fallen below the average young American man standard?

Judge Molloy will tell you that it is the *defendants* that have the *burden* to come forward with the *evidence* to convince you that the plaintiff is unworthy to recover damages. Mr. Briney has told you that Godare had been drinking and that that is the reason he didn't see this hole in the road in the dusk. But where is the evidence that Godare had been drinking? Mr. Briney didn't show you any. Sure, my client had a brandy bottle on him, but where is the broken bottle? It's not in *this* court.

The cap would have told you that Godare is telling us the truth when he testified that the bottle had never been opened. Surely, someone retrieved the pieces, because when I got out in the gulley, two weeks later, I found the broken brandy bottle, but there was no neck and cap of that bottle there, which would have shown it had never been opened. We have only Godare's sworn testimony that he had not drunk a drop of the brandy and was cold sober when this tragic accident struck him. So under Judge Molloy's instruction, you've got to give this young man in front of you the benefit of the doubt, because his sworn word is *all you have.*

As Udall talked, an ugly thought came to mind. Did Udall, when he was out there having his picture taken, standing in the bottom of the arroyo, find the neck of the bottle and dispose of it? Did jurors have the same question? If so, we all answered the question with a resounding "no," because of this man's personality. Deceit just didn't fit this man of pioneer Mormon parents. This is what carried him to the pinnacle of political success—his warm sincerity giving the lie to any accusations of deceit.

Udall was in his glory when he got on the subject of Godare's damage. In those times, contrary to what we now have, there were no standard jury instructions, devised by a committee of the Fraternity, to fatten verdicts—which now goes through a litany of possibilities of hurt, suffering, and loss.

Udall had to deal with a very nonenthusiastic instruction from me, as judge, then in vogue in our courts. My instruction on damages pretty much stopped after telling the jury that, if it found the defendant liable to the plaintiff, it should award such damages as would "fully compensate" the plaintiff for injuries "proximately caused" by the defendant's negligence.[72]

But, the Great Persuader made the most of that language.

His argument covered the out-of-pockets methodically—the

---

72. Today's juries hear the judge solemnly give them a litany of around a hundred words, ticking off the elements they should include in their damage award, such as "pain, discomfort, suffering, disability, disfigurement, and anxiety" and "loss of love, care, affection, companionship, and other pleasures of the [marital] [family] relationship," etc., etc.

medical bills, the lost wages, and future loss of earnings. He detailed these on the blackboard, and then totaled them. He was up to $84,000 (PV04 $527,685). His eloquence was greatest when he placed price tags on pain and suffering, and disfigurement, which brought the total above $250,000 (PV04 $1,419,850). Finally, he came to the last big addition: "And how much is it worth to be able to have children? If you have never been a parent, how much would you want in exchange for giving up all right to ever have a child?"

He let this question hang in the silence of the courtroom, looked at each juror in the eye, and then looked again and again at his paralyzed client. Defense counsel Briney was riveted to his chair. There was no objection.

There had not been one scintilla of evidence on the subject of fertility, or sexual relations. After the drama of the pause was about to wear off, Udall wrote on the board "$100,000" (PV04 $638,850). And then he looked up again to the jury: "Is this enough? How much would you take to be totally deprived of this precious privilege?"

The jury was out two hours or so and brought in a verdict of $210,300 (PV04 $1,343,510). That was in March 1959. I know it is hard to believe, but *there had never been a verdict for as much in a personal injury case in our part of the world up till then.*

There was no appeal—the judgment was paid in full—a result that we trial judges take as a certificate that we had performed our job well. Rumor has it that Godare proceeded to sire two children.

Soon after this case, Morris ran for and gained the position that his brother, Stewart Udall, had held for three years—Arizona representative to Congress—this when Stewart was appointed secretary of the interior by President Kennedy. Morris became one of the most influential members of Congress and ran for president of the U.S. in 1976. If he had been accorded both the first and last arguments in that contest, he rather than Jimmy Carter surely would have won.

Now, back to what "negligence" is all about.

If there was a difference in the quality of the conduct that brought these two cripples to their grief, between Riley and Godare, it was certainly as to the nonessential.

What brought about the difference in result was the *difference in the ability of the trial lawyers who tried their respective cases.* And this difference is playing out in every courtroom in America, as you read.

But, even when the best lawyer wins, the Fraternity does not like defense verdicts. Reason: *defense verdicts are not conducive to raising lawyers' fees.*

Results such as in the Riley case—no recovery for a badly injured person with a competent lawyer—caused the Brethren to change the law so that juries in both of such cases would have been given quite different instructions on contributory negligence if the cases had been tried just a few years later.

In our State, the ancient law of England on contributory negligence was changed, not by our legislature, where the legislative power is reposed by our Constitution, but by the Fraternity, in a 1962 judicial decision—*Layton v. Rocha.*[73] This case determines the rule to be that the jury, in each case, will decide whether or not contributory negligence on the part of the plaintiff will defeat recovery—in other words, Arizona juries are granted the power *in each case* to decide what *the law* on contributory negligence should be for that particular case.

While acting as a trial judge I had denied in at least a dozen trials a plaintiff's request for an instruction that would have given the jury this prerogative. One of the most assiduous protagonists for such a new law was a plaintiffs lawyer by the name of Norman Herring. He requested such an instruction in cases tried in my court enough times so that it was somewhat humorous:

> *Molloy:* "Norm, are you requesting it again?"
> *Herring:* "Sure."

---

73. 90 Ariz. 369, 368 P.2d 444 (1962).

Molloy: "Denied. You can make your record with the reporter during the next recess."

Herring: "Sure, I'll just tell Jim [my court reporter] to copy my objection to your denial of my instruction in the last case. I'm going to reverse you on this one, Judge."

Molloy: "Norman, you're just wasting your time. Juries don't make the law in this state, and you know it."

Herring: "You're so wrong. It's just a matter of time. You judges need to be reversed once in awhile."

But, it wasn't me who got reversed for refusing to give an instruction opening the gates to negligent plaintiffs, but my friend Jack Ogg, Superior Court judge in northern Arizona. Even though it was not directly reflective of my won-lost record—yes, trial judges are sensitive as to how often they are reversed—I resented the *Layton* decision.

Maybe it was because I had guessed wrong as to what our Constitution meant, but I believe it was because of a religious [yes, I, too, have my religion] belief that the law should be more sacrosanct than letting jurors decide, in each case, what the law is. These are all carefully screened-over jurors, picked by trial lawyers. They have just been required to listen to the oratory of those who have devoted their lives to the art of persuasion. And then, are they to determine what the law is in the particular case? The answer now in our part of the world, in a negligence case, is clearly "yes."

In my dislike of this new law, my religion clashed head-on with that of the Brethren, for if each jury can decide what the law of the particular case is, *the persuasive powers of the trial lawyers are much, much more important.* And so it is in this state, and throughout our land the Fraternity has continued its attacks on this doctrine of contributory negligence, devising concepts of "comparative negligence" and the like—to increase plaintiffs' recoveries, and the Fraternity's fees.

As my days on the trial bench were nearing their end, I was busy judging in a jury case on November 22, 1963, when our president, John Kennedy, was shot. My bailiff came up to the bench and, in an agitated whisper, said: "*The President has been shot!*" There was stir in the courtroom unlike any I had ever heard before or since.

I repeated to the stunned court room what I had just heard. Then I announced: "We are at recess." It is my recollection that it was then about eleven o'clock, and that I allowed the jury to retire until 1:30 that afternoon. I have been accused, by those who exaggerate my proclivity to force work, of allowing only twelve minutes for this recess. The author of this version seems to get some kind of twisted amusement out of my reputed one-track mind.

It was about this time that my authorship actually benefited the Brethren of this part of the world. It was by a change in our Rules of Civil Procedure. In the history of courts of law, legislatures have historically conceived that, as the lawmaking body, they had the duty to draft the regulations that controlled the dispensation of justice in our courts. Legislatures had for hundreds of years drafted the procedural rules by which courts were governed. But the Brethren considered this unseemly because, of course, these legislators, many of whom are mere laypersons, are clearly incapable of knowing what proper rules of procedure are for the religious ceremonies being conducted by the Brethren.

So, we lawyers have taken it upon ourselves, more and more, to determine what the rules will be in our courts. This we do by "rules committees"—committees often appointed by the presidents of state bar associations—which committees recommend and in some states virtually *enact*, the rules governing our courts of law. Such recommendations are given, in some states, to the legislature for adoption, or, in other states, sent directly to the state's highest court for adoption. There is seldom resistance in legislatures, or in Congress, to these lawyer-recommended changes, because laymen have difficulty comprehending their meaning or realizing their importance.

But those rules of procedure determine the outcome of many, many cases.

In some states, as in Arizona, the highest judicial court has acquired, by constitutional amendment lobbied through the electorate by the Brethren, the exclusive right to make these rules of procedure. This occurred in 1960 in Arizona with the "modern courts amendment," a law adopted by an initiative petition,[74] drafted and promoted by the Great Persuader, Morris Udall.

Legislators appear to be oblivious to the dramatic changes in law that can be brought about by mere amendments to "rules of procedure."

Example: As a good member of the Fraternity, I was involved in changing these rules so that the Arizona Brethren could hale into our Arizona courts more out-of-state defendants, from wherever. It is very advantageous to reach out across state boundaries and summon wealthy defendants from other states to defend against large damage claims in Arizona, or, even better, to reach out across oceans to bring in rich defendants from foreign lands. These "hauled-in" ones are delicious meat for a hungry legal meat-grinder, directed by Arizona's lawyers.

When I had started practicing law, plaintiffs had to be satisfied solely and exclusively with defendants who could be served— personally handed documents by an official process server—while they were physically present within the boundaries of our state.[75]

There was one exception—when property of that defendant could be found within the state and brought within the jurisdiction by a court order (i.e., a garnishment or sheriff's attachment). In such cases the property attached or garnished alone could be affected by the court's decree—such a judgment could not be levied against any other property of the defendant.

---

74. Arizona is one of the few states in which new laws can be created by initiative petition when signed by 10 percent of the voters and adopted at the next general election by majority vote. Art. 4, Pt. 1 § 1, Arizona Constitution.

75. This is the law of *Pennoyer v. Neff,* 95 U.S. 714, 24 L. Ed. 565 (1877).

But these limited extensions of lawyer power did not present themselves often enough to satisfy the Fraternity. This inability to sue out-of-state defendants, especially when they were big, fat corporations, was aggravating to say the least.

So a great deal of that aggravation was eliminated by the Great Court in 1945. This is when the Nine Intrepids changed the games that we lawyers play in a most pervasive way—more than the injection of the three-point-basket rule did for America's favorite sport.[76] According to this wonderful (for the Fraternity) decision, suing a citizen of another state is perfectly all right if such procedure does not "offend traditional notions of fair play." This is now the gospel of this great land, established by the Holy Nine in *Washington v. International Shoe.*[77]

Since the adoption of this wonderful (for lawyers who make their money from litigation) but nebulous standard, lawyers have been suing defendants scattered from Hell to breakfast, and all of the courts of this country have struggled in one case after another to determine what "traditional notions of fair play" may be in a vast array of particular situations. Once this has been laboriously determined for the pariticular case, those courts then have struggled to determine what conduct might "offend" such "notions." This they do humbly, without question, for minor priests do not question what comes down from Mount Olympus.

Typically, twenty-page briefs from each side are needed to assist a trial court in reaching its final guess as to what the Great Court may have had in mind when applied to a particular fact situation. And, of course, there is no guarantee that what that particular Nine meant when it churned out *Washington v. International Shoe* is what it will hold the next time the problem gets before it, which is every once in awhile.

---

76. Old-timers may remember the first three-pointer ever shot in basketball—that was on November, 29, 1980, by Western Carolina's Ronnie Carr. Up until then, the most allowed for any basket was two points.

77. 326 U.S. 310 (1945).

Many times the pretrial jousting by lawyers over these nebulosities takes up more time and effort than the trial itself.[78] But the stakes are high. Once a plaintiff has done enough so that out-of-state service of process does not "offend notions of fair play," any judgment entered in that action must be enforced by the law officers of every state of the union, under the "full faith and credit" provision of our Constitution[79]—provided, of course, that one has a good lawyer who knows what papers to file.

Temporarily limiting *International Shoe*'s leap into what is "fair play" were various procedural rules of the individual states, which specified only a few fact situations when one could serve process on a defendant residing in another state. Such was the deplorable situation in Arizona when yours truly, as a good member of the Clan, set about changing it.

I worked with John Frank, a member of a prominent Phoenix firm, and drafted a new rule that would permit suing a defendant in Arizona anytime that the defendant had "caused an event to occur in this state out of which the cause-of-action arose." In drafting this rule by which members of our Fraternity, with carefully drafted procedures, could drag into our Arizona courts defendants from worldwide, we were not consciously trying to draft a rule with which only anointed members of our Fraternity could cope, but, nicely, that was the fortunate—for the Fraternity—result. Plaintiffs-without-lawyers would seldom cope with this gem of new law.

Our rule was forthwith adopted by our Supreme Court, and a wonderful new way to sue out-of-staters was in place, usable

---

78. For example, see *Burger King Corp. v. Rudzewicz*, 471 U.S. 462, 105 S. Ct. 2174 (1985). Here, six years of litigating elapsed from the time these defendants were sued in Florida (for delayed payments to Burger King) to the time of the ultimate decision regarding Florida's personal jurisdiction over them. Only then could a trial finally proceed to determine what is important—who was at fault and the extent of the damage. Lawyers paid by the minute never complain about such things.

79. Art. 4, § 1, U.S. Constitution.

by members of the Fraternity, but pretty much beyond use by the noninitiated. The possibility of representing oneself without a lawyer, as in the days of Daddy, was, nicely for yours truly and other practitioners, getting more difficult.

And the delightful thing about our new rule was that we had accomplished this gain for the Fraternity without even bothering our mostly non-lawyer legislature with it. Our Fraternity would now bring all of these out-of-state defendants in for an Arizona working-over through this neat change in our Rules of Civil Procedure—adopted by our Supreme Court—on the recommendation of our enterprising committee of two. You may have noted that all concerned in this magnificent accomplishment were loyal members of the Fraternity.

Thus did our Brethren gather in as much litigation as possible for our state and, as a side benefit, a greater opportunity for the Fraternity to interrogate witnesses, to write briefs, make arguments, and do all kinds of other things so as to have determined when "traditional notions of fair play" are being "offended"—services performed, of course, at the regular hourly rate, or perhaps at a premium rate from the wealthier clients, because of the technicality of this "jurisdictional" work.

By this time, the "Egregious Eight years" were in full swing. Decisions to gloriously enhance the role of lawyers proliferated in the Warren Court—the Court of of Warren, Black, Douglas, Clark, Harlan, Brennan, Stewart, White, and Goldberg—all loyal members of the Fraternity.

Of these Dictators of our law, only one, just one—Brennan— had ever sat as a trial judge (for just one year in New Jersey). It must be acknowledged, however, that one of the these Fearless Nine had had the talent to play professional football—Justice Byron White.

One after another pontifically written decisions came from that court to increase the need for the services of the Brethren, from these individuals who had proven their worth only politically or athletically.

Among such breakthroughs coming from the Nine was

Gideon,[80] the case that mandates that lawyers be appointed, and *be paid by taxpayers,* for every person charged with anything in the way of semi-serious crime who does not have *sufficient(?)* assets.[81] *Gideon* overrules a 1942 decision of this very same Court,[82] which had respected the wisdom and humanity of our trial judges to look after the less endowed when accused of crime. So, in just twenty-one years, our Constitution had marvelously changed so as to make paid-by-the-minute lawyers essential in a vast, mind-boggling number of additional cases.

It is my observation that this injection of lawyers into more proceedings in response to *Gideon* and similar decisions, has in no way reduced the chance that an innocent person will be convicted of a crime. National news stories in recent months have been concerned with innocent defendants reputedly convicted of crime.[83] Every one of these cases, of course, came long after *Gideon.*

Whenever we make a lawyers' game out of the ascertainment of truth—and the suppression of confession evidence invariably promotes such—confusion is more of a possibility. And, when things are confused in our criminal courts, the innocent come into jeopardy.

Decided on the very same day as *Gideon* was another very re-

---

80. See *Gideon v. Wainwright,* 372 U.S. 335 (March 18, 1963).

81. We have used the word "sufficient" as being the measuring stick of when one gets a tax-paid lawyer. *Gideon* is less than definite on this subject. Jackson's majority opinion uses various words to describe the gate-opening condition, i.e., "without funds," "too poor to hire a lawyer," and "poor man charged with crime." This probably explains why, now that the *Gault* decision has permeated our juvenile courts, our local courts are appointing counsel for every juvenile who does not affirmatively employ counsel.

82. *Betts v. Brady,* 316 U.S. 455 (1942).

83. "Defendants Who Face Death Penalty Often Poorly Represented," by Dirk Johnson of the *New York Times,* in the *News and Observer,* Raleigh, NC, February 6, 2000; "Flawed Trials Lead To…," by Mills, Armstrong & Holt, *Chicago Tribune,* June 11, 2000; "A Deadly Distinction: Guilty…or Merely Proven Guilty?" by James Kimberly, *Houston Chronicle,* February 6, 2001.

warding decision for the Fraternity[84]—one enshrining the power of federal courts to issue writs of habeas corpus (labeled the "Great Writ"in this decision) as to those convicted of crime in a state court. The power is insisted upon even when the accused has failed to use remedies available to test his conviction in the state court—where writs of habeas corpus have historically been available.

We need to go back in our history and get a bit technical to understand the enormity of this decision. We started out with thirteen independent, sovereign states that, in a compromise document (the Constitution), gave up many, but not all, of their powers. One of the powers *not* delegated away by the states to the new sovereign was the right to punish those committing crimes within their state—to bring miscreants before judges such as Judge Kelly, whom we had elected from amongst us. Sure, there were to be guaranteed fundamental rights, but the Judge Kellys of the world respected them, and then, if some Judge Kelly was autocratic (and we could take care of him at the next election), there were always judges of the state supreme court who also had to be elected from time to time to review and straighten things out. But now, after *Gideon*, hailed by the Fraternity with "trumpets,"[85] the Abe Fortas's who manage to get appointed to high courts from New York law firms can overrule all of the Judge Kellys in all the courts of the land as to when police officers can detain those charged with crime.

Another wonderful step forward for the Fraternity was taken the next year, in a decision imposing upon all of our state courts the federal definition of what a "voluntary" confession of crime might be. This is *Malloy v. Hogan*,[86] in which Hogan is a sheriff contesting the release of a good Irishman, Malloy, accused of—I must point out, as a half Irishman—the less-than-villainous crime of gambling. This decision completely reverses the prior

---

84. *Fay v. Noia*, 372 U.S. 391 (March 18, 1963).

85. Book review by Y. Kamisar, 78 Harv. L. Rev. 478 (1964).

86. 378 U.S. 1 (1964).

law of the land as to what a voluntary confession is, precluding juries from learning about what most would consider avenues to truth. This decision is protested vigorously by four of the Nine— by Justices White, Harlan, Clark, and Stewart, but to no avail. The decision adds nicely to the weaponry of the criminal defense lawyers of our country.

Another really great leap forward in making lawyers important in these fecund Egregious Eight years is *Massiah v. U.S.*[87] Its holding is to the effect that once a criminal has retained a lawyer, and a law enforcement officer knows this, investigators must stop listening to his admissions of guilt unless that lawyer is present.

Fat chance for a litigation-stopping confession in this setting!

And what a gate-opener for the rites conducted by the Fraternity—the jousting over guilt and the augmenting of lawyers' fees! With *Massiah*, lawyers became the Great Immunizers from criminal investigation, indispensable adjuncts for the professionally criminal. Nothing else has done more to expand the power of the Chosen Few—the few who have passed our bar examinations.

So, the easy, direct doors to Truth are closed, so that lawyers can play their games. Let's take a look at how *Massiah* came about. Perhaps there are facts to justify such a strange, unsocial result.

Massiah, arrested for possession of heroin, had been released on bail. While he was thus at large, a police informer met with him with a hidden recorder and taped a conversation that narrated facts which totally implicated Massiah in the crime with which he was charged. There is no suggestion in any of the voluminous legal writings that followed that Massiah was not putting the absolute truth on this tape or that there was any coercion whatsoever used to get the information.

But at trial, clever defense counsel objected to the admission of this tape in evidence. The trial judge, in keeping with the then well-established law, permitted the jury to learn about the confession. Thereupon, Massiah was convicted, and the Infallible

---

87. 377 U.S. 201 (May 18, 1964).

Nine—after two full years of legal proceedings—gave him a new trial, and probable freedom to recommit his offenses, because of the *just-then discovered dogma* that once a person has designated a lawyer, a confession of guilt by that person, in the absence of that lawyer, is forbidden by our Constitution.

Massiah was written by Justice Potter Stewart, whose judicial experience before being appointed to an appellate bench consisted of being a vice mayor of Cincinnati—"judicial" in the sense of perhaps passing upon a zoning appeal, or something of the sort. There were three dissents, led off by Justice White—dissents never to be resurrected by a grateful Fraternity.

The High Court's printing presses were still turning out *Massiah* when the Bravest of all Courts proceeded to make lawyers even more important. This it did in *Escobedo v. Illinois.*[88] This 5-4 decision holds that once an accused person who is in the custody of the police *requests* a lawyer, *all* questions to that person forthwith must cease, *until* he has his own lawyer present, or, if such person cannot "afford"(?) a lawyer, until the government has provided him with one.

What an effective way to make it more difficult to ascertain truth and to make the Fraternity more important! Today it is Gospel that every lawyer advise a guilty client not to talk.

Even Justice Stewart, who had written *Massiah*, dissented from *Escobedo*—taking the view that the Great Court was using his words in the previous decision far beyond their intent. Justices White, Harlan, and Clark also dissented vigorously, pointing to the public damage the decision was sure to do.

The difficulty of proving guilt, especially the guilt of professional criminals with their retained lawyers, increased dramatically with these "breakthrough" decisions of our religiously inspired court. As the priests of the ancient Jews ordered human sacrifices, so do our judicial priests in Washington. And, as in so many cultures, when the priests have spoken, no one dares to question, but

---

88. 378 U.S. 478 (June, 1964).

only to bow down and genuflect.

Though these landmark decisions were all by close votes with strong, vitriolic dissents, their mandates have suited the Brethren so well that there has been scant effort to upset them. Every lawyer in the land, whether practicing criminal law or not, has felt more important after these ridiculous pronouncements.

And ridiculous they certainly are. Just imagine trying to run a business, if you had to go through *Escobedo* nonsense in order to find out what happened when an accident occurred to one of your delivery trucks. Just suppose you couldn't ask your driver what had happened! Or, in a family setting with children, couldn't ask questions to determine how mother's crystal goblet got broken!

As a trial judge I never noticed that *Escobedo* affected my work *because*, before our local law enforcement officers really understood this wayward decision, I had gone on to another job—on our new appellate court. It actually took some time before most police understood the enormity of *Escobedo*'s holding, but they have had to learn to adapt to it—through criminals being turned free time after time after time.

And, it was at this time that my politically bitten life was affected by growths in litigation, coming from the new and wondrous legal remedies being discovered by the Fraternity. Such was the magnitude of this growth that in 1960 it was thought that an intermediate appellate court in my State was needed, to screen-out the over-abundance of appeals going to our Supreme Court. So, a constitutional amendment was adopted and the first judges of this new court were elected by popular vote at the November, 1964, elections.

Considering the profound changes in our laws being dictated from appellate benches, I felt a strong urge to run, and did, and was elected. In my new job, I felt a delicious sense of power elevating my soul. I had taken one step up in the hierarchy of the Anointed! For the next four years and eight months I tried my hand at declaring the law of the State which Daddy and my Swedish ancestors had selected for me.

CHAPTER SEVEN

Appellate Judge—The Lawmaker
1965–1969

The state of Arizona in January 1965 was not physically prepared for my ascendancy from the "inferior" to the "higher" court. The quarters gerrymandered for our new court were skimpy at best. I no longer had the dignified physical plant that the trial court had provided. We newly sanctified appellate judges were assigned as our courtroom those quarters that had been the hearing room for the much, much less important—in the inflated estimation of this newly anointed court—hearings of the Arizona State Corporation Commission.

There was no entrance at the back of this bench for the dramatic (with black robes flowing) entrance that had characterized my Division One lodgings. The three of us had to make our supposed-to-be dignified entrance trooping in single file through a door in the side of this room. The "bench" was elevated just somewhat above tabletop height in a large room that had normal-height ceilings—to the point where the ceiling was a little too close to the top of our heads as we sat on our thrones behind the bench and tried to be impressive. There was barely room for about fifty or so in the audience—and we hardly ever had that many, except for the installation of the court, when we filled the space with the Brethren plus the families of the installees on January 5, 1965.

The very first Court of Appeals, Division Two, State of Arizona. L to R: Herbert F. Krucker, John F. Molloy, and James D. Hathaway.

I could never have sentenced Bobby Fenton to death in this setting—it did not have enough dignity. He would have gotten off with a " life" sentence and then would have been back on the streets in less than a decade. In this setting I came to realize why religious groups around the world build impressive temples and laminate their icons with gold. This is to give an aura to make it more appropriate to enforce idiotic disciplines involving draconian measures—beheading, perhaps—to carry out concepts of what is Holy and Sacred.

As I commenced this new work of grading other judges' papers, I could sense that there were thousands upon thousands of words within my psyche craving for an audience. I was assigned a law clerk. Traditionally law clerks do a great deal of opinion-writing for judges. But I was not ready for this. I would use a law clerk to dig up citations, but I would write the decisions. Having read every Tarzan book Edgar Rice Burroughs had ever written—while in grammar school—I was prepared for this new role. I was ready to write!

During my tenure on this appellate bench—just short of five years—I authored 301 published opinions—meaning that I was responsible for writing a semi-lucid (hopefully) explanation of 301 disposals by our court of serious controversies. Also, in four cases, decided by the Supreme Court of our state, I was called on to write the final opinion for that court.

And then there were a number of dissenting opinions of which I am just as proud, but the number of which is lost—for my computer does not bring up dissenting opinions—plus I must brag about uncounted (perhaps a hundred) written opinions disposing of special writs, which were not published.

During this time there came an effective blow from Above to create more work for the Profession. The case was *Griffin v. California*,[89] a murder case, in which the defendant refused to take the stand and tell any story to the jury. In accordance with the California Constitution, the prosecuting attorney was permitted to argue to the jury that the jury could take this failure into account in assessing whether he was guilty or not. This is what prosecutors had been doing for the almost two hundred years since the Fifth Amendment to our Constitution had been adopted. But the Fraternity had better things in mind for us, and for itself.

The jury argument made in this *Griffin* trial had been expressly approved by our Highest of Courts in 1947.[90] If one is really seeking truth, this prosecuting attorney's argument makes a lot of sense, but not if one is motivated to make a game out of criminal trials and the talents of trial lawyers more important.

---

89. 380 U.S. 609 (1965).

90. In *Adamson v. California*, 332 U.S. 46 (1947).

Justice White, the ex-football player, again had the good sense to dissent from the abomination of *Griffin*. After this case, prosecuting attorneys throughout this land must refrain from even mentioning the fact that the defendant has failed to take the stand—thus leaving the impression with the jury that it is not unusual for innocent defendants to do so. And, thus we proceeded with this understanding of what our constitutional fathers had intended by their wording of the Sacred Fifth—until the Godly Ones struck again, in 1981. This later abomination falls in our next chapter.

But, before this next Revelation from on High as to the *real* meaning of the Fifth Amendment, another stimulating blow for the Fraternity was struck in 1967, in the case of *Spevack v. Klein*.[91] Here, a member of the Fraternity was saved from disbarment. This lawyer took the Fifth Amendment in a judicial proceeding, refusing to produce records that a court had ordered him to produce and refusing to answer questions, all on the basis that to do so would incriminate him. The State of New York thought that it had the right to discipline members of its bar for so acting—the association assumed that a profession that prides itself as being "officers of the court" should expunge from its membership lawyers who refuse to tell the truth to those very same courts. In so believing, it had a long history of this being the practice in state after state, including a recent (just six years previous) decision of our Highest Court itself holding that it was proper to sanction lawyers for refusing to testify about their behavior when called into question officially.[92]

But, religious dogma adjusts as the Priests consult with one another, and this lawyer was reinstated to his profession without having to disclose what nasty things he had been doing. Four of the Nine, Justices Harlan, Clark, Stewart, and White, had the good sense to dissent, but again their voices have had no echo.

---

91. 385 U.S. 511 (1967).

92. *Cohen v. Hurley*, 366 U.S. 117 (1961).

Thus, our Great Court has made it difficult to take criminals off of the streets, has forced prosecuting attorneys to overcharge defendants in criminal cases so as to intimidate them to "cop a plea," and has given assurance to lawyers that they will not be professionally disciplined if they refuse to testify in court because their testimony will incriminate them.

But criminal law is depressing, so let us return to the civil cases I helped decide.

An example of my wavering between my duty to the Fraternity and my revulsion at creating more lawyer-work was my reaction to the judicial creation of the new cause of action for "defective products," which has become so lucrative throughout this country for plaintiffs and their lawyers. Let's look as to how the Fraternity accomplished this.

As a relatively new lawyer, I had attended an Arizona bar convention at which William L. Prosser, dean of the University of California Law College at Hastings, gave the principal address. It was an evangelistic speech about an "Assault on the Citadel"—an "assault" in which all lawyers and judges were exhorted to participate. The "citadel" was the legal barrier to lawyers getting judgments against sellers-of-merchandise, a barrier that, historically, had insisted there be a relationship (privity) between the injured person and the defendant being sued—such as the plaintiff being a buyer from a defendant-retailer.

This was the common law of England, which our country had adopted and used for hundreds of years. What Prosser was advocating was a massive change for more damage awards: that any seller of any product that had a "defect" that caused injury to any user was to be held "strictly" liable for the injury—regardless of whether the user was careless (negligent) in using the product and even if the user had solemnly renounced the right to claim for any injury when the product was purchased. The proposed change in our law was prodigious and revolutionary.

Many constitutional scholars of the time believed that a change in our law as monumental as this would certainly have to be made by legislative bodies, if at all, for if courts can pass laws such as this, what has happened to the separation of powers mandated by our Constitution?

But Prosser did not go to the legislatures of this country to change this law—where there are many non-lawyer legislators who would not profit from its adoption. He knew a better way. He went to the Fraternity itself.

The Brethren were quick to realize the potential of Prosser's assault—in this technological and gadget-oriented society of ours, there are vast numbers of accidents caused by *things* that break or malfunction, and this can happen years after the product was sold, and after it has been in many hands. A diamond-rich mine was being discovered for the Fraternity!

So this change in our tort law was adopted by the American Law Institute, an association of lawyers, unknown by most people, but which has had a vast influence upon the lives of all of us. The Institute has recruited for its membership the most prestigious legal scholars in this country, in other words, the intellectual heroes of the Fraternity. Many of its members are academicians, like Prosser, who have published extensively in textbooks and university law reviews and the like. Many of these selected ones are practicing lawyers and a few are judges.

A judge so anointed by the Institute at the time was Justice Roger J. Traynor of the California Supreme Court, whose written decisions were at the very forefront of where the Brethren was taking our law in the direction of giving damages to injured users of products.

The avowed, and clearly stated purpose of the American Law Institute is to summarize the mainstream of the existing case law of this country as previously determined by the appellate courts of our land.[93] But this is not what it did here. The prize to be gained was too lucrative to resist. So here is how this opening of the gates to millions upon millions upon *billions* of dollars in damage

---

93. For an example see *Porter v. Porter*, 416 P.2d 564 (Ariz. 1966).

awards came about.

For each of the principal areas of law from which litigation comes, the Institute appoints a committee to write the Restatement of the law in that field. Each committee has a reporter who is charged with putting to writing the findings of the committee. Prosser, as dean of a prestigious law school, who had written a casebook on the law of torts, was a natural for the position of Reporter for the Restatement of Torts, Second. And there he wielded his longing for power.

His wonderful (for the Fraternity) revolution in our law came in Section 402A of the *Restatement Second of Torts*, published in 1965, which decreed that *all* "sellers" of products are liable for *all* injury caused by any "defect" in the product, *even though* the product might be manufactured with the best of technical knowledge and skill known, and *regardless of* whether the injury was caused by the buyer's own negligence(!).

This "assault" went so far as to decree that even *if* the seller required the buyer to sign a written release of all liability *before* allowing the buyer obtain the product, this will *not* reduce in any way whatsoever the liability of the seller!

Prosser unabashedly referred to his new doctrine as "strict liability" and hailed it as a great "leap forward" in jurisprudence. It is safe to say that no legislature in this land would have adopted this law—no legislature in this country has ever gone this far in imposing liability—and several have attempted to cut down on the liability so imposed. But, *by its very publication in the Restatement,* it became the law of this country.

For such a radical departure to be published as a "restatement" of existing law, one would expect that there be *at least one* judicial decision *somewhere* in this land—perhaps even in some reported decision of a trial court—to support the innovation. Not so in this case. At the time of Prosser's breakthrough there was no case law that went so far in laying down this dogma of the strict liability to pay damages without fault—though some of Judge Traynor's decisions in California had come as close as any.[94]

But, such was the Fraternity's fascination with opening up such a huge door to litigation that appellate judges—urged on by the Brethren—jumped aboard the "strict liability" bandwagon in droves, *sometimes even before there was a case before them calling for the application of the new law.*

Our Arizona courts chose this route to assault the citadel. The court upon which I was sitting as an appellate judge accomplished this great feat—on the court's own initiative—before the plaintiff's counsel in this case had even asserted the new law. I was the dissenter, and my two colleagues were in the driver's seat. We are talking about the Pogo Stick Case.

This case involved a ten-year-old boy who was jumping on a pogo stick when it came apart, and a piece of the device hit the child in the eye, doing serious damage. For the uninitiated, a pogo stick is a jumping device—basically a metal rod with stirrups for the feet and a handle near the top, with an internal heavy metal spring. By holding onto the top of the stick with one's hands, with feet on the foot pedals below, and jumping, the user, with average balance, may bounce around enthusiastically for an indefinite time.

The trial court had applied the existing law which required *some* proof that the defendant had violated *some* standard or done *something* that a jury might consider as a lack of ordinary care. Finding none, the court had directed a verdict for the defendant manufacturer of the pogo stick. The case came to our court on appeal. The case was assigned to my judicial colleague, James Hathaway, who wrote an opinion reversing the trial court—predicating his opinion upon the newly discovered product liability law. This was accepted by the other judge on our court despite my agitated dissenting argument thus expressed:

---

94. To support his thesis that § 402A came from existing authority, Prosser cites a group of decisions similar to Traynor's *Escola v. Coca-Cola Bottling Co. of Fresno,* 150 P2d 436 (Cal. 1944). But this case and every other of the "authorities" Prosser gives has absolutely nothing that negates the defense of contributory negligence, as the new § 402A does. See Comment "n."

There is no testimony that the toy was *not* used by anyone else other than the two Bailey [plaintiffs'] children.
There is *no* testimony that any portion of the toy failed
or broke—*only that it came apart.* ...And there is no
testimony as to what caused it to come apart. There are
few mechanical assemblages which will frustrate the
disassemble genius of a small boy.

*   *   *

The new doctrine takes the tranquilizing view that strict
liability in tort reaches a just result because it passes back
to the manufacturer—where it 'really belongs'—the liability for a defective product. This 'passing back,' of course,
will only be possible to the extent that proof is available
to trace the defect back, and only to the extent that the
original supplier is financially responsible. If passed back,
inexorable laws of economics do not permit the loss to
rest with the manufacturer. It will be a rare manufacturer
of any size who will make less profit at the end of the year
because of the new doctrine. Big manufacturers will pass
the loss on to the consumer. Products liability insurance,
another tranquilizing thought which has appealed to
some of the proponents of this doctrine, is of no real con-
sequence in determining the final debtor in this shifting
of losses, as the cost of the liability insurance must in turn
pay a profit to the insurance company, all of which must
be paid in the final analysis by the consumer.

*   *   *

Under the strict liability concept, neither contributory negligence (Comment *n* of Restatement (Second),
Torts § 402(A), nor a contract limiting liability (Comment *m* of Restatement (Second), Torts § 402(A))
are to detract from full recovery. Under this doctrine,
then, the negligent consumer, and the consumer who

has deliberately limited his right to recovery by solemn contract, are to recover their losses from all other consumers, non-negligent and contractually unencumbered as they may be. In the process of passing these losses along, there will be substantial wastage in the costs of litigation, and by reason of the small entrepreneurs who will fall by the wayside, thus frustrating this equalizing process from full achievement.

*   *   *

The supplier-consumer relationship is the most ubiquitous in our society, not even excepting the sexual relationship. A concept that contemplates equalizing most of the accidental loss arising from the consumption of goods demands a vast conveyor belt of judicial machinery to redistribute losses. One might pause to reflect whether a conveyor belt rolling on wheels provided by an adversary system, which expends so much energy in friction heat, will be sufficiently efficient to meet the demands of this brave new world.

In one great respect, my dissent—against the adoption of the new law which my Brethren were so hungry for—was totally wrong. Saying that "It will be a rare manufacturer of any size who will make less profit at the end of the year because of the new doctrine" clearly was a false prophesy. The bankruptcies of such industrial giants as Johns Manville (manufacturer of asbestos products), A. H. Robins (manufacturer of the Dalkon Shield), and Dow Corning (manufacturer of breast implants) have been attributed to this judge-created products liability law.

What I had hoped for by the above-quoted railing against my court's decision was that our Supreme Court would grant review and pull away from this rush to change the law, which would do so much good for the Brethren but which, I thought, would be a detriment to our society. The result was a "denial of review" of the

Bailey decision[95] (which amounts to approval), and the embalming and perpetual interment of my dissenting opinion, according to me the best expressed of all my renditions.

As I retrospect on the Pogo Stick Case, I condemn myself for not taking a more religious tone, to passionately condemn this raw and ugly violation of our *sacred* Constitution, for if there is any one principle that is clear in reading that document it is that our forefathers did not intend to grant to the courts the power to legislate.

I had other dissents—equally ineffective. In one I railed against the decisions of the Nine Priests in the criminal law field. The decision prompting me to speak out on this subject was a petty theft charge with a prior felony conviction against a James Randall.[96]

Under Arizona law and that of most other states, a prior conviction within a certain period of time of a later offense increases the possible penalty that can be imposed for the later crime.

The petty theft here involved twenty-five coils of copper wire that had been stolen from an industrial plant. The manager of the plant came upon the defendant's car stuck in a wash near the burglarized plant with the stolen wire in his backseat. The defendant earnestly promised the manager that he would return the wire if the manager would, "please," just not call the police. Nevertheless, the police were called, and a prosecution resulted—a prosecution that was to cost the public coffers a pretty penny.

My futile dissent from what happened to this defendant came after his second jury trial and conviction for this very same theft. A previous conviction by a jury had been set aside on appeal because of a failure by the trial judge to observe some protocol commanded by the Nine Exalted Ones. With this background, I was handed a proposed opinion circulated by my fellow appellate judges holding that this defendant had to be tried yet again!—this time solely because the defendant had been charged under the name of "James Randall, aka Robert Clayton Malone" ("aka"

---

95. *Bailey v. Montgomery Ward*, 6 Ariz App 213, 431 P.2d 108 (1967).

96. *State v. Randall*, 6 Ariz. App. 73, 443 P2d 434 (1968).

is the abbreviation for "also known as"). This "aka" was the *exact* name under which the defendant had been previously convicted of a felony, and the county attorney had, simplistically perhaps, believed that the defendant should be charged under the same name as that used by the defendant in his prior case.

I argued against the opinion drafted by another member of our triumvirate, which ordered yet another, third trial. My dissent conceded that a technical violation of state procedural law may have occurred by leaving the "aka" in the complaint, but I pointed out that Arizona's Constitution provided: "No cause shall be reversed for technical error in pleadings or proceedings when upon the whole case it shall appear that substantial justice has been done."[97]

To me the result reached in the trial court reeked of substantial justice—two separate juries had both found him guilty beyond a reasonable doubt—and, bottom line, we were not dealing with the death penalty. A suspended sentence was a distinct possibility. Trying to get converts, I wrote the following in dissent:

> It is my opinion that a review of this record by rational men will indicate the defendant was given his day in court and was fairly tried and convicted.

> * * *

> By the time this action is retried, one must estimate there will be several thousand man-hours of the time of our citizens devoted to the question of guilt here presented. We may soon reach the place where it is just not worthwhile to charge anyone with anything but the most heinous of crimes. Owners who have been victimized by thefts, and policemen on the beat, may come to the point where they turn their backs on many offenses rather than become involved in the entanglements of a modern criminal trial.

---

97. Arizona Constitution, Art. 6, § 27.

My words brayed into the wind. The majority opinion was well-received by the Brethren, for it rewarded counsel for skill in playing the game well and provided opportunity for more lawyer-skills in the coming, third trial of this case.

About this time, I wrote an opinion for our court in another area in which the Brethren were moving the law—to put lawsuits into the home. It was in a case in which plaintiffs' lawyers were challenging the then well-established law that parents are immune from being sued by their children for carelessness in the course of the family's affairs. Then the case of *Purcell v. Frazier*[98] came along. In retrospect, the Fraternity might contend that I should have recused myself from this case as having a conflict of interest, six of them in fact. (There will be no more to report—Josephine and I were out of production at this point.) But I didn't recuse myself; instead, I wrote the decision for our court.

English common law had held for hundreds of years that husbands could not sue wives, nor wives sue husbands, nor children sue parents, nor parents sue children, for accidents occurring in their mutual homes. To these early judges, it just seemed right that these intrafamily matters were better handled otherwise. These judges had in mind that there is a compensating body of law dealing with domestic relations that permits all kinds of court orders—such as orders of support and alimony and the like, which can be enforced by jail sentences—to remedy intrafamilial injustice. And families themselves can bring pressure to bear to straighten out unfortunate occurrences without lawyers being involved at all. And, of course, many families have health and accident insurance, to at least partially handle such problems.

But the Fraternity champed at the bit of such a limitation to their power. After all, there are all kinds of and many, many accidents that happen in homes, and why cut these bonanzas off from personal injury lawyers? When my chance came to create more work for lawyers in this area of family, my court was presented

---

98. 7 Ariz. App. 5, 435 P.2d 736 (1968).

with the fact that the Fraternity's assault on this citadel of family immunity had succeeded five years before, in the "progressive" state of Wisconsin,[99] and was gaining ground in the courts of this nation inexorably.

I managed to only slow this "progress" down for a short time in our state. In this, the *Purcell* case, three children, five years, four years, and seventeen months of age, were suing their father for negligently driving the family car in which they were passengers. I refused to adopt the new law lobbied for by the Fraternity:

> We are here concerned with a common activity in the typical American family. Children are often "ferried" about by their parents. It is our belief that such a function is conducive to the well-being of both the children and the parent and is intimately connected with the welfare of a family. The family unit has been weakened by various economic and social changes in our modern world. This court is reluctant to take any step which might bring additional centrifugal force to bear upon the family structure.
>
>   *   *   *
>
> If a person does not realize that a civil action, brought when there is no insurance coverage [it was not spelled out in the briefs in this case whether or not there was such insurance, but there was little of such in our population at the time], by a child against a parent for a mistake made in attempting to carry out ordinary family activities, is disruptive of family unity, then we can only suggest that that person knows little about family living.

This decision by a unanimous court had a three-year life. My pontifications in *Purcell* managed to get passed a petition for review

---

99. *Goller v. White,* 20 Wis. 2d 402, 122 N.W. 2d 193 (1963).

to our Supreme Court, but, from there on, the Brethren hacked away until there is only its ghost left today.[100] As holdings such as *Purcell* have been wiped out by the Fraternity, the cost of liability insurance has risen despite the gargantuan increase in the volume of such premiums—arising from the universal fear of being sued.

I had been an appellate judge less than eighteen months when the devastating case of *Miranda v. Arizona*[101] came down from the Nine Priests. We've mentioned this case previously in this tome as being one that, if a rendered few years earlier, might have allowed Robert Fenton to escape sanction for his killing.

Miranda topped off the *Massiah*, *Escobedo*, and accompanying monstrosities of the Warren Court—to further impair the ability of juries to find truth. This decision withdraws from law enforcement the quick solutions of crime that have, since the beginning of civilization, resulted from someone just asking questions. Since *Miranda* there have been few simple solutions to *any* crime that was not committed in the manner of Ruby's killing of Oswald (after President Kennedy's assassination)—which occurred on national TV with tens of millions watching.

The *Miranda* decision insanely holds that before police officers can question those suspected of committing a crime as to "What happened?" they must first go through a litany of warnings that, with any sensible guilty person, will result—before the police officers have learned anything—in a lawyer being present to tell the person not to talk. To add insult to injury, these lawyers must be paid at public expense if the questioned person is indigent.

A dozen words in our Constitution have now been stretched and expanded by this *Miranda* decision to constitute these many mandates:

---

100. It was severely limited by *Streenz v. Streenz*, 471 P.2d 282 (1970). Another decision of Arizona's Supreme Court taking a hunk out of *Purcell* is *Broadbent v. Broadbent*, 184 Ariz. 74, 907 P.2d 43 (1995).

101. 384 U.S. 436, 86 S. Ct. 1602 (June 13, 1966).

The warning of the right to remain silent must be accompanied by the explanation that anything said can and will be used against the individual in court.

*   *   *

...an individual held for interrogation must be clearly informed that he has the right to consult with a lawyer and to have the lawyer with him during interrogation under the system for protecting the privilege we delineate today. As with the warnings of the right to remain silent and that anything stated can be used in evidence against him, this warning is an absolute prerequisite to interrogation.

*   *   *

If an individual indicates that he wishes the assistance of counsel before any interrogation occurs, the authorities cannot rationally ignore or deny his request on the basis that the individual does not have or cannot afford a retained attorney. The financial ability of the individual has no relationship to the scope of the rights involved here.

*   *   *

In order fully to apprise a person interrogated of the extent of his rights under this system then, it is necessary to warn him not only that he has the right to consult with an attorney, but also that if he is indigent a lawyer will be appointed to represent him.

*   *   *

Once warnings have been given, the subsequent procedure is clear. If the individual indicates in any manner, at any time prior to or during questioning, that he wishes to remain silent, the interrogation must cease.

Any sensible person has to ask: Where do judges get the power to thus make this new law for us? And: What does all of this ritual accomplish for our society, other than to create more litigation?

The above are sweet words for the Fraternity. These all-encompassing Warren pronouncements mean that there will be vast additional need for the services of lawyers. The incredible part of this amendment to our Constitution is that all of the above is being presented—not as something that these lawyers who have been appointed judges have invented—but as something put into our Constitution by its framers back in 1789!

The damage done by this decision is insidious and pervasive. If our society were having a problem with coerced confessions, surely it could be solved in a better way. We have already observed the practicality and the actuality of allowing large jury verdicts for oppressive conduct by police officers. Marshaling public opinion through jury education and otherwise to purge out of police institutions any person who abuses a prisoner would be another approach. But, surely not the denying to juries the right to learn truth.

England, from whence we took the inception of our legal system, has reached a more sensible stance. Their lack of a Sacred Constitution has served them well. Parliament has adopted controls over police interrogation that can be easily amended by that legislative body, as pragmatic results indicate the proper compromise between the need for privacy and the need for law enforcement, e.g., England's Police and Criminal Evidence Act of 1984 (PACE).[102]

A much simpler solution to this specter of police intimidation, —conjured up by the Fraternity for its own purposes—would be to legislatively require all police interrogation to be in front of cameras and to insist that videos of confessions be available for jury perusal. But such a solution has a basic defect in the eyes of the Fraternity—*lawyers would not be required to implement it.*

---

102. See Wolchover and Heaton-Armstrong, *The Questioning Code Revamped,* Crim. L. R. 232–33 (1991).

And, above all else, the Nine Mighty Ones would do well to remember that we have a jury system to an extent far beyond that in any other criminal justice system in the history of this world. They should let this tremendous force do its cleansing of the postulated police misconduct that caused the Warren Court to become psychotic. Let juries hear about the indignities the police have inflicted on the accused, in every sordid detail, if there be such. Let juries decide these matters, not the political appointees who have usurped powers that belong to Congress and the legislative bodies of our states.

And, these Nine appointed Ones should permit the trial judges of this country to do some of the monitoring of police activity as to which they express such concern. Trial judges, most of them elected by their fellow citizens, sit next to the jails and police quarters where the Nine speculate all this intimidation is going on.

There will always be greater knowledge at the trial bench level as to what is going on in the police stations of this country than in that marbled castle in Washington, DC, where these Nine politically appointed Lords sit. Trial judges can do many things to discourage the kind of conduct that the Warren Court was neurotic about.

But, for it to impose *Massiah, Escobedo, Miranda,* and other asininities on our people is devastatingly wrong.

When *Miranda* came down, I, along with many other trial judges, was amazed; the impact of the decision on the criminal justice system took a year or two to be felt. Prosecuting attorneys tended, at first, to ignore it. But, subjection has been beaten in by reversals of thousands of cases, at horrible public expense.

Four of the Nine in *Miranda*, as in *Escobedo*, led by Justice White, the ex-professional football player, had the common sense to dissent vitriolically from this extension of the Gospel. Justice White's dissent prognosticated that "in some unknown number of cases the Court's rule [Miranda] will return a killer, a rapist or other criminal to the streets...to repeat his crime whenever it pleases him."

An analysis of *Miranda*'s perversive effect has been summarized

30 years after its rendition: "[E]ach year *Miranda* results in 'lost cases' against roughly 28,000 serious violent offenders and 79,000 property offenders and produces plea bargains to reduced charges in almost the same number of cases."[103]

We will look at the plea-bargaining disaster that has taken over our criminal justice system a few pages down the road, but, in passing, as a member of my Fraternity, I must pay homage to what the Great Court has done—what wonderfully important personages we lawyers have become under *Miranda*-like decisions!

Miranda himself did not finally escape conviction, and in this, I played a small role.

After the Infallible Nine had invalidated his conviction, Miranda was tried again before an Arizona jury, this time *without* permitting the jury to learn about the confession he had made to the police. The jury nevertheless convicted. This conviction was appealed to Arizona's five-judge Supreme Court, where I was invited to sit as a visiting judge and to write the dispositive decision.

In reviewing the record of Miranda's second trial, I found that during this eight-day retrial of Miranda, there was but one day of actual testimony. The rest of the time was devoted to legal argument. During all of these arguments the jury was confined *incommunicado*.

After being so inundated with argument, the trial judge had permitted the raped girl to identify Miranda to the jury and had also let the jury learn about a confession made by Miranda to his regular girlfriend. Most of the pontificating, and oratory by Miranda's lawyers to our court was focused on the "Fruit of the Poisonous Tree Doctrine"[104]—that pernicious doctrine invented by the Fraternity to keep juries from knowing about facts discovered

---

103. From Paul G. Cassell, *Miranda's Social Costs: An Empirical Reassessment*, 90 Northwestern University Law Rev. 387 (1996). A previous analysis is entitled *Handcuffing the Cops? A Thirty-Year Perspective on Miranda's Effects On Law Enforcement*, by Paul G. Cassel and Richard Fowles, 50 Stanford Law Rev. 1055 (1988).

104. First promulgated in *Nardone v. U.S.*, 308 U.S. 338 (1939).

by the police as a downstream sequel to failing to observe one of the New Rules coming from the Nine. By its very quaintness in expression, the "Fruit" doctrine has tempted judicial activism.

Among Miranda's "poisonous tree" contentions on this appeal was that his outright admission of guilt to the police (previously determined by the Nine Glorious Ones to have been illegally acquired) had "caused" him to give a similar confession to his girlfriend, and thus this later confession was the "fruit" of a "poisonous tree"—the "tree" being the original police interrogation. This and several other assorted problems came before the Supreme Court of our state sitting *in banc*, with me as the invited jurist writing the final decision. There were extensive and impassioned arguments to our court by some of the best (and most expensive) lawyers in Arizona.

You probably know me well enough by now to predict that there was no need for another trial. I have previously indicated that my dissenting opinion in the "Pogo Stick" case is the opinion of which I am the most proud. Now, after rereading my *Miranda* decision, I change my mind.

Painstakingly, because this case had achieved national notoriety, I dealt with the eight contentions of error raised by three of the best lawyers in our state. Lead counsel for Miranda was John J. Flynn, who specialized in high-profile criminal defense and who had previously gained the revolutionary *Miranda* decision in the U.S. Supreme Court. Another Miranda lawyer on this appeal was none other than John Frank, who had worked with me a few years back to draft a new rule of procedure so that Arizona lawyers could sue out-of-state defendants.

In this appeal, Miranda's trio of able lawyers argued vehemently that our court should set aside his conviction of rape—a rape that the defendant had testified under oath during the course of these proceedings that he had committed.

This acknowledgment by Miranda was given, *in the absence of the jury*, in the course of pretrial wrangling. The acknowledgment of having raped arose out of one of the defendant's contentions on appeal—that there had been improper cross-examination in the pretrial proceeding because, in these extended hearings, the judge had permitted a question to be put to Miranda as to whether the confession of his guilt that he had given as to having committed this rape was "truthful," and Miranda had responded to the court, under oath, that it was!

It required eight full pages of my best rhetoric to steer around the rocks and shoals of thirteen different pronouncements of the Holy Nine that were relied upon in Miranda's briefs—including that of the "fruit of the poisonous tree" gospel.[105] The few who read this last *Miranda* decision may accuse me of hypocrisy, in that there is no scorn expressed as to the pronouncements of the Anointed Nine in what I wrote, but rather a degree of reverence for what they had pronounced in their decisions. I hope that you can accept that at that time, I, too, was a Believer.

Pursuing Miranda's history from press releases after this decision was rendered may be of some interest. After this conviction, Miranda served eleven years before being paroled in 1972. Thereafter he was arrested and returned to prison several times. Miranda died in 1976 at age thirty-four after being stabbed during an argument in a bar. The police arrested a man suspected of Miranda's murder, who chose to remain silent *after being read his Miranda rights*. The suspect was released and no one was ever charged with Miranda's killing.[106] So, if justice cannot be administered by our courts, then....

It was during my appellate court stint that the tragedy occurred that destroyed the juvenile court system of this country. That system had been successful in stemming delinquency in this country—partly because of its swift reaction time, but also for its nonadversarial (*sans* the Fraternity) method of determining the problems before it.

The determination of the facts of a particular case in the

---

105. *State v. Miranda*, 104 Ariz. 174, 450 P. 2d 364 (1969), cert. den., 396 U.S. 868 (1969).

106. <www.courttv.com> by American Lawyer Media, L.P. and Little, Brown and Company, Inc.

pre-*Gault* juvenile court took a matter of hours or days rather than months or years, as in the typical adult criminal court. This procedure permitted correction and sanction to be imposed on the juvenile soon enough to be effective.

But the pre-*Gault* court system had a *major* problem in the minds of the Brethren—*the system did not require lawyers*. This obnoxious situation was to be corrected, not by going to the ballot box, nor to our state legislatures, where our Constitution contemplated that such changes would be made, but by appealing to the Fraternity, specifically to those Brethren sitting on the High Court.

And that Court proceeded to destroy the obnoxious system that required no lawyers, with Justice Abe Fortas writing the killer. This was *Application of Gault*.[107] Here it was decided that all juveniles involved in conduct which, if they were adults, would be a crime, are entitled to a lawyer, and a trial, with the same basic rules of the game as in the adult court, i.e., not having to say anything to investigators if it would "tend to incriminate" them. Despite *amicus curiae* pleadings by the juvenile court judges of the country, frantically trying to explain to the Nine Know-It-Alls in Washington as to how a juvenile court works, Justice Fortas had a field day in belittling the procedures followed by my friend Judge Robert McGee, who served just up the road from Tucson in Gila County.

Fortas excoriated Judge McGee vigorously for failing to give to this "defendant"—the very use of this term indicating Fortas's ignoring the juvenile court system[108]—"due process." The exalted personage who wrote this opinion and mercilessly whipped Judge McGee with language emanating from Above had never been a juvenile court judge nor any other kind of a trial judge. He had been the head of a Washington, DC law firm and had been Lyndon Johnson's personal attorney, thus qualifying him to destroy

---

107. 387 U.S. 1 (May 1967).

108. At this time—pre-*Gault*—files of juveniles were titled as In re Matter of _____[name of juvenile], similar to probates, adoptions and the like, and the subject juvenile was never referred to as a "defendant."

the juvenile court system of our country.

After writing this destructive opinion, hailed by the Brethren—it created vast amounts of lawyer-work—Justice Fortas resigned from the High Court under fire on May 14, 1969, accused of taking a $20,000 bribe from an indicted stock manipulator.[109]

Surely, Fortas, if he had had the opportunity to comment on my Boy Killer Case, would have excoriated me thoroughly—for failing to insist that these two fifteen-year-olds have lawyers to defend them, and, above all else, for failing to inform them that they had the right to remain silent without any prejudice as to whether it could be determined that they had killed someone.

Before his embarrassing resignation, Justice Fortas—apparently being regarded by the Nine as *the* authority on the subject—wrote another decision involving juveniles, *Kent v. U.S.*[110] This opinion reverses and sets aside a remand order (permitting prosecution of a juvenile in the adult criminal court) entered by a juvenile court judge in the District of Columbia. The remandee was a sixteen-year-old boy. The remand order was rendered after the many administrative procedures of that juvenile court had been followed, but there had been no formal hearing at which his lawyer could do what lawyers do. The Fortas decision strikes down the remand order for failure to accord the juvenile "due process"—that magic phrase which gives members of the Fraternity so much to be paid for.

On reading of this *Kent* decision, shortly after it was written, yours truly, as a fee-collecting member of the Fraternity, agreed with what was happening. After all, if my profession is to have the importance that it is supposed to have, then before such an important step as a remand order of a juvenile is entered, most clearly there has to be a hearing at which opposing lawyers can be allowed to demonstrate their litigation skills.

But now, in my senile years, as I look again at this *Kent* decision, I see it as another mandate that there be a horrendously

---

109. See *New York Times*, May 14, 1969, front page.

110. 86 S. Ct. 1045 (March 21, 1966).

large—counting all of the similar cases arising in this country—expenditure of public funds paid to members of the Fraternity, and not much gained of public good. The facts resulting in the *Kent* remand order, not unlike thousands upon thousands of cases presented to the juvenile courts of this country, are set forth in this very same Fortas[111] opinion, as follows:

> Morris A. Kent, Jr., first came under the authority of the Juvenile Court of the District of Columbia in 1959. He was then aged 14. He was apprehended as a result of several housebreakings and an attempted purse snatching. He was placed on probation, …On September 2, 1961, an intruder entered the apartment of a woman in the District of Columbia. He took her wallet. He raped her. The police found in the apartment latent fingerprints. They were developed and processed. They matched the fingerprints of Morris Kent…. Kent was taken into custody by the police. Kent was then 16 and therefore subject to the 'exclusive jurisdiction' of the Juvenile Court,… Upon being apprehended, Kent was taken to police headquarters where he was interrogated by police officers…he admitted his involvement in the offense which led to his apprehension and volunteered information as to similar offenses involving housebreaking, robbery and rape.

What took place then, as further detailed in the Fortas opinion, was that this young man was examined at the juvenile judge's direction by two psychiatrists and a psychologist who came to the opinion that he was "a victim of severe psychopathology." Thereafter, based upon the recommendation of the Juvenile Court staff, and relying upon the social service file relating to the boy, plus a report submitted by the juvenile probation department staff the juvenile judge entered an order permitting prosecution of this lad

---

111. See note 110.

as an adult—yes, just permitting prosecutors to file—if it was determined there was enough proof.

Mistake!

Most people would consider this a reasonable decision. But what this juvenile court judge did in the *Kent* case was absolutely wrong, according to the Fortas decision, because, despite all of the staff work performed, the judge had acted without a formal hearing at which a lawyer representing this young man could have argued (and been paid for such). Such an affront to Lawyering could not be tolerated by these Selected Members of the Fraternity, and the *Kent* disposition was reversed, four and a half years after this rape occurred, so that the legal gyrations could commence all over again.

State legislatures have not been pleased with the *Gault-Kent* mandated lawyer expenses entailed in these juvenile court hearings necessary to make the decision of whether to prosecute a juvenile as an adult. So a good many state legislatures in recent years have modified the law so as to take away from juvenile courts the prerogative of determining this, trying to turn that decision over to prosecuting attorneys and adult-court judges.

In response to the Great Court's taking away this discretion from the elected judges of this country, twenty-eight states have adopted legislation removing from the jurisdiction of these new juvenile courts many criminal offenses. Other states greatly extended the discretion of public prosecutors in selecting juveniles to prosecute; a group of still other states lowered the age of the juvenile status to fifteen years. Only five states of the union as of 1998 relied on the decision of a juvenile court judge to determine when a juvenile should be criminally prosecuted as an adult—the kind of discretion that all of the other juvenile court judges of my time exercised.[112]

---

112. See *Juvenile Offenders in the Adult Criminal Justice System,* by Donna M. Bishop, in vol. 27 of *Crime and Justice* (University of Chicago Press, 2000).

As far as the record reveals, *not one* of the All-Knowing Ones who joined in Fortas's revolutionary decisions on the juvenile justice system of this country had ever been a juvenile court judge, nor had ever witnessed such a court in operation. But this did not stop the Almighty Ones from laying down, in an appendix to the *Kent* decision, no less than eight detailed—in a thousand words—"determinative factors" that all of the juvenile court judges of the land must follow in going about the deciding of when to remand a juvenile for adult prosecution.

What a demonstration of how power corrupts! These mandated eight "factors" are pure, unadulterated legislation. In *Kent*, again we have dissents coming from the four who some—well, at the very least, yours truly—regard as the wiser heads—Stewart, Black, Harlan, and White.

So far in this presentation, you have been reading only about the wrongful legislation coming from Above. Well, there are monetary detriments as well. The flow of decisions from the High Court has resulted in mind-boggling additions to the expenditure of tax money in this country. When I left the trial bench in 1964, my county had five judges. Each of us had a secretary, and, by alternating the job of administering the court, these five judges and the five secretaries handled all of the scheduling and administrative problems of the court. We had no "commissioners" (lawyers appointed to do substantially the same work as judges), which are now used in addition to our judges.

Today there are thirty-one Superior Court judges in our county, plus sixteen court commissioners (lawyer-appointees who do the work of judges).[113] This provides 9.4 times as many judges as in my day, in a county that has grown in population by a factor of 2.94. To appreciate how amazing this growth is, one needs to know that each of these judges and most of these commissioners has an individual secretary, *and* an individual bailiff, and, in addition, there

---

113. Statistics are the courtesy of Mr. Kent Batty, Court Administrator of Pima County's Superior Courts.

is a court administrator's office of 190 employees to administer this new system. It takes these 190 to do the work that the five secretaries of the five judges did! And our county still pays individual secretaries for its judges![114] I have never heard that Pima County's magnificent growth in judicial numbers is unusual; the rest of the country appears to be on the same track.

In reviewing this chapter, I realize that I may have given the impression that as an appellate judge I was a brave dissenter, always leaning against the tornadic winds of the Fraternity's movement toward more litigation and more lawyer-profit. The written record gives lie to such a claim.

Most of the three-hundred-plus plus opinions that I authored pleased the Brethren. During my tenure I was even elected president of the Arizona Judges Association (1962–1963), an honor that would never have been bestowed had I been the rebel that I would like to portray myself as being. My decisions were sufficiently predictable by my Brethren that they were able to live with them, and, more important, make money off them.

I decided to do the same and mailed in my resignation to the governor on August 18, 1969 (my fifty-second birthday), to be effective on September 5, 1969.

---

114. The 1964 population of Pima County was 309,000, and in 2003, 910,950, according to the Arizona Department of Economic Security, Population Statistics Unit, found on the Internet at <*www.workforce.az.gov*>.

CHAPTER EIGHT

From Judge To Lawyer
1969–1971

So, in the second week of September 1969, I went back to the top of the no-longer-tallest building in town—because several taller ones had come into Tucson's downtown, with higher per-square-foot rents—to the very same offices that my law firm had occupied twelve years before and where I had always been under the tutelage of Judge Hall.

My last three opinions for the Court of Appeals were released on that same day. I had served an extra five days so that I was sure I had put in the minimum of twelve years to be eligible for the generous retirement pay provided by my state. When I got back to the old offices, some things were the same, but in many ways it was an entirely new world, a much better world for my profession if net income is the gauge.

Judge Hall was dead—he had passed away in 1968—but his name was still on the door; it was considered a client-getter. So, the firm name, as I walked in to meet my new partners, was Hall, Jones, Trachta, Hannah, Coolidge, and Birdsall. These were the names of *all* the lawyers in this office except that of one lowly associate. One of my new partners was Stanley Trachta, a retired Marine aviator, whose combat path and mine had crossed in the Pacific. Stanley had joined my old firm three years before. Russell Jones, a law graduate whom I had recruited out of law school for the old firm, was the only one still there from my prejudgeship firm.

There was no discussion of what the firm name would be. It fell into place. My name up front as that of an ex-judge was considered essential. Names were also departing from the firm as I came back. Ben Birdsall, who had been added as a partner in the Hall firm, was changing roles to fill the vacancy on the Superior Court left by the resignation of Superior Court judge Larry Howard, who was resigning his position as a trial judge to take my vacating spot on the Court of Appeals. It was a game of musical chairs.

The new firm consisted of the five partners and one associate. Molloy, Jones, Trachta, Hannah, and Coolidge was the title that went up on the front door, on the court pleadings, and on the stationery. We were soon being referred to as Molloy Jones. Seeing my name on all this gave me exquisite—almost sexual—satisfaction. I had no sense of loss as to the powers exercised by judges.

In these halcyon days there were no "paralegals" and no "profit centers" in the firm. These wondrous moneymakers were to yet come.

My new financial arrangement on coming back was simplicity itself. The firm had agreed that I would draw the same salary that I had been receiving as an appellate court judge—$22,500 per year (PV04 $115,185.) I considered that good pay—I had gotten used to judges' pay, which had *just* been increased from $18,500.

Making the agreement favorable to yours truly, my new partners informed me that after one year at this stipulated salary, I was to be a full partner, sharing equally in the ownership of the substantial accumulated assets of the firm—i.e., in the accounts receivable, in the "work in progress" (unbilled time of lawyers), and in the furniture, equipment, library, etc., etc. There was to be no "buy-in" other than that. I was to learn that this was in stark contrast to practices common at other law firms. The system from which I benefited was the one that Judge Hall had used in building this firm. It is almost unheard-of in the lawyer-world of today.

I was told that I was to occupy the Judge's old office. As I moved my things into his massive desk, it seemed sacrilegious. I felt uncomfortable, and yet it made me realize that I was expected to provide leadership. I knew I would never keep his desk as clean as he had. I hoped that I would have his ability to lead as gracefully and as wisely as he had for the dozen years I had been under his leadership.

And, as I resumed my role of a lawyer, I found that the amount of pretrial "discovery" work had increased during my tenure on the bench. The practice of litigants "discovering" their opponents' evidence before trial had blossomed into an intricate art/skill at which "trial lawyers" had become adept. Not satisfied with the systems prevailing in other civilized countries of the world—in which litigants for the most part take whatever evidence they have to court[115]—the Fraternity invented this fascinating game of "discovery."

"Discovery" consists of submitting to opposing parties "requests for admission" of various carefully worded statements, and of submitting "written interrogatories" to them—required to be answered in writing under oath within certain time limits—and of taking oral depositions (out-of-court, verbal questioning of witnesses—very often of the party himself—under oath, with a verbatim record made by a court reporter). These wonderful lawyer tools had all become available in this country with the adoption of the Federal Rules of Civil Procedure in 1938. Thereafter, the use of these lawyer-weapons blossomed with the years.

The mandates of these rules to make full pretrial disclosure to one's opponents—provided always, or course, that the opponent trial lawyer knows what to do—are enforced by court

---

115. See *International Business Litigation & Arbitration*, vol. 1, Practicing Law Institute (2001), p. 102; and *Boreri v. Fiat S.P.A,* 763 F. 2d 17, 19 (1st Cir. 1985).

orders, which include having litigation-concluding judgments rendered against the party failing to satisfy these penetrating procedures.[116]

This power of lawyers to discover their opponents' evidence had its birth seventeen years after Daddy had tried his last case.[117] Daddy missed an awesome power! Most of my victories in litigation came from the damaging admissions that I extracted from my opponents during oral depositions.

After my twelve years on the bench, in returning to active practice I found that "discovery" had become the paramount ingredient in achieving success in litigation. The Judge Hall technique of proceeding to trial as soon as possible was long gone. Oral depositions, which during my prejudge years seldom had lasted more than a few hours, now often lasted more than a day. Written interrogatories to one's opponent had blossomed from three to ten pages, and growing.

So I came back to these marvelous tools to serve my inquisitive/avaricious nature. I could examine opposing witnesses hour on end—sometimes for days—asking questions that I would not dare to ask in front of a jury for fear of antagonizing jurors. There is an innate repulsion in most humans against probing into another's most private matters and so, without a jury to observe, I could probe until witnesses, in exhaustion, would tell me what my clients desperately wanted to hear.

As I went back to being a lawyer, I felt awkward. I had gotten used to seeing everything from both sides of a dispute, and then trying to find something fair to both. Now I had to pursue the most advantageous course for my particular client.

---

116. See Kozolchyk and Molloy, *United States Law of Trade & Investment* (Hein, 2001), chapter 7, §§ 48(f) and 51.

117. Oral depositions were available to my father, but under the statutes of his day, only four situations allowed such a procedure—generally to preserve the testimony of a witness who would not be available at trial. The cross-examination of your opponent and/or his witnesses was not a proper ground for the taking. See §§ 2506 et seq., R.S. Ariz. 1901.

Returned to the lawyer role, I was delighted to find myself being called Judge by most of my fellow lawyers and by my newly acquired clients. I was careful not to discourage this, although I made it a point to never give myself the label. Every ex-judge I have known has done the same, except some, who, themselves, volunteer the title. Why not?

As I returned to the practice, the firm was in the process of changing its legal organization—as other law firms were doing—from a partnership to a "professional corporation." The reason for this change was to avoid personal liability. The law of partnership, universally, is that all partners are personally and fully liable for all damage caused by the negligence of a partner, or of an employee of the partnership, if that person was acting in the course of the partnership's business. There was no effort made by law firms undergoing this metamorphosis from partnership to corporation to inform their clients of any change in their liability. Whatever else, lawyers are not stupid.

Fees charged to our clients were not as much the result of a weighing of factors (i.e., success or failure) as they had been when I left in 1957. Fees had become a matter of the time records that I had inaugurated for our firm—and in my latter years have come to detest. When I left the firm to do my judging, this record of minutes and hours had been kept less than religiously. Judge Hall, our leader, had never paid much attention to it. And, when we had filled the form in, in those days it had received less than full respect, because time simply was not considered the measure of a lawyer's worth.

But by 1969 the records of time were getting much closer, on a progressive scale, to being *the* measure of the lawyer's bill—like measuring water or gas.

I was no longer to be ashamed of keeping a secret record of what I personally had brought into the firm, as I had in Judge Hall's day. There was no need. Each lawyer, whether he liked it or not, was made aware by monthly reports from bookkeepers as to what their billings had been, and their time "logged" for each and every day. As the years rolled by, the information became more detailed, and ever-more-worrisome for any lawyer who had not brought in their "share."

Very occasionally, during these pre-computer days, we took pains, in shareholders' meetings and the like, to acknowledge that time was *not* the only measure of a lawyer's worth. Service in community organizations, we said, contributed to the prestige of the firm, but we heard less and less of that as the years went by.

At first, in these precomputer days, if any lawyer in the firm failed to hand in a time sheet, he was politely reminded by the head secretary of the firm, but, no one dared suggest, yet, the withholding of a paycheck. This would have been considered beyond the pale of tolerance, but, this was to come!

Each of our lawyers had a set "billing rate," but we had not yet, in 1969, thought it appropriate to bill out the time of anyone other than licensed lawyers. The word "paralegal" first came in the practice in our part of the legal world in the early 1970s. There were no particular qualifications to be such, and for the most part "paralegals" were nothing more than experienced legal secretaries. Over the years since, lawyers all over this country have collected vast amounts of money by promoting "secretaries" to "paralegals."

When I returned to this firm, $40 dollars (PV04 $205) an hour was considered nice pay for an "a" rated lawyer—which top rating I was forthwith assigned by *Martindale*.[118] This ranking came although I had not been a practicing lawyer for twelve years, and, before judgship, had been only a "b" rated lawyer. Thus is the unity of the Fraternity—that of the lawyers and judges of this country—recognized.

After taking over Judge Hall's impressive leather chair, the

---

118. *Martindale* refers to the publication *Martindale-Hubbell,* which provides information about the law and the practicing lawyers of this country. *Martindale* assigns to the "upper half" of practicing lawyers a letter-rating of relative merit, i.e., "a", "b", or "c". To the many practicing lawyers evaluated as less competent, no specific grading is assigned. This grading is available, for all those interested, on the Internet at <*http://www.martindale.com*> and <*http://aolcom.lawyers.com*>.

assertion that lawyers were "not plumbers, to charge by the hour" was no longer heard. Time records had become of the essence. But still, at this stage of development of the Fraternity there was no computer to keep time records, time was manually recorded on "time slips." This left just a little room for considering factors other than the elapsed time on a particular case. Our lead secretary passed these slips out and religiously gathered them in on a weekly basis. We had no "office manager" as law firms of today. The idea never occurred to any of us that there was any need. The concept smacked too much of running a "business," and we proudly regarded ourselves as "professionals."

A year after I came back to the firm, the game of musical chairs continued. Our fellow "shareholder," Richard Hannah, accepted an appointment to be a judge of our Superior Court, and then his name came off our door. The fact that our firm was a producer of judges was established, and our clientele flourished in the atmosphere of being right next to where the decisions were being made.

But not all of our clients were lucrative sources of fees. I always seemed to end up with an odd client or two for whom the new, wonderful, hourly fees didn't seem right. One of them was Horton "Snortin'" Weiss.

Horton was a prosecuting county attorney who got in big trouble with a trial judge because he tried, during a murder trial, to get around some of the decisions rendered by the Infallible Nine, which our local trial judge was meticulously following— decisions that made it much more difficult to prove the crimes that Horton was prosecuting. So, soon after I came off the bench, Weiss became a part of my life for the next three years as I battled in court to keep him out of jail.

It began one morning as I was sitting in one of our then seven Superior Courtrooms for "law and motion" day, a court session with multifarious legal motions being heard by the judge. There, as I sat inside the bar (where only the Fraternity and victim-clients—when under treatment—are permitted), Horton approached me to tell me that he wanted me to defend him against contempt charges that one of our locally best-regarded trial judges had brought against him.

The protocol for holding a lawyer in contempt for conduct in the courtroom had changed since I had sat as a trial judge. The one time when I, as a trial judge, had found a lawyer in contempt, I had simply summarily put him in jail for one day. Such conduct was no longer permitted, as the Fraternity had moved in with a decision of the Infallible Nine[119] to protect its Brethren from such high-handedness. The new approach to hold in contempt required, before any such could happen, more lawyer-work.

Under this new, formalized procedure, Horton had been cited by a written order from trial Judge Roylston—for no less than five acts of "contempt" allegedly committed during a murder trial. In each of these five "counts," my client was accused of continuing to argue after being "overruled" by Judge Roylston. The trial in which Horton had transgressed was that of the locally notorious Atwood Murder Case.

An agitated Horton informed me that the hearing on this citation was set for the following Monday morning and that he just knew that the judge was going to put him in jail. I had read about the Atwood trials in the press, as had everyone who read a newspaper in our part of the world, and had discussed the matter with my partners even before Horton approached me. Our firm had a special relation to the case.

The man murdered had been a client of the firm, William Atwood, a retired industrialist. Mr. Atwood had been shot dead at the front door of his luxurious home in an exclusive Tucson subdivision—either by his ex-wife, Rachel Voyles, or by his son, Anthony. These two, it seemed, had jointly called upon him,

---

119. See In *re McConnell*, 370 U.S. 230 (1962). In case some of you may consider my jailing one of the Brethren for a day without a hearing as being very high-handed, please accept that the conduct censored was deserving of the penalty, and that if I had gained the reputation of being "high-handed," it would have made it much more difficult to keep my office in the next election.

together with one .38 caliber pistol. The killing had resulted in separate trials for Rachel and Anthony, with Horton as the prosecuting attorney in each. The separate trials, rather than a joint trial for both, before the same jury, had resulted from clever maneuvering by astute defense counsel. Understandably, the well-heeled defense had employed John J. Flynn, the lawyer who had done so well for his client in *Miranda*.

After achieving the separation of the trial of these two, Flynn used *Miranda* in Rachel's case to withhold from the jury incriminating statements made by her immediately after her arrest. And at this trial of his mother, the Atwood son claimed mental illness to avoid testifying. Rachel thereupon—without being impeached by what she had said when she was arrested, which was excluded by the court in rulings upon Flynn's well-written briefs—testified in such manner that it appeared that it was the son who was responsible for the old man's demise. So, Rachel walked free.

Having lost the ex-wife's case, Horton then took on the job of trying a murder trial against the son, and he proceeded to lose that one, too. In this son's trial—not surprisingly—the mother testified in such a way that it appeared that she may have made a mistake and shot her ex-husband.

The "not surprisingly," above, stems from the fact that the Constitution (in its sacred Fifth Amendment) prevents the ex-wife from *ever* being tried again for the crime of which she had been acquitted, so, in effect, she had nothing much to lose in suggesting to the jury that it was she who had done this bloody job.

It should be noted here that there are very, very few criminal complaints filed against perjurers. There are literally thousands of defendants in criminal cases, year after year, who take the stand to testify falsely, and, not being believed, are convicted. Yet, I have never heard of—though it must have happened someplace—any one of them being prosecuted for perjury. It is pretty much accepted by prosecuting attorneys of this country that defendants lie to juries to try to try to save their skins, so that perjury is, in effect, just a part of the game played perpetually in our criminal courts.

So, it was, with perjury thick in the air, that Horton, in futile attempts to convict *somebody* of this cold-blooded murder, got in trouble with the court. Horton had talked persistently, and with heat, in attempting to get Judge Roylston to change his mind on some rulings on the admission of evidence—more persistently than Judge Roylston would tolerate.

When I had heard about the separation of this murder charge into two jury trials, it had seemed like a very awkward way to determine who, between these two—mother or son—had pulled the trigger. In a joint trial, as in the old days, it would have been a simple matter of a jury's hearing both mother and son testify in the same proceedings, and the truth would have been evident. But, what a travesty of deprivation of lawyer-work that would have been!

So, Horton's desperate persistence in Rachel's trial infuriated Judge Roylston sufficiently so that on five separate occasions he pronounced Weiss in contempt of court and ruled that Horton would be sentenced for his conduct after the trial was concluded. So, Horton was seeking my good offices to try to keep from going to jail—a less-than-enjoyable event that had not yet graced his life's history.

Sucked in by our firm's interest in this whole unfortunate affair (the deceased Atwood had been a good client), I agreed to be Weiss's lawyer to try to assuage Judge Roylston's ire and the fine and/or jail sentence that might follow.

Thus began a three-year saga of trying to keep this energetic prosecutor out of jail. At the contempt hearing before his Honor Roylston, upon requesting the opportunity to present matters in explanation, I was told by a stone-faced judge that I should take "just as long as you want." I put on the county attorney to testify that Weiss was her most overworked trial attorney and that he was exhausted from a heavy trial schedule at the time of the Atwood trials. I had Horton himself take the stand to apologize for his "overstepping." And then I made what I thought was one of my best arguments for leniency. When I had finished, the judge confirmed the fact with me, and then proceeded to pull out from under his black robes a sentence, all written out in advance, by which Horton was found guilty of five different counts of contempt and sentenced to a fine of three hundred dollars on the first count, and then to consecutive sentences of one, two, four, and eight days in jail for the next four counts—a programmed sojourn in the local Bastille of fifteen days.

My client was devastated. He informed me that some of those, in that same jail where he would be incarcerated, he had "put" there himself, and that they would be out to "get" him.

My special writ to our Court of Appeals (my old court) resulted in a unanimous decision that what Horton had done was *not* contempt—it was nothing but the "advocacy"of a lawyer trying to serve his client—the State of Arizona.[120] But, alas, the state's attorney general, at Judge Roylston's urging, filed a petition for review to the Supreme Court of our State, which surprisingly took the case (it accepts only about one in fifty among such special writ petitions). This court proceeded to reverse my old court and held that Horton's arguments, on all five of the occasions picked out by Judge Roylston's order, constituted contemptuous behavior. Horton was ordered to pay his fine and serve his jail time.[121]

I took a writ of habeas corpus to the federal district court, where my ex-student (he had taken the Molloy Bar Review preparing for his state bar examination), Judge Carl Muecke, held that there was *nothing* but *contempt* in the record before him. He refused to use his power to interfere with the Supreme Court of Arizona's decision. Seeing the desperate look on Horton's face as he thought of spending time in the jail where he had sent so many of its sojourners, I applied to Justice Douglas of the U.S. Supreme Court for a stay of execution and a review. You should understand that I had more sense than to select Justice Douglas from among the Holy; he just happened to be the "duty" justice. I had read

120. 472 P.2d 950 (July 1970).

121. 480 P. 2d 3 (Jan. 1971).

enough of his opinions to know that he would not be particularly sympathetic to a prosecuting attorney. I was right; that petition was summarily denied.

I thereupon took an appeal to the Ninth Circuit Court of Appeals in San Francisco, where I argued the case so extremely eloquently—well, this is my version—that the court came down with an opinion[122] that eventually got Horton out of his troubles, *except* for the one count for which a one-day sentence had been imposed.

Thereupon, I applied for a writ of certiorari to the United States Supreme Court, which, in its majesty, did not deign to be bothered with one prosecuting attorney going to jail for one day. So, in sum, the only person going to jail after a cold-blooded killing was the prosecuting attorney. Such are the confabulations resulting from the Law emanating from on High.

It was in these times that the Holy Nine was at work, rendering decisions such as *Bruton*, which requires all the courts of this land to provide separate trials for jointly charged defendants whenever one of the jointly charged threatens to "take the Fifth."[123] No trial judge who had sat for any time in a courtroom where criminal jury trials take place would join in the asininity of *Bruton.* The Almighty Court that made this decision had not one single person amongst its members with any such experience to handicap it.

Bruton is worth looking at to see if there was some special reason for imposing this monstrosity on our society. The *Bruton* case involved two defendants, Bruton and Evans, who had been jointly charged with armed robbery of a post office. Evans gave a complete confession to a postal inspector, and at the joint trial of Bruton and Evans the jury was allowed to hear this confession, which unavoidably, in order to tell the story that *Evan's* testified was the truth, spoke of *both* of the two being involved in the crime.

---

122. 484 F.2d 973 (May 21, 1973).

123. *Bruton v. U.S.*, 391 U.S. 123 (May 20, 1968).

This testimony, of course, provided a window for reasonable persons to learn what had happened when this robbery occurred.

But in this trial, Evans refused to take the stand, claiming his Fifth Amendment right to remain silent, and therefore neither the prosecutor nor Bruton's attorney had the opportunity to cross-examine him. The trial judge carefully, in careful obeisance to prior pronouncements of the Holy Nine, instructed the jury to completely disregard this confession of Evans insofar as it might implicate Bruton.

Only eleven years previously, in *Delli Paoli v. U.S.*,[124] the All-Knowing Court, in a full-scale opinion by Justice Burton, had held that it is proper to do just exactly what this trial court did. Mistake! In this later, 1968, revelation of the true intent of the Founding Fathers, our Holy Nine held this procedure to be a violation of that Sacred Document.

Thus the Fraternity created more need for its services throughout this land, for there is a tremendous need in this country for additional lawyers to try the additional trials that result when lawyers make the right moves at the right times.

As a sidelight on this bollixment of criminal justice, it should be noted that, on appeal, Bruton's coconspirator, Evans, was turned loose[125] because he had *not* been read the litany of the new rights put into the Constitution by Warren's incredible *Miranda* decision!

Ever since *Bruton*, in this entire country, defendants like Mrs. Atwood and her son, a myriad of them, are given separate juries whenever there is a confession of a jointly committed crime, and the one who has confessed threatens[126] to "take the Fifth."

The potential for obtaining a conviction decreases dramatically in the separate trial situation, as the Atwood case demonstrates. The possibility of confusion is also increased, shifting the

---

124. 352 U.S. 232 (1957).

125. *Evans v. U.S.* 375 F2d 355 (1967).

126. But this does not *commit* them—they may change their mind at the trial and take the stand.

odds somewhat so that the outside chance of an innocent person being convicted also increases.

Besides *Gault, Kent, and Bruton,* American legal systems were impacted by several other revelations from on High during my tenure as an appellate judge. One such coming-down-of-the-Gospel arrived just as I was itching to get back into the law practice so as to take advantage, as a practicing (and charging) lawyer, of the new laws that the Fraternity was inventing. We look at *McCarthy v. U.S.*[127]

McCarthy was the last of the opinions written by Chief Justice Earl Warren to make it more difficult for states to impose criminal sanctions. Perhaps the good justice had a twinge of conscience just before he wrote this one, possibly realizing that the decisions of his Great Court had driven the prosecuting attorneys of our nation to resort to coercive plea-bargaining to obtain guilty pleas.

McCarthy has to do with what judges must do before accepting a plea of guilty. *McCarthy* requires that, as to each defendant to enter a guilty plea, the sentencing judge must read, verbatim, every criminal charge to which the charged person has agreed to plead guilty; *and* must explain to the defendant the constitutional right to remain silent, *and* the right to have a lawyer at government expense to defend; *and* must explain the elements of each crime to which the defendant seeks to plead guilty, *and,* after all of the above, must inquire to be sure that the defendant acknowledges to committing each element of each such crime.

To an observer not indoctrinated into the Fraternity, these scenes, now occurring in every courtroom in this land—as mandated by *McCarthy*—closely resemble a judge pleading with a defendant to withdraw his guilty plea and plead innocent so that the State can have the pleasure of putting judges, lawyers, and juries to work. All of this routine is done in a full-regalia courtroom scene, with judge, with clerk, with prosecuting attorney, and with defense lawyer(s) present. A verbatim record is made by a court

---

127. 394 U.S. 459 (1969).

reporter.

All of these fees and salaries of the court personnel—with the exception only of fees of lawyers of the few defendants with *"sufficient(?)* assets"—are paid by the public. All of this so that the accused can listen to the judge tell him what has already been explained by his own lawyer.

The *McCarthy* procedure has had practically no effect as far as freeing anyone from a criminal charge. Once an accused has been coerced into a plea of guilty by threats of overprosecution and has been coached by his lawyer on how to react to this litany of questions, there is hardly ever a recantation. On any occasion when an accused might not accede to all of the *McCarthy* bench inquiries—and I have personally never witnessed or heard of such—then, when the defendant leaves the courtroom, this person is faced with the same Hobson's choice as before—to stand trial against every possible offense that trained prosecutors can conjecture from a set of purported facts—or to plead guilty to some reduced charge so as to eliminate the horrible risks of multiple, consecutive sentences to prison, and including, on rare occasions, the threat of death. If the courage was not previously there to take on a trial with the threatened horrendous penalties, it will probably not be there on the second go-around. On a second *McCarthy* examination, the defendant will be able to pass the test to get the plea agreement accepted—to relieve the defendant of fear and the court of its congestion.

If *McCarthy* had come down ten years earlier, its mandates, along with a few other innovations dreamed up by the Holy Nine during these years, would have required my Monday morning criminal calendar to consume a good part of my week as assignment judge rather than the few hours that got the job done.

After the Egregious Eight years had run their course with *McCarthy*, the Fraternity remained active, to give lawyers more to do, but nothing to compare with the horribles of those years.

One subsequent decision stands out. It actually cuts down somewhat on the work of lawyers. It achieves this by setting up a procedure to induce defendants to plead guilty to criminal charges. It had become apparent to all that the obstacles to law enforcement imposed by the Great Court's suppression of searches and confessions was creating a problem. So, the Great Court went about eliminating trials by giving approval to prosecutors using threats to induce confession of guilt.

It did so by permitting all criminally charged defendants in this country to be threatened by prosecutors with many charges, duplicitous in nature, but carrying a total of life-extending penalties, and then permitting the coerced defendant to plead guilty to a lesser charge with a limited penalty involved. This clever way to avoid factual trials received the imprimatur of the Great Court shortly after I left the bench in 1969.

This was the *Alford*[128] decision, which sanctioned prosecutors' bargaining with defendants to get them to plead guilty. The decision blesses the threatening of defendants with multiple counts in criminal complaints, and then the dropping of charges in exchange for the accused's agreeing to plead guilty to some crime(s), with perhaps a promised lenient sentence as additional inducement. Here are the words of *Alford*, which give sanction to this shameful bargaining with people's lives:

> Plea agreements are consistent with the requirements of voluntariness and intelligence—because *each side may obtain advantages* when a guilty plea is exchanged for sentencing concessions, the agreement is no less voluntary than any other bargained for exchange [emphasis added here].

This "bargaining" argument could justify almost any conduct—for anything can be bargained after threats. So, from *Alford* onward, the pursuit of truth in this land of ours has been a bit more warped, as prosecutors, driven by won/lost records, and

---

128. *North Carolina v. Alford*, 400 U.S. 25 (1969).

with collaboration in many instances from trial judges, shamefully overcharge criminal defendants and then bargain to get guilty pleas and/or testimony.

If such threats are not enough to get a guilty plea to *something* that will be politically acceptable—prosecuting attorneys generally have to run for office every few years—then individually one or more of the defendants is approached with an offer that hopefully the recipient cannot refuse. This means that one defendant is promised that if he/she will testify against a codefendant, then that he/she will get a lighter sentence, or, if the case is one hitting the front pages and the prosecution is desperate for evidence, then the promise will be made that the "canary" will not be prosecuted *at all* for what they have done if they just will "sing."

There is an additional ugliness arising from this "canary" situation. Such "immunized" witnesses are given to understand that they can be prosecuted for perjury if they get on the stand and lie about the transaction. Such a "promised" person, when testifying, is thus under pressure to tell the "truth" in the manner that the prosecutor wants to hear it. The witness cannot hurt himself with the prosecuting attorney by overstating the incriminating facts as to the defendant on trial.

And then there is a concomitant evil. If the witness, in his eagerness to please the prosecutor, overstates the facts and is caught in a lie, the jury is turned against the prosecution. There is no quicker way to lose a jury case than to be caught presenting false evidence to a jury, and thus a guilty defendant may go free.

Thus, the truth is distorted and our judicial system dishonored.

Most reasonable persons, if they had the opportunity to compare—an opportunity that, under the present mandates of the Nine, they will never get—would prefer the fresh air of the pre-*Gault* juvenile courts. There, no witness was promised any reward to testify, and what had actually occurred became crystal clear compared to the lawyer-manipulated obfuscations now coming out of our courts.

Plea bargaining has now become so common that we think

that this is the way justice has always been dispensed in this country, but it was not until these lawyer-dominated modern times that we have permitted coercion to so determine guilt.

Among the subsequent gains for the Fraternity was the decision of *Bivens v. Six Unknown Named Agents of Federal Bureau of Narcotics*.[129] And, perhaps our country may benefit from *Bivens*'s creations—I can argue both sides of this one.

What *Bivens* does is to create out of whole cloth a new cause of action for the Fraternity to pursue in our courts. To some of us older-schooled in what the federal Constitution is all about, *Bivens* is a blatant violation of the well-expressed intent of our Founding Fathers that the legislative branch of our government—not judges—should have the prerogative of making new law.

However, *Bivens* proclaims that anytime there is a search by police officers that violates the restrictions such as the Infallible Nine have set, the person so searched has a cause of action for damages against those officers—a cause of action that had been hidden in our Sacred Constitution for centuries, now, gloriously to be discovered.

One of the *Bivens* dissenting opinions, by Justice Burger, attributed the motivation for this blatant piece of judicial legislation on the total failure of the egregious *Mapp v. Ohio*, and its progeny, to do any good whatsoever:

> Suppressing unchallenged truth has set guilty criminals free but demonstrably has neither deterred deliberate violations of the Fourth Amendment nor decreased those errors in judgment that will inevitably occur given the pressures inherent in police work having to do with serious crimes.[130]

Another dissent in *Bivens*, by Justice Blackmun, expressed dismay that courts should be openly making law rather than staying with the function delegated by the Constitution to our courts:

---

129. 403 U.S. 388 (June 21, 1971).

130. Quote from Justice Burger's dissent, 403 U.S. 388, 418.

Why the Court moves in this direction at this time of our history, I do not know. The Fourth Amendment was adopted in 1791, and in all the intervening years neither the Congress nor the Court has seen fit to take this step.[131]

From the page references to the above quotations you can glean that it took no less than forty-two full pages of rhetoric to accomplish *Bivens*'s result, demonstrating that the All-Powerful at least had the decency to employ thousands of words to try to justify its usurpation of the power of Congress. A few years after *Bivens*, Congress accepted that it had to live with this new uncharted, judge-created civil action and proceeded to codify *Bivens* in the Civil Rights Act.[132]

The potential good in *Bivens*, of course, lies in answering the question of whether unlawful searches and seizures are really a problem in this country. Personally, I haven't been exposed to such, nor have any of my acquaintances reported such. Perhaps you have had a different experience. If there is such a problem to be solved, then *Bivens* clearly is the way to solve it—giving those aggrieved by a wrongful search a cause of action for damages. But, most certainly the turning of criminals free to continue to commit crime—as the abominable exclusionary rules devised by the Great Court are doing day after day after day throughout this land—is not in anyone's interest except that of the Fraternity.

So, having covered these depressing leaps forward by my Fraternity, let's go back to practicing law, and the building of a law firm, where things were going very, very nicely for me.

---

131. Quote from Justice Blackmun's dissent, 403 U.S. 388, 430.

132. 42 USCA § 1983—R.S. § 1979; Pub.L. 96–170, § 1, Dec. 29, 1979, 93 Stat. 1284.

CHAPTER NINE

Maturing of a Law Firm
1971–1978

We come in our litany to two far-reaching events occurring in close succession. The first was in distant Washington, DC—an event destined to have a pervasive influence on every resident of this country.

I am referring to the appointment of William Hubbs Rehnquist to the All-Mighty Court. This selection was by President Richard Nixon on October 21, 1971. Mr. Rehnquist was a Phoenix lawyer, an aspiring leader in the Republican Party. As is the case for so many appointees to the Great Court, he had had no previous judicial experience. With this purely no-trial-judging experience, he was to be appointed chief justice of the Court by yet another Republican, President Ronald Reagan, in June 1986, and as such, was destined to be the leader in choosing a Republican over a Democrat to be president of this country.

The other far-reaching event was very close to home. On November 1, 1971, the Molloy Jones firm merged into the firm of Robertson & Fickett and became the firm of Robertson, Molloy, Fickett & Jones, P.C. At the time of this merger there were six

Brethren in Molloy Jones and eleven in the Robertson firm.

The Robertson Fickett firm occupied a full floor in the newest and tallest building in our town. It contained one lawyer noted for his managerial skills—Thomas Childers. The mechanics of our Great Merger were structured by him.

One of Tom's ideas for our newly formed firm, which he had acquired in attending legal seminars for law firm managers, was to divide it up into "profit centers." There were to be "Commercial," "Tax," "Probate and Trusts," "Collections," and "Trial" Departments. To our little Judge Hall-trained firm, "profit center" was a strange word.

In Tom's structured merger, most of the old Molloy Jones group went to the nineteenth floor of this new building, with a prestigious dinner club occupying the two floors immediately above, to which our firm's offices were connected by our own private stairway. Plush!

But the Trial Department, with me as its newly appointed "head," was assigned by Childers to occupy the twelfth floor of this same building. There, with my new title, I should have been no hindrance to the many Childers organizational methods—too busy trying cases to be bothered with "administrative" matters, which were to be Tom's province. But it did not work out so; perhaps I was too hungry for power, getting my inspiration from the Infallible Nine.

Childers had ambitions to make our firm the most efficient and the most profitable in the state. One of his ideas was that legal secretaries were to be organized into "pools"—one for the "Trial Department," one for "Commercial," etc. Under this system, when one wanted a secretary, one "rang" the pool, and whoever was available came to do the lawyer's bidding—a very efficient use of secretaries' time, on the surface, at least.

But the system lost a lot of ground by not having a secretary working on files with which she[133] was familiar. I had come to depend upon my own well-qualified secretary for many things. Accordingly, I found the secretary "pool" idea to be straight-out repulsive. Knowing my proclivity to forget appointments and give bad dictation, I needed one of the best secretaries in the firm, and that is what I was going to get. Actually Tom was just a few years ahead of his time. He would have found his element after the Last Merger, which you will be hearing about.

The Childers-Molloy clash lasted but a few years, ending when Childers resigned. Looking back, I regret my intransigence. Bottom line, I was shortsighted in my refusal to let Tom govern.

During this period of changing leadership, our firm's governmental structure changed drastically. Soon after the Great Merger of 1971, it was apparent that the old system of the "partners' meetings" to make decisions—which had occurred even to consider whether to buy one of the new electronic typewriters—was not going to work. The *time* of all these lawyers had become too precious for such "waste."

So, we created an executive committee, the "E/C." The E/C was given the power to make all decisions except: (1) the hiring and/or termination of a lawyer, (2) compensation of lawyers, (3) changing office locations, and (4) "major policy decisions." These four limitations on power, reserving them for "partners" meetings (which had legally become, for reasons of limiting liability to clients, "shareholders" meetings), were to erode over the years as power centralized in certain individuals in our midst.

During these years of growth, our firm was recruiting top graduates out of Arizona law schools, and that meant offering competitive salaries—there were many firms recruiting as the law business flourished under the wonderful decisions coming from Above.

Unfortunately for heads of law firms, the salaries needed for this recruiting opened up in the veteran lawyers' minds the realization of what magnificent salaries they should be earning for their own vastly superior talents. So, as the president of our legal

---

133. No apology here for using the feminine, because in this era, secretaries were, almost without exception, all females, and, with a few more exceptions, all lawyers were males.

structure—a title that Tom Childers had ceded to me from the onset—I had work cut out for me in making finances fit. And, of course, there was only one place to get the funds to make it work—from as many clients as we could possibly entice into paying the highest fees possible.

Fortunately, the clients that had been recruited by the Robertson Fickett firm, and were now clients of our now-merged firm, had a continual need for legal services, and of substantial order. Early in the new firm's conception, I acquired a case in which my evidence-suppression skills came in handy.

I was representing three men burned as the result of a defective valve on a propane tank situated in a recreational vehicle. The defective valve resulted in an explosion, and three war veterans were badly burned. The case was a natural for our new lawyer-created product liability law, which I had so stupidly refused to foster as an appellate judge. But, there was one downside to this case—my three clients were all smoking "pot" (marijuana) when this accident occurred.

Conceiving that I might lose a juror or two with the marijuana scenario, I convinced the trial judge that such smoking had nothing to do with this accident and was granted a wonderful order *in limine*, precluding the jurors trying this case from knowing about the recreational activity of my clients.

Such motions—based on rules the Fraternity has put in place—result in every trial court in this land issuing orders to prevent juries from learning facts about cases. This jury-blindfolding process works like this (providing you have a good trial lawyer): The lawyer files a motion—asking that the judge enter an order suppressing certain evidence. The reason for the motion is often based on a new ("new" to me—perhaps not to you—so let's say a "since 1960") judicial interpretation of the U.S. Constitution—such as the meaning of the Fourth Amendment's prohibition of "unreasonable searches and seizures," or the Fifth Amendment's prohibition of requiring a person to testify against himself. E.g., a search warrant has the wrong address and a police officer discovers the stolen silverware under the defendant's bed.

Under the exclusionary rule now forced on all of our states by our All-Knowing Court (e.g., *Mapp v. Ohio*,[134] the blockbuster case of 1961), a jury trying such a stolen silverware case would never learn about this interesting discovery. Thus are juries kept ignorant of evidence which would be very, very helpful in separating the innocent from the guilty as far as stolen silverware is concerned.

A case such as this, incidentally, was actually tried in my court shortly after the *Mapp* decision came down from Above. The defendant in this case was charged with a house burglary. Prize silverware of a family had been found by the police under the defendant's bed. The police had entered the defendant's room in a boardinghouse without a search warrant. Unfortunately for this defendant, it sometimes takes a little time for a decision such as *Mapp* to filter down through the ranks of the legal fraternity, especially in 1961, before the advent of computer research.

In my case, defense counsel made no objection to the testimony of the police as to where the stolen silverware had been found, presumably thinking it obvious that somehow the client would have to explain its presence or be convicted. Without the proper objection, trial judges "admit" evidence—which means that this jury was permitted to learn about the finding of this silverware. It did not take this jury long to convict—a travesty of justice to those indoctrinated in the New Order, but very satisfying to homeowners, especially those with silverware they cherish.

But all was not arguing to juries and judges in these days of my life. I had other concerns as the head of a money-hungry group of lawyers. There followed fifteen years of growth during which I was the leader—titularly at least—of an organization which became more and more profit-oriented. On January 1, 1973, the firm opened its first branch office, in a shopping center some twelve miles north of downtown Tucson. At this time we employed several new lawyers. It was during these times that spe-

---

134. *Mapp v. Ohio*, 367 U.S. 643, 659 (1961).

cialization by lawyers in particular segments of law practice was taking over the legal profession.

I myself focused on trial work; intuitively I hated to be an administrator. I tried a potpourri of cases and learned to roll with the punches in the courtroom. Our new firm grew and prospered, ascending plateaus in the dog-eat-dog world of competing law firms.

My "salary" in 1972 was $51,000 (PV04 $224,162.) My nameplate-shareholders' (Jones' and Donahue's) salaries were both at $50,000 (PV04 $218,840), and the rest of the "salaries" stood at lower levels, with the lowest paid of the twelve shareholders' salary set at $35,000 (PV04 $154,030), and the seven associates being paid from $23,500 (PV04 $103,420) to $13,200 (PV04 $58,090). In addition to these "salaries," there were quarterly, very substantial bonuses paid to shareholders—10 percent of the annual wage on several occasions—plus additional substantial amounts being put into two trusts, one a "profit-share trust," and the other a "retirement trust" for the benefit of the partner-shareholders. We were doing well—financially at least—but no better than many other firms, and our earnings were a fraction of what lawyers in Wall Street firms were getting.

During these times there was an inexorable change occurring in the practice of law—not only resulting from the momentous decisions of the jerks of the Holy Nine, but with a gradual and insidious movement—*always* toward more commercialism in what had been Daddy's profession.

In April 1976 our firm moved from its sumptuous but separated—by six floor levels—offices to even more sumptuous quarters, with two thousand more square feet of total space in the very top two floors of a new building, the new tallest building in town, across the street from the courthouse. But we were still not completely into the new ways to make money. In 1976 our firm's hourly records were still being kept by written "slips" written out by the lawyer, or, by the delegated secretary of the lawyer, and there were only a few paralegals to add to our revenue.

In December 1977 our firm "progressed" to an IBM System

32, "suitable for 40 timekeepers"—under a two-year lease of this equipment. I yearn to tell you that I vigorously resisted this selling-of-our-soul act, for with this expense, it had to be used vigorously and implacably. But, alas, a review of the minutes of the E/C of the firm indicates that, if anything, I was leading the charge. I still had not realized my sin in introducing timekeeping to the firm.

It was during these times that the class action, that awesome weapon in the hands of a skilled attorney, came into its own as a glorious tool for the Fraternity. In my prejudge years, class actions were rarely heard. They had been provided for in the revised Federal Rules of Civil Procedure of 1938.[135] But it had taken some time for the Fraternity to appreciate their wonderful significance, and, even today, they present intricacies of procedure with which some lawyers hesitate to cope.[136] But for the initiated and clever, class actions are bountifully rewarding—for lawyers—but always destructive for defendants. You may remember that we have mentioned what happened to Johns Manville, A. H. Robins, and Dow Corning.

Since these hits, the tempo of the class action scene has accelerated dramatically. Major corporations throughout America now consider these actions a threat to existence itself. A recent article in a national magazine reports that in the calendar year 2003 alone, just two lawyers who specialize in such actions collected, in class action settlements, the tidy sum of $2.372 billions of dollars (yes, $2,372,000,000.00!).[137]

To understand how this wonderful milieu for enterprising lawyers could develop, we go back to December, 1975, when a new Priest was installed on the Court of the Holy Nine. John Paul Stevens was elevated from the ranks of the Fraternity by appointment of President Gerald Ford. This appointee, like so many before him,

---

135. Rule 23, Uniform Rules of Procedure.

136. There is a six-volume set, annotated, to assist lawyers in the filing of such actions. See Newburg on *Class Actions,* 3d ed. (West Group, 2000).

137. Forbes, February 16, 2004, "Mr. Class Action," pp.82–90. There were seven defendant corporations who coughed up this tidy sum.

had never sat on a trial bench. He had been a principal partner in one of Chicago's leading law firms, and this had served as his qualification for being selected some years before by President Nixon for appointment to a federal intermediate appellate court.

And then came a great leap forward for the Fraternity. The "no-no" against lawyer-advertising, which the legal profession had placed upon itself,[138] was destroyed by the Nine Gods in Washington, who all understood the need for lawyers to advertise—being themselves all members of the Fraternity. They had no trouble finding that our Founding Fathers, mostly non-lawyers, had most providently, in our venerable Constitution, guaranteed lawyers the right to commercially proclaim their wares.[139] So thus, belatedly, and very profitably for some, the sacred document was amended by lawyers for the benefit of lawyers.

Soon after this 1977 decision, lawyers' ads came to gloriously dominate the yellow pages of phone books and to vibrate in our homes though the media. This is one minor reason legal fees have been raised—to accommodate this expense.

The 1978 *Martindale* directory listed our firm with twenty-one lawyers. There was still one firm in Tucson with more lawyers—the Bilby firm with twenty-three. But we were to overcome, yes, we were to overcome!

---

138. In Daddy's day the American Bar Association, in 1908, adopted a Code of Ethics which, in Canon 27, banned all advertising by lawyers, with the exception of "simple professional cards and…publication in reputable law lists…" The 1969 Model Code of Professional Responsibility had a similar provision.

139. *Bates & Van O'Steen v. State Bar of Arizona*, 433 U.S. 350 (1977), holding that a lawyer's advertising of his/her wares to be "commercial speech" protected by the First Amendment, thus recognizing that the legal profession had degenerated from a profession to a business.

CHAPTER TEN

The Golden Years
1978–1982

There followed some golden years, in which I was able to produce for the firm as I was expected to do, and our firm prospered in size and earnings, and in pride in itself. Our Phoenix office came in December 1978 with a publicized "merger." "Merger" is somewhat of a misnomer, because while it is possible legally to merge professional corporations, in our case we merely issued new stock to a new shareholder in our existing corporation.

This 1978 Phoenix "merger" pertained to my old fraternity brother Herbert Mallamo. Mallamo had become a well-recognized litigator in Phoenix. Our firm became Molloy, Jones, Donahue, Trachta, Childers & Mallamo, P.C. The Phoenix office then proceeded to add three more lawyers.

Up until then the firm had been a semi-fraternal organization. All shareholders and associate lawyers had met once a month for breakfast to discuss recent decisions of our courts and once a month for a cocktail party, once a year for a Christmas party, and at least once a year for a weekend "retreat" at a hotel-resort. It was written firm policy not to take a malpractice case against any lawyer without consent of the E/C (otherwise our practitioners were on their own in taking on clients), and unwritten policy not to take such internecine cases at all.

Our regard for our fellow shareholders was not founded upon whether each was "producing" as much as he should, under "goals" established by a "billing committee." These abominations came about in the next few years.

Insidiously, business concepts crept in, and the Judge Hall concept that all lawyers should be able to run their own practices pretty much as they pleased became long-gone. Firm protocol—administered by an "office manager"—came to govern minutiae, i.e., whether any particular secretary got a new typewriter.

Like a cancerous growth, the amount to be billed to clients became more and more controlled by the time records and the financial demands of the Brethren. The September 1973 minutes of the E/C reveal that we had five paralegals, "all now completing time slips in the same manner as attorneys," and besides charging assiduously for each minute the paralegals logged, we had learned to charge for each copy of any writing we produced for a client. "No more freebies," we said.

Then, a most insidious and pervasive invasion of professionalism occurred. In order to consider the setting of our salaries for 1977, our E/C directed the office administrator to provide us with an analysis not only of the "billed hours" that each lawyer had tabulated but also of the "collected hours" of every lawyer, and the "collected hours" of every paralegal in the firm, and the "originated fees" of every lawyer, and the "office expense" attributed to each. We were told that "all successful firms" were doing the same.

This disgusting report was ordered by the E/C for calendar years 1974, and 1975 and up to November 30, 1976 (the E/C meeting was held in early December of this year), to account for not only fees generated by each lawyer but also the secretarial expense of each lawyer, and minutiae, such as the square footage of office space occupied by each lawyer and the cost of any special equipment used by that lawyer.

What a crass way to be a professional!

The "origination" of fees became a matter for petty bickering between lawyers. The theory was that if a client first came to our firm by reason of some contact or relationship with one of our lawyers, then this client's fees thereafter, no matter by which lawyer earned, were to be recorded as "originated" by that first lawyer, to thus affect that particular lawyer's salary. We were told that all firms were doing the same.

But what if there were a conversation on the golf course in which one of our stalwarts recommended a fellow lawyer in the firm, and extolled, of course, that lawyer's expertise? And then, one month later, the recipient of this touting happens to meet the client in the clubhouse over cocktails and thereafter the first office visit occurs. So, which lawyer "originated" this client?

In the Judge Hall firm, we would have considered that it made absolutely no difference. In my new firm, it became a disturbing problem of dollars-in-whose-pocket?

In similar ways, each step taken in this path from a "profession" to a "business" drove one more possible wedge between members of our segment of the Fraternity. You would have thought that to someone trained in the Judge Hall tradition, where a lawyer was ashamed to admit he was keeping track of his personal intake, such commercialism would have been obnoxious.

Not so. Our E/C minutes show that I complimented our staff on their work.

But, even then, there still remained some small remnant of the spirit that said that time spent was not the total measure of a lawyer's worth. The March 1976 report of the billing committee, headed by my partner Jack Donahue, ended with this language— which was heavily underlined:

It is also recognized that the suggested billing rates may be too high to charge individual clients because of their financial circumstances and, accordingly, in those cases, the rates must be reduced.

This memo proved to be a milestone that marked an irreversible boundary. Never after this was there ever a scrap of paper coming out of the executive committee, the billing committee, nor, I'm sad to say, from the president of this money-hungry firm, which in any way suggested that billings should be anything but on a time basis, unless, of course, there were "special circumstances" to support a higher bill. We were infatuated with the flow of delightful cash.

I had no pangs of conscience in giving up the philosophies of Judge Hall, because "everybody" was doing it. As the head of my firm, I was attending meetings of state and national bar associations, where there were conferences such as those conducted by the ABA's Committee on Economics of Law Practice, and this is what we were taught to do. Our firm was just keeping up with other "successful" firms.

On January 18, 1980, our E/C established a monetary fine for any of our timekeepers (lawyers and paralegals) who were late in handing in a time sheet. And, we were expanding in the Phoenix area with our new business methods. In March 1981 we leased the entire eleventh floor of the Title and Trust Building in Phoenix, an office building close to the county courthouse to make it easy to get to court, and because a few loose clients might be in the area.

It was during these days that I was doing well as a trial lawyer—putting to use some of the tricks of the trade I had observed from the bench. One of my more interesting litigations arose out of the fatal crash on March 25, 1977, of a Cessna 210 aircraft on the island of Martinique in the eastern Caribbean. This is one of several of our cases made profitable by the law of the Pogo Stick Case.

The pilot of the aircraft was Kenneth Ferguson, who owned a cable TV system serving the environs of Sierra Vista, a city some seventy-five miles southeast of Tucson. There were two passengers plus the pilot aboard this six-seat plane. All three died when their plane impacted on the side of Mount Pelée, a dormant volcano rising out of a gorgeous tropical island with a fascinating history.

The three had been searching for a proper location for a

missionary radio station, to convert the "heathen" of the Caribbean to Christianity. They had explored this possibility on the island of Barbados and were on their way to Antigua, another English-speaking island, when their explorations ended as they passed, high in the sky, over Mt. Pelée, on the French-speaking island of Martinique.

My client-widow, Betty Ferguson, told me that the Cessna plane had been recently bought by a flying club of businessmen in Sierra Vista. As I was first exposed to it, there seemed only a remote possibility of a viable case. But at this point in my life, product liability, from a plaintiff's standpoint, was part of my religion. As a Judge Hall trainee, I took the case on the usual 25–33⅓ percent contingency.

The complaint filed joined as a defendant Hotton Aviation Company, a Tucson fixed-base operator. Hotton had sold this airplane to Ferguson's flying club and hence there was that marvelous product liability doctrine—which I, as an appellate judge, had foolishly tried to block—working for us! Our real target was Cessna, and we were acquiring jurisdiction over that company in our Arizona courts under the very rules that I had codrafted— "long-arm" rules permitted by the Great Court's innovations. Thus did we impale Cessna, a Kansas corporation, on the sharp edge of the wonderful products law, which our Arizona courts had adopted over my foolish dissent.

We, of course, joined Hotton Aviation, the retail-seller, as a codefendant for the purpose of "anchoring" the case in our state court. Under federal law, in order to remove a case to the federal district court—where most defendants prefer to be—there must be a complete (all defendants from all plaintiffs) "diversity" of citizenship. The defendant, Hotton, nicely, was an Arizona corporation, so "diversity" was lacking and we stayed in the state court, where verdicts generally come higher.

This joinder of Hotton was on solid legal grounds. Arizona by this time was married, by judicial ceremony, to the new product liability law. Following the Pogo Stick Case, several other product cases had been decided by the Arizona Supreme Court.[140] So, without question, the retailer (Hotton, in this case) was liable for any "defect" in the airplane that it had sold, but it was entitled to recover indemnity from the manufacturer if it could establish that the "defect" was there when the plane had been received from the manufacturer.

Inasmuch as our *Ferguson* case was based entirely on a design and manufacturing defect, Hotton really had little to worry about. It could serve as our state court anchor without fear.

The wonderful new product liability law was a powerful sword in hand as I began getting ready for trial against Cessna. I proceeded to employ an aerospace engineer from California State Polytechnic University as my expert, Joseph McKinley. I was soon "loaded for bear" with theories of defects supplied by him—more than enough to get me to a jury to argue damages. Among McKinley's principal theories was that this particular plane, at certain altitudes, has a propensity to vibrate, or "flutter," to its destruction.

Under McKinley's directions I set about finding out everything there was to know about what caused this plane to come to its end. This took me on two different occasions to the island of Martinique.

There, my encounter with the French legal system jolted everything I had come to know about the rights of plaintiffs to discover evidence. My first denouement occurred at a restaurant, over glasses of fine wine, where I was attempting to interview the two gendarmes who had filed the official accident investigation report as to this plane crash. This clever ploy of mine, a *tête-à-tête*, so to speak, with *the* sources of knowledge of my case, netted me absolutely nothing!

These officers politely but firmly informed me that, under French law, they could not even talk to me about the case. Under their law, it seemed—incredibly—the written report of the

---

140. For example, see *Estabrook v. J. C. Penney Company,* 105 Ariz. 302, 464 P.2d 325 (1970), and *Byrns v. Riddell,* 113 Ariz. 264, 550 P.2d 1065 (1976) embracing enthusiastically Dean Prosser's assault on the citadel.

investigating officers is the *only* source of information available to civil litigants. I have learned since that this French law is followed by many "civil law" countries—countries that trace their law back to the Napoleonic Code of 1807—which countries include most of Western Europe and Latin America. A great way to save the public from paying policemen while they talk to lawyers, but a dismal scene for lawyers, particularly a plaintiffs' lawyer like me.

I found out that under French law, I could not even take their depositions! Having always practiced under the wonderful U.S. system, which permits us to pry out vast amounts of information from opponents and whomever, it was extremely puzzling to learn that international law supports many restrictions on the "discovery" that American lawyers savor and which fuels the magnificent dollar awards that we can provide to our clients.[141]

But—praise the Lord for our U.S. law—I proceeded to camp out in Wichita, Kansas, to take depositions of Cessna's personnel, and there I used all of the gamut of procedures that trial lawyers in this country have invented to find out the closely kept secrets of opposing parties.

In May 1980, I deposed: 1) William "Ted" Moody, the chief engineer of the team that had designed the cantilever wing for the 210 aircraft; 2) Arden Bloedel, an engineer responsible for the structural integrity of the 210 design; 3) Donald Ahrens, an engineer who had helped design the 210, and 4) five other Cessna personnel selected by Cessna to testify on its behalf in response to my notice of deposition that required Cessna to produce knowledgeable witnesses on seventeen designated "deposition subjects" (e.g., on the "structural strength of the wing of the 210L model aircraft," etc. etc.).

---

141. Restrictions of the Hague Evidence Convention, Articles 12(b) and 23, permit a foreign state to refuse to respond to a discovery request from the U.S. Many foreign countries refuse to permit depositions. See U.S. Department of State Circular, "Obtaining Evidence Abroad" (April 13, 1987). And see Kozolchyk and Molloy, *U.S. Law of Trade and Investment,* chapter 16, §§ 83–86 (William S. Hein, 2001).

Opposing me as counsel representing Cessna were Robert Lesher and Richard Kleindienst. Lesher was an experienced defense attorney who had served a stint as a justice of the Arizona Supreme Court, and Richard Kleindienst, as a very few of you may remember, had been United States attorney general under President Nixon and was considered to be very competent as a trial lawyer, serving in that capacity for a leading Phoenix defense firm both before and after his unfortunate sojourn in Washington.

After tenderly milking information from the top guns in the Cessna organization, I then proceeded to depose some subordinates whose names I had gleaned in the course of those first probings. Most were engineers. I had come to appreciate that engineers tend to be vulnerable to a well-conducted discovery deposition. Their profession is fact-oriented; they have accepted certain physical laws about which they find themselves unable to intellectually quarrel. Laws of physics can sometimes be a trial lawyer's lever to bring out wondrous statements for juries to ponder.

The depositions in Wichita went on for weeks. Key Cessna witnesses were grilled for days on end to garner a few wondrous (for my plaintiffs) words as to certain built-in propensities of this aircraft that a jury might determine, after my able argument, were "defects." These "defects," which my expert seized upon as causes of this accident, can be attributed in great part to the need of Cessna to meet and beat its competition.

Cessna was competing against, and, in the field of six-place private aircraft, was selling more aircraft than, Piper, Beechcraft, Mooney, or any other manufacturer in the world market. The statistics of cruise speed (how fast will it go?) and range (how far will it go on a tank of gas?) are what sell aircraft. The 210's statistics had made it the best-selling in the world in its class.

But, fortunately for members of the Fraternity, jurors do not think the same way as manufacturers of products and are not very sympathetic with any dilution of safety to garner sales, especially when the case is properly argued to them by counsel who has attended a few seminars to learn to how to get juries excited.

This Ferguson case went to trial on July 10, 1980. The jury came in with verdicts on July 15, 1980, after a full day of deliberation (again agony time) for the plaintiffs and against Cessna, in the total sum $1.765 million (PV04 $4,003,608). In today's courts, jury trials of cases of this nature *always* last much longer and have a propensity to result in higher verdicts.

There are other of my cases that I would like to tell you about, but the point to be brought home here needs no more illustration. The Ferguson case was won, not because I was a great trial lawyer, because I was not—perhaps just average among those who specialized in trial work—but because of the magic of the rules of discovery that have been put in place in U.S. courts by the Fraternity. These rules, unique to the world's legal systems,[142] permit the prying out of the most confidential information of your opponent to gouge out bountiful money damages in our courts.

About this time in my trial career, two other Cessna crashes came my way, attracted, perhaps, by the publicity of the Ferguson case. These subsequent cases involved four other deaths, in which I used some of the discovery in the Ferguson case, supplementing it with additional days of deposition to glean more "jewels" of confession with which to regale a jury. These cases were satisfactorily settled for my clients, for sums that cannot be revealed by reason of restrictions expressed in settlement agreements.[143]

It was in these times, in July 1981, that the Greatest of Courts

---

142. See Newman and Zaslowsky, *Litigating International Commercial Disputes*, §§ 83–96, chapter 16, in *United States Law of Trade and Investment* (Wm. S. Hein, 2001).

143. Such a nondisclosure requirement is typical of settlements with knowledgeable defendants, so as not to encourage other lawsuits. Not long after these cases—all single-engine cases—Cessna announced that it was terminating the production of all single-engine aircraft because of "the proliferations of product liability litigation" (quote from the Cessna web page <*cessna.textron.com*> The renewal of such production came ten years later, after the passage of the General Aviation Revitalization Act of 1994, 49 U.S.C.A. § 40,101, which established a statute of repose—barring claims for damages on product defects more than eighteen years in existence.

received its first, in a long time, recruit who had actually had some experience on a trial bench, Sandra Day O'Connor, appointed by President Reagan. Justice O'Connor had, after reaching prominence in Arizona's Republican Party, actually served as a trial judge in Phoenix for five years—the most such experience for any appointee to that Great Court in its entire history. Despite her judicial background, and perhaps influenced by her political background, she also was destined to favor the selection of a Republican over a Democrat to be president. She chose to do so in the most inconspicuous way possible—by joining in *per curiam* decisions written by unidentified persons.

But we are again ahead of our story, so back to October 15, 1981, when further commercializing of our firm occurred. It was then that a memo of the E/C ordered all law clerks to add to their bills to clients—always based upon every minute devoted to a client's case—a new special charge for using a computer in research. After all, computers cost the firm money.

And, our firm was adding paralegals to all "departments" of our firm—by 1982 we had twelve paralegals vigorously billing out their time.

In these days, for riding on this wave of success without really trying to control the direction of the wave, I had the highest salary in the firm of $125,000 (PV04 $240,800), plus regular annual bonuses. My salary was comparable to that of the president of the U.S. The 1982 *Martindale* directory listed our firm as having twenty-five lawyers, more than any other in southern Arizona. We had passed the Bilby firm! We had a support staff of another fifty or so.

The cash-producers of this "staff" were the paralegals—our firm was one of the leaders in our part of the world in employing these new income-producers. So, as the thirteenth year of my return to practice was filling out, in 1982, I found myself at the head of the fastest-growing firm in our part of the world—we were very pleased with ourselves. We considered ourselves—nay, we were—the premier law firm in southern Arizona.

Looking back at this history, there is a milestone on February 12, 1982, when our executive committee voted to buy an IBM 5520 computer to keep track of billing time. Big as a large desk, this computer cost $192,000 (PV04 $371,846). Its acquisition did not change the mechanics of our billing, we had already sold our soul to the Devil—to a leased computer—but somehow, this purchase was a philosophical event as well as a monetary commitment. A leased system could be dropped, with no big loss. But now, there was no going back! The computer had to be paid for; it had to earn its keep, with the money that it would produce from the bills it would generate.

From then on, logged time became such a controlling force that any preaching of being "professionals" or suggesting that a lawyers' charges to their clients should not be measured by the hour because such was "for plumbers" would have been ludicrous. Such profanity was never uttered, nor even thought—by me or anyone else in our profit-seeking firm. Granted, the firm's billing committee subsequently came up with several recommended ways to "value bill," but these were all ways to increase the hourly rate whenever there were "special" circumstances. A fee computed by the hour had become the rock-bottom floor.

And fees were inexorably rising. The firm's records indicate that my billing rate went from the $40 (PV04 $188.66) per hour that Russell Jones had told me I should charge when I came off of the bench in 1969, to $75 (PV04 $243.44) per hour in 1976, and then to $140 (PV04 $271) in 1982.

Our firm was not alone in this metamorphosis. The pure, pervasive urge to *make money,* more and more, dominated the thinking of lawyers. And this new concept of value permeated the thinking of those on the bench. Lawyers trained in this concept—that time is the measure of a lawyer's worth—were appointed to the judiciary. In that regard, as you may remember, our firm had contributed two appointees to the bench, just since I had shifted roles in the Fraternity.

As I was closing out this financially rewarding chapter in my life, the Nine High Priests were continuing to receive inspiration from their gods as to the true meaning of the Fifth Amendment. Much of what they did can be traced back to the decisions of the Egregious Eight years.

The case of *Carter v. Kentucky*[144] was one of these in which a conviction was overturned—so that the Fraternity could continue to earn fees—for the sole reason that the trial judge had not affirmatively instructed the jury that a defendant's failure to give any testimony: "*...cannot be used as an inference of guilt and should not prejudice him in any way.*"

This was one step beyond *Griffin,*[145] which had come down just sixteen years prior—preventing a prosecuting attorney from actively arguing that the silence of a defendant is evidence of guilt. But there was nothing in *Griffin* to stop jurors from using their common sense when a defendant failed to take the stand to tell them what happened. *Carter* now proceeds to massage the Constitution again, so as to make it more difficult to convict, providing, of course, that the defendant has a competent member of the Fraternity to make the right moves.

Carter received little notice from either the Fraternity or the press because the Great Ones had already taken our society so far in the direction of insisting that lawyers' games be played in our courts. After all, when decisions such as *Miranda* are part of our most *sacred* inheritance that were given to us by our brave forefathers, what is a little impediment to law enforcement such as *Carter*?

It had taken hundreds upon hundreds of pages for our High Priests to explain these drastic—and magnificent for the Fraternity—changes in the meaning of the simple language—"*...nor shall be compelled in any criminal case to be a witness against himself...,*" but it was accomplished!

The simplest ways to determine guilt versus innocence, used

---

144. 450 U.S. 288 (1981).

145. 380 U.S. 609 (1965).

in law enforcement since the beginning of civilization, have been eliminated from our system of justice. Unfortunately, any time one makes a game out of determining who has committed a crime, the possibility of accusing/convicting an innocent person is increased, for there is a natural drive in our society to punish when an ugly crime has been committed.

Here is the bottom line: What is wrong with holding that every person has a duty to help in the pursuit of the truth, as our juvenile courts had proclaimed before being destroyed by Fortas's *Gault* decision?

CHAPTER ELEVEN

Sunset
1982–1992

Sunsets in Arizona are spectacular. First the sky turns somber, flashes of magnificent color follow, and then the night closes in.

The sad tales that follow will convince you that Judge Hall was right in his speech at my installation ceremony as a trial judge, when he mentioned what a hardworking lawyer I was, without much of a concession of any degree of acumen or intelligence.

I will not give you the details of what followed. It would be too painful for both of us. Shall we just say that I proceeded, over the course of two years, to lose two big jury cases that had taken months upon months to try before juries. Those were contingency cases, taken on by me in keeping with the Judge Hall tradition. In those two cases our firm had invested several hundred thousand dollars in out-of-pocket costs (depositions, etc.). And these cases kept me in Phoenix, laboring away in the trial court there, for six months at a stretch.

And while I was thus suffering convulsive defeats, the leadership of my firm passed to others, and, in what seemed like a short time, I had retired and the largest law firm in southern Arizona had disintegrated.

A good part of what propitiated my demise was my resistance to the very same profit-making concepts that I had embraced in their inception, but which became nauseant as they evolved in their crassness.

I will hit only on the highlights of the schisms that destroyed my leadership and subsequently the firm itself. To give you a picture, I have refreshed my memory from the firm's corporate records and quote from them occasionally. I like to believe that among the reasons for the disintegration was my revulsion against the firm's focusing always on profit—the truth may be that I was just getting old.

Those were years of metamorphosis in which clients had to pay in order to receive service—always moving to increase the dollar intake into the law firm. One of the new moves that disturbed my reconstituted conscience was a "client profile" and an "intake procedure," put in place over my objections by the new leadership of our firm. These new standards were carefully designed to guard against the disaster of getting a client who could not afford to pay our ever-rising hourly fees.

Our reorganized firm was now to focus, according to this "profile," on "banking," "construction," "real estate," and "publications." Clients seeking our services who did not fit into these categories were to be turned away, with certain exceptions when there was a clear potential of large, collected fees. Clients with domestic relations problems should be accepted only when the divorce involved "very substantial property." Plaintiffs with employment discrimination cases were in the "per se" class, to be rejected—but defending such cases was acceptable, providing the client was "substantial."

Areas that the firm must "avoid" were: 1) "small personal injury cases," 2) representing "very small businesses," and 3) "simple wills for small estates, and guardianships."

No. 3 in this list of "no-nos" eliminated the jobs of two of our younger associates whom we had recruited to join our "full-service" firm to handle domestic relations matters for our clients. Every now and again one of our principal clients had need of such services for a family member or a key employee, but such matters were, admittedly, not a lucrative source of fees and hence, according to the new regime, should be purged from our area of service.

An important change was made as to the taking on of any "new matter" by any of our lawyers. The new "intake procedure" prohibited any lawyer in the firm from accepting a new client, or even from accepting an additional case from an old client. All such were to be passed upon by an "intake committee" appointed by the E/C.

What a contrast to the individualism of the Judge Hall firm!

Seeking protest material, I inquired as to what other firms were doing, and was appalled to find that our firm's new mandates were typical in the new lawyering world being structured by the Fraternity. These changes seemed to make sense to the younger, talented recruits, whose interests were focused on how much money could be made out of their activities as soon as possible. All of which has economic virtue because of its business efficiency, but, there are some poignant downsides—centering around impediments to the average citizen's obtaining lawyer service.

Clients designated to be purged from our firm had been the mainstay of the Hall-type of firm. A significant virtue of this kind of clientele is that there are lots of them, and if you cater to them, you have a broad base of income. As the new order took over law firms, these persons found it much more difficult to obtain the kind of the lawyer-client relationship that they had enjoyed.

And, of course, my reconstructed firm was totally sold on the money-is-time theme. With me, as the years had rolled by, charging by the hour had become somewhat less entrancing. And, of course, this was a good part of my "has-been" status.

I noticed that, under this time-is-money system, my *individual* noncorporate clients nervously tried to save themselves from what they considered to be oppressive fees. This would cause them to hurry to tell me about their case—to "stop-the-clock" on their bill. This anxiety, on a rare occasion or two, resulted in the client failing to communicate something of legal significance, resulting in detriment to their case. Fortunately, our *corporate* clients (our targeted clients) didn't seem to have the same problem—somehow corporate employees (including their in-house lawyers) just don't have that same nervousness over taking up the time of a lawyer.

For me personally, the new regime tended to isolate me from my type of client, and my precious contingency cases, which I had always accepted routinely à la Judge Hall.

And it was in these times, in June 1986, that another lawyer who had never judged a single case from a trial bench was appointed to our Highest Court—Antonin Scalia—by President Reagan. He had previously been elevated to the Court of Appeals for the District of Columbia by Reagan, coming from a career as a recognized conservative-minded law professor—previously a resident scholar at the American Enterprise Institute, a conservative think tank in Washington, DC.

Scalia was also destined, not surprisingly, to select a Republican over a Democrat to be the president of the United States.

At the time of my loss of leadership of my firm, *Martindale* listed our firm as having thirty-six lawyers—four of whom were in the Phoenix office. We still continued to grow in the early post-Molloy era. But, though the lowest paid, newly recruited law graduate in our firm was earning $27,500 (PV04 $46,557), according to our new leadership all the "better organized" firms were doing "much better" in this regard and we needed to dedicate ourselves to bringing our firm up to its "true potential."

A new concept of who should be allowed to be a shareholder was placed in a memorandum coming from the sans-Molloy executive committee. It proclaimed that shareholders, "of course," had to be "av" rated in *Martindale*. Remarkably, at time of this proclamation, all of the "shareholders" in what had been a Molloy-led firm *were* "av" rated in *Martindale*, the top rating of this national "bible" of the profession, and our firm was listed in *Martindale's*

"The Register," reserved for the elite law firms of this country. But we had never insisted that before one became a shareholder, this status of recognized merit must have been achieved.

The real blockbuster in the new protocol was that, to be a shareholder, one had to excel at being a "business-getter." One shareholder, the new dogma stated, must be able to keep two associates busy with the "business"—an odious word to those trained in a Judge Hall firm—that the shareholder must have generated. The previous structure, when there had been more "partners" than "associates," was to be a thing of the past.

Amazingly, and ominously, as this revolution in the firm proceeded, my name was left as the lead name in our banner. The firm name was even changed to Molloy, Jones, Donahue, P.C. (dropping the names of Trachta, Childers, and Mallamo). This occurred on October 15, 1986. With my name in the very front, others were steering the firm's course. Looking back, it was like placing me in the nose cone of a space rocket steered by others.

My total derailment from the power structure occurred in March 1987 at a specially called meeting of certain selected stockholders in the firm—selected by the new leadership as being "producers." When the meeting convened, I learned that the purpose of the meeting was to work out the procedure to eliminate four lawyers in our firm who were labeled as "nonproducers." One was a shareholder, a "partner" in the pre-corporate organization.

What a violation of the Judge Hall "marriage" philosophy!

With heart pounding, I made a passionate speech in opposition. I brought up the history of the firm. I used the word "fraternity" to try to express the spirit that I felt was being violated by the meeting. My total misuse of this word was prompted by thinking of my college fraternity and its spirit of loyalty and support for each other, even for the less endowed amongst the brethren.

My trouble was that I was dealing with a different kind of a Fraternity, religiously dedicated to increasing the earnings of the gifted few. My passion in delivering an argument that the four lawyers to be eliminated had all committed their lives to the firm—that one of them had waited years for membership in our firm, and that we had talked about the act of taking in a new member as being analogous to a "marriage"—received a cold, bored response from this audience of those that I had helped recruit because of their high grades coming out of law college.

And that was the end of my leadership. The New Order, I was subsequently told by its new leader, was to be that I was still to be the nominal president, but with power only to sign documents, and then only when directed to do so. I was to be able to attend E/C meetings, ex officio, but I was *not* to have a vote! My salary, set at the annual meeting of the board, would continue, at least temporarily.

The firm's bylaws were amended so as to take away the management of the firm from the board of directors, which under our historic structure consisted of all the shareholders, and to vest it in the executive committee—which meant those who had led the sanctification by which my leadership ended.

After this meeting at which I was defrocked, I went home and spent the night debating with myself whether to leave the firm and take a few lawyers with me—or stay?—with what in outward appearances was a burgeoning firm—the largest law firm in southern Arizona. My perennial lack of courage controlled—I stayed.

Afterward, I attended many meetings of the E/C and, when given a chance, spoke against concentrating the firm's client efforts on large corporations and against discouraging small businesses and individual clients from coming to the firm. My opinions were politely listened to by the E/C and then ignored.

The members targeted for elimination were treated "appropriately." Those selected as "deadwood" were eased out of the firm, usually with an "either-produce-or-leave" ultimatum. A memo from the E/C dated March 30, 1987, described what would happen in the future when lawyers in the firm did not meet "expectations":

> Those individuals should be informed of the specifics,
> and a timetable for the changes developed with them.

They should be informed of the nature and prospect of future action which will be recommended by the Executive Committee to the shareholders if changes do not occur.

*   *   *

The Executive Committee will communicate to each individual clear performance standards which address the discrepancies, with a requirement that the standards be met within a nine-month period. Each of the individuals will be asked to agree, or the shareholders will be asked to approve separation of that individual from the firm if the standards are not so met. Earlier separation will be discussed with those individuals who do not feel able or willing to meet the standards proposed.

My ejection from control caused no immediate downturn in the firm's prosperity. The New System worked very profitably, that is, for a while.

Though the stock market had suffered its biggest loss in history on October 19, 1987,[146] lawyers were needed in ever-increasing droves as the Fraternity continued to change the rules of the games by which the Brethren play so as to provide more for the Brethren to do to earn fees.

In February 1988 there was another appointment by President Reagan to the Highest of All Courts—again a lawyer totally without trial-judging experience—Anthony M. Kennedy. Some years previously Kennedy had been appointed to an appellate bench as the result of being involved in Republican politics, and thus obtaining the endorsement of the then California Republican governor Ronald Reagan. No one was surprised when Justice Kennedy con-

---

146. To be exceeded only by the loss taken after the terrorists' destruction of the World Trade Center on the morning of September 11, 2001—a drop, then, of 684 points on the Dow when the market reopened on September 17.

tributed to the choosing of a Republican as our president.

Another appointment to the High Court came on October 9, 1990—by President George Bush (The First). This was David Hackett Souter who was so anointed. Remarkably, this appointee had *actually* served as a trial judge for five years (in New Jersey)—tying Justice O'Connor's precedent-breaking record in this respect. Despite the source of his appointment, and I like to think because of his judicial background, this justice did not join in making his anointer's son our president.

But, the Team of Five to get this accomplished was almost assembled, for, in October 1991, President Bush (I) made his second appointment to the Great Court—Clarence Thomas. As per the historic practice, again he picked a lawyer with no experience as a trial judge—a lawyer recognized for his conservative leanings. It is not in the least surprising that Justice Thomas did join in selecting his appointer's son as our president.

Then, after a second year under the New Order, the firm, which had taken twenty years to build, came apart.

Profit motivation proved to be more of a separator than a glue. It seems that if the focus is always on making more money, there is much to dispute as to who is going to take less when the firm's profit turns into less. By this time a good part of our income was concentrated in the "big" clients, many of which were banks and savings and loan associations and others who met our new standards. Unfortunately, the year 1991 was a year of depression for banks, and particularly savings and loan companies.

A 1986 Tax Act, passed by a Reagan-inspired Congress, had eliminated the advantage of owning nonprofitable real estate. The advantage had come from the ability to take, on personal income tax returns, depreciation losses from ownership of buildings and the like so as to subtract such from income generated from other sources. The value of real property, particularly in Arizona, where we had had a surge in values over the past ten years, plummeted. There were many foreclosure sales. Lending companies had to foreclose on vast amounts of property. New money for loans became scarce and interest rates went sky-high.

Savings and loan associations were hit the hardest. They had been mandated by federal law since their inception to place most of their money into long-term real estate loans at low interest rates. What they had done, of course, was to lend out their depositors' money, and when interest rates went up and they had to pay as much, or more, for depositors' money as the interest rate on the loans they had made, they went bankrupt by the droves. And these were the clients that our newly led firm had been "focusing" on as we dropped the less lucrative ones. So it was then that two of our major clients, both S&Ls, were taken over as insolvent by the Resolution Trust Corporation (RTC), the U.S. government agency specially created to try to temper the damage being done by the nationwide collapse of S&Ls.

Of course, the RTC did a land-office business in foreclosing mortgages, but our newly constructed E/C decided that we would not represent the RTC because it paid too little *by the hour.* By this time this measuring standard was more common for lawyers than for ditch-diggers. Then, to add to our woes, our largest client, our only bank client that had not gone defunct, was acquired by another bank, based in Phoenix, our state's capital, and, as often occurs after such an acquisition, our firm was replaced by Phoenix counsel for the acquiring bank. So we lost our biggest client to go along with our other losses of clients.

An emergency meeting of the shareholders was called by the new leadership for August 17, 1992. At this meeting our well-paid administrator told us that our problem was "cash flow," which was not coming in fast enough to take care of the "payroll." An imposing percentage of this bothersome "payroll" was the "take" of those whom I considered partners—but who were, of course, now all "shareholders."

At this meeting, lasting an hour or so, I had the temerity to argue that we, the shareholders, should all take an appropriate cut in salary to make up the gap. There was dead silence after my impassioned presentation. None of these shareholder-non-partners volunteered to cut any "salary" to help the firm in its crisis. An across-the-board cut in everyone's take, including associates, secretaries, and all, was discussed for about five minutes and then discarded—because it was recognized that the better secretaries and staff might leave to go to more prosperous firms.

At this time, seeing that I was contributing nothing to this money-hungry organization, I resigned, on my seventy-fifth birthday, indicating that I would come back to the firm *only* if I was given the leadership that I had once had. This proffer was promptly declined.

Disintegration followed immediately. The "business-getters" left, to be employed by firms who had been more fortunate in retaining their clients. There remained in the old offices, with an oppressive lease commitment, just eight practitioners and staff. Bankruptcy was a distinct possibility. I could see quite clearly my name as the lead in such a filing. But the eight who had not deserted for greener pastures labored on, and discussion ensued about my returning to the firm.

After months of negotiation between myself and members of my disintegrated law firm, amazingly, a few remaining shareholders of the firm signed a "creed" I authored. In consideration of this signing, I agreed to leave my name in the firm. Though my active leadership was disdained, the ex-judge name on the door was still an attraction. On the firm's letterhead, still emblazoned with my name as lead, I was listed as being "of counsel."

The creed included these wonderful provisions:

CREED

As a shareholder ("Member") of Molloy, Jones & Donahue, P.C. ("Firm"), I accept and intend to act according to the following statement of principles:

1. The objective of the Firm is to provide excellent and ethical professional services to clients in the Firm's chosen areas of practice for reasonable and fair fees.

2. The members of the Firm commit to deal with

one another as partners, with undivided loyalty to the Firm and to each other and with the intent that such commitment shall continue indefinitely.

3. In fulfilling the Firm's ethical obligations toward its clients, each Member commits to the following [italics added in the following, to indicate the portions that "bothered" some of the remaining firm members who had come to think that billing by the minute was the only way]:

A. Retainer fee agreements incorporating fixed fee, contingent fee, *reduced rate or other alternative billing arrangements* shall be considered at the inception of the undertaking of a new legal matter, whether for new or existing clients.

B. In all instances fees charged by the Firm shall be fair and reasonable to the client as well as the Firm, *giving full consideration to the value of the services to the client as a primary factor, and the time spent by the lawyers performing the client's work being billed shall not be considered as the sole factor* in determining the amount of the bill.

4. Upon admission to the Firm, new members shall sign this Creed.

DATED August 5, 1993.

The creed was signed by the remaining seven (one more of our group had departed since the original breakup). This was all that was left out of 27 shareholder and 15 associate lawyers. The rest had all deserted to greener (the color of dollars) pastures, but these sturdy seven, along with some of the secretaries and paralegals, stayed with the firm long enough keep it out of bankruptcy, despite the continuing lease on three (we had picked up another floor since we had moved) whole floors in Tucson's high-rent district. I was naive enough to believe that with this creed, this firm would come back to the vibrant organization it had been. But, it did not, not even close.

Part of the problem was that my name no longer drew in clients, as in the old years. There is nothing like being an ex-judge to attract clients, but the "ex" has to be from more recent press than mine. As much of a problem as anything was that the signers of this creed *didn't really believe in it*. They had "gotten on the tit," so to speak, of hourly fees, and they saw no point in giving up the monetary milk that flowed as they recorded every minute of their time on the computer. Most had come to believe that their worth was really measured by their time—they could not mentally focus on billing by what they had accomplished for the client. Time sheets were draconically required by firm protocol, and the computer still measured the bills sent to clients despite the creed.

No one in this regurgitated firm ever consulted me as to how to prepare a contingency contract with a client; I was always ready with the Judge Hall 25–33% formula, or a variation thereof. But, survive they did, and my name was saved from bankruptcy by the tenacity and professional skill of the small group of lawyers who stuck with this disintegrating firm, and—I hate to admit—the computers billing by the minute.

Onto this dismal scene came the last merger, with the then very successful Phoenix firm of O'Connor Cavanaugh. The Tucson office became O'Connor Cavanaugh Molloy Jones, P.C., on September 1, 1996. The creed forthwith became history, unknown history—forgotten as ridiculous trivia.

And what were the Holy Nine doing during these turbulent years, you ask? (You better, for we are coming to the end of this chapter, and that is where you should have become conditioned to expect this sort of thing.) Well, the answer is a number of things, and, as you might suspect, things moving our culture always move into the clutches of the Fraternity.

I select three cases in this time frame for comment to illustrate the progress that the Fraternity was making for Itself.

Cleveland Board of Education v. Loudermill[147] is an illustration of

---

147. 470 U.S. 532 (1985).

the wonderful (for the Fraternity) finding of *new* rights in *old* constitutional language to provide more for lawyers to be paid to do.

Mr. Loudermill was a security guard at a school. In his application for his job, he stated that he had never been convicted of a felony. When the school board learned that he had, in fact, been convicted of the felony of grand larceny, they felt it appropriate to terminate Mr. Loudermill's employment as a school employee.

Bad idea!

Before discharging him, the school board had given Loudermill ample opportunity to disprove the record of his conviction, in accordance with the procedures of the civil service provisions of Ohio law, but Loudermill declined to do so, because he had, in fact, lied about his record in his application. Ohio law had created this position as one of "civil service," but, in the very statute creating the job had provided for certain procedures to be followed before a holder of one of these jobs could be terminated—all of which procedure had been followed by the school board in the process of its discharging of Mr. Loudermill.

Nevertheless, the Greatest of Courts proceeded to hold that, even though the procedure for termination provided in the creation of this job was carefully followed, nevertheless the termination was *constitutionally wrong* because the full panoply of "due process" procedures—meaning much lawyer-work—which the Holy Nine has managed to find with glorious prose in the Fifth Amendment, were not followed.

The new religious dogma of *Loudermill* is now inextricably a part of every job created by law when that law gives the employee any rights at all to be free from arbitrary termination. In effect, it holds that there is no such thing as a partial civil servant, any more than there is a partially pregnant woman. Either the employee is entitled to all of the panoply of procedures that all civil service employees are held to have as "property rights," or none[148]

---

148. Until the Fraternity shifted the law again, as it did in the "whistle-blowing" cases, giving the employee a cause of action against the employer if fired for reasons against "public policy." See Kozolchyk & Molloy, *United States Law of Trade & Investment,* 2001, chapter 14, § 70 (c).

(because no limitation upon the employer's right to terminate had been promised). This result is reached by prolix, obtuse writings of our Great Court, which but few lawyers can understand, with five separate, "learned" (which means with much law clerk time involved) opinions.

It is doubtful that *Loudermill* will cause any lessening in the number of legal firings in this country, because most employees who lie about a felony conviction to get a job in a school organization will probably still be fired, but be assured that *there will be substantially more legal fees paid to accomplish this.*

Another case of this time is *Ake v. Oklahoma.*[149] This is a murder case, with the death penalty being imposed by the trial court. I realize, of course, that about half of you are inclined to accept *Ake* as a step in the right direction, because of your feelings about the death penalty. But perhaps you will appreciate that this case represents an unnecessary diversion of public monies to the Fraternity.

Ake had been examined for mental capacity prior to trial in the usual course by psychiatrists of the state mental hospital and been found competent to stand trial. Defendant's counsel declined to call any one of these psychiatrists to testify at trial, but, instead, moved for the appointment of still another psychiatrist, at state expense, to examine the defendant for the purposes of trial testimony. The motion was denied by a trial judge with much more experience in these matters than those who were to overrule him. The trial judge made his decision in obeisance to the previous law laid down by the Great Court[150] which left this matter in the discretion of the States. But in doing so, this trial judge erred, for the Fraternity was moving our law even further in its pursuit of a lawyer-oriented perfect justice.

Ake's lawyer, of course, during the jury trial of this case, had argued that his client did not have sufficient mental capacity to

---

149. 470 U.S. 68 (1985).

150. *U.S. ex rel Smith v. Baldi,* 344 U.S. 561 (Feb. 9, 1953).

form the necessary malice aforethought to be convicted of murder. The jury, after listening to the evidence and observing the defendant in trial, decided otherwise.

It is fairly easy to raise an insanity defense, and, when the facts are blackest for a defendant, astute members of the Fraternity do just that. Every state has a mental health procedure, with which trial judges across this land are well-acquainted. These procedures are regularly used to protect the mentally incompetent. To impose upon this nonpartisan structure the addition of a publicly paid psychiatrist—for the special purpose of testifying at an adversary trial—may make the games we lawyers play more interesting for TV cameras, and more lucrative for lawyers, but achieves nothing of public good.

There was no problem in the Ake case that needed fixing. Trial judges simply do not want to sentence mentally incompetents to prison or death. What Ake's lawyer, with the help of the Great Fraternity, achieved, was an absolute mandate that *every time* an indigent defendant throws in the issue of his competence to stand trial, the state must—on top of having examined his mental state by qualified professionals—pay for a special witness to examine said defendant and to testify at the trial. And, of course, if the defendant's counsel has anything to do with the selection of the examiner (and *Ake* would seem to encourage this),[151] the defense lawyer is *not* likely to pick a doctor who has a reputation for being conservative in finding mental illness or for being a poor testifier on the witness stand.

Thus, permanently and inextricably (for *Ake* places this principle in the holiest of documents), the games of lawyers' skills are made more necessary, and one more chess piece is put on the board for the defense to checkmate the prosecution.

There is one more pontificated "breakthrough" in these times that we should look at: *Minnick v. Mississippi.*[152] In this discovery

---

151. See M. Goodman, *The Right To a Partisan Psychiatric Expert: Might Indigency Preclude Insanity?* 61 N.Y.U. L. Rev. 703 (Oct. 1986).

152. 498 U.S. 146 (1990).

of new meaning in the Constitution, our All-Knowing Court extended the idiocy of *Miranda*. This defendant, Minnick, had had considerable experience with law enforcement procedures—having previously been convicted of robbery in Mississippi and assault with a deadly weapon in California. In this case, Minnick stood charged with yet another serious crime in Mississippi. He was assigned a competent, state-paid lawyer, with whom he held several consultations.

This lawyer, like any good defense lawyer, advised Minnick not to talk to law enforcement officers. Despite this, Minnick proceeded to tell a Mississippi deputy sheriff, who had come to California to talk to him, about his participation in a double murder in Mississippi. Whereupon, Mississippi authorities thought it appropriate to extradite and prosecute, thinking they could use this sheriff's testimony to enlighten a jury as to what had happened. And in this way we had another very costly, for the public, mistake!

For, after a conviction in Mississippi, the Great Court stepped in to reverse a result achieved after years of litigation. *Minnick* comes down with new Scripture to the effect that once an accused has designated a lawyer, that person has acquired an impenetrable shield to being questioned in the absence of that lawyer. And what a magnificent (for the Fraternity) impediment to learning truth!

Lesson: *Perhaps the most important to be learned in this life—get yourself a lawyer as soon as possible.*

Thus the Fraternity tightens its grip on the dispensation of justice to its lucrative benefit, as it will continue to do, unless the hypnotic spell that causes our people to accept the Brethren's religious dogma can somehow be broken.

CHAPTER TWELVE

Twilight
1992–2004

While this all was going on, in November 1992, William Clinton was elected our president, and a Democrat finally got an opportunity to put someone on the High Court. So it was in August 1993 that this nation acquired the then *only* member of the Great Court appointed by a Democrat—Ruth Bader Ginsburg. (The last Democratic appointment had been that of Thurgood Marshall, in June 1967.)

But Clinton had no more regard for trial judging experience than had his predecessors. Like so many of her colleagues, our new Justice Ginsburg had never been a trial judge, but did have a fine academic career at several of our leading law schools. She had also served on an appellate bench, the Court of Appeals for the District of Columbia—a President Carter appointment—twelve years prior to her ascendancy to the Ultimate Plateau. As might be expected, in view of her political affiliation, Justice Ginsburg was to dissent from selecting the Republican to be our president.

And, in August 1994, the second justice selected by a Democratic president came to the High Court—Stephen Breyer. He, too, had a distinguished academic background before he had been appointed, some fourteen years before by Democratic president Carter, to the U.S. Court of Appeals. He, too, had had absolutely no experience participating in the dispensation of justice at the trial level. And, again not surprisingly considering the source of his appointment, he dissented vigorously from the Rehnquist selection of George W. Bush to be our president.

Changes at these highest of levels are contrasted by changes in our local courts—where political connection is much less important and selection by voters is more prevalent. But these decisions coming from above have taken their toll on our local court system, and I was recently personally exposed to that influence.

As retired judge, I serve occasionally in our Superior Court when the assignment clerk is desperate to keep up with a busy calendar. Recently while on such duty, I picked up a piece of literature on the clerk's counter—apparently designed to be given to any juvenile charged with a crime. It informs them that they have these "rights":

> 1) If you are a suspect in a crime and are detained, you have the right to remain silent. 2) Police officers may question you; however, you have the right to remain silent. 3) You have the right to have your parents notified of any hearings at which you may have to appear. 4) The Juvenile Court or Superior Court will provide an attorney for you upon request if you are charged with an offense in these courts and your parents cannot afford to hire one. 5) You have the right to an attorney in all court proceedings (your parents may be assessed attorney's fees.)

Little wonder that juvenile crime in this country today is such a problem! Of these "rights" in my *vintage* juvenile court—operating under the gospel as massaged by the Fraternity to that time—juveniles had, of these five enumerated "rights," only "right"#3 (the right to have ones' parents notified of "hearings"). In the process of thus making lawyers so much more important, very precious rights of both parent and child, which our juvenile court considered sacrosanct, have been eliminated.

In the pre-*Gault* court we religiously provided 1) the right of parents to be notified promptly whenever their child was arrested (why, oh why, would this now be left out of the clerk's literature?); 2) the right to have police reports checked out by trained professional social workers—sympathetic, but realistic, toward juveniles—who would present to the juvenile judge an analysis of the problem at hand; 3) the right to have an elected judge determine what had happened, without any testimony against any child being coerced by threats of punishment and/or by promises of leniency; and 4) the right to have the principal energies of the court and staff expended in the task of correcting problems—rather than in the "who-done-it?" exorcisms for lawyers to demonstrate their skills and to receive compensation for same.

And, as the second millennium closed out, the last merger of the largest law firm in southern Arizona fell apart. The assemblage of lawyers, assiduously recruited from the top of their classes out of law schools, fought with each other over who was to get the most of the more, and the firm of O'Connor Cavanaugh Molloy Jones, P.C. split into fragments, with me observing from the sidelines, interested but unaffected.

So in this manner, the Tucson firm that Judge Hall had created went completely "down the tubes." Lawyers who had practiced together for years went to various other law firms—where they could earn hourly rates more than I ever dared to charge—and could look across the halls of their offices to those of their fellow stockholders to wonder whether they were really earning as much as the firm was paying them, and whether in comparison they should not be paid more.

The glorious ability of the Fraternity to gather in fees is illustrated in the story of the murder prosecution of Timothy McVeigh. For months on end McVeigh made the front page of every newspaper in this country and every newscast on television. There was a final magnificent extravaganza of coverage on June 11,

2001, when he was given a lethal injection. This, of course, was in addition to the top coverage that he had been receiving for the six years since he had bombed the Federal Building in Oklahoma City on April 19, 1995. The Brethren managed to collect $15.1 million of tax money to defend this man whose guilt was hardly in question![153] And this sum, of course, does not cover the many dollars of public funds expended on the salaries of judges, court attachés, and the like to deal with the legal manipulations of McVeigh's court-appointed lawyers. This is money that could provide a great deal of education to worthy young ones or relieve tax impositions.

Cases such as *McVeigh* should cause any reasonable, unbiased person to question whether this system, which so favors members of the Fraternity, should be changed. The bottom line is that the purpose of every criminal justice system on this Earth is to discourage criminal conduct. What else? The purpose certainly is not to make work for lawyers, and if this make-work-and-profit for lawyers is an of-the-essence ingredient of our present system, and if this system does no better a job than the systems of other countries, which do not provide ghastly fees to their lawyers, perhaps it should be replaced or modified.

So, let us look, just for a peek, at the other systems existing in this world of ours.

Each country has its own legal system, and it is extremely difficult to accurately compare the effectiveness of these various systems insofar as they discourage crime, because there are no recognized measuring sticks. There are, of course, international crime statistics,[154] but no international standard of what a "crime" is, or even what a "burglary" is, for example.

"Crime" encompasses a vast variety of behaviors—jaywalking may be a "crime" in the statistics of one country and be ignored in the statistics of other countries. However, there is one crime that

---

153. Associated Press wire stories of July 20, 2001, and October 26, 2001.

154. Two such publications are *The Illustrated Book of World Rankings* (Sharpe, 5th ed.), and *Statistical Abstract of the World*, 3d ed.

has a common denominator—that of murder. So perhaps if we compare murder rates among countries, we will have a flavor of how well our criminal system discourages crime.

These world tabulations of this crime show that the United States ranks 42nd in the world as the most murderous, less than the homicide rate in countries such as Rwanda, Colombia, and Nambia. But it ranks after countries that do not even come close to our standard of living. For example, Mexico ranks much safer at 56th in the world, Denmark 72nd, France 75th, Italy 76th, Sweden 80th, Spain 109th, the United Kingdom 115th, and Switzerland 117th.[155] The murder rate in Sweden is one-half of that of this country, and that of Switzerland one-half of that again![156]

Getting us out of the quagmire where the Fraternity has taken us is not a small task. Congress, where our Constitution intended the legislative power to be vested, recently tried to undo some of the madness imposed by the Holy Nine by enacting a statute[157] which made the admissibility of confessions depend on whether or not they were voluntarily made, i.e., without coercion. Sound reasonable? But this legislation was nothing but a futile effort!

In *Dickerson v. U.S.*, Chief Justice Rehnquist straightened out a Congress that thought it had the right to legislate on such matters. *Dickerson* preempts Congress from tampering with meaning or intent of the magic words used in the *Miranda* decision, because, as the majority opinion explains, that decision had been placed by the Great Court in the Constitution itself, where Congress has no right to transgress.

The sheer audacity of this decision causes members of the Fraternity to glow in the pride of sharing an awesome power. As the dissent of Justices Scalia and Thomas points out, this majority

---

155. *The Illustrated Book of World Rankings,* Schedule 22.5

156. The U.S. had 9 murders per 100,000 persons; Sweden 4.5 per 100,000, and Switzerland 2.3 per 100,000.

157. 18 U.S.C. Sec. 3501.

decision appropriates for the Nine "an immense and frightening antidemocratic power" arising from "an illegitimate exercise of raw judicial power." Among this dissent's cogent language is:

"Today's judgment converts Miranda from a milestone of judicial overreaching into the very Cheops' Pyramid (or perhaps the Sphinx would be a better analogue) of judicial arrogance."

And, as this, my own diatribe, is closing down, we have seen the Fraternity displaying how really awesome its power has become—by selecting our president.

It came about because of the near-tie in the Tuesday, November, 7th, 2000, popular vote for the presidency of the United States. The winner was either Al Gore or George W. Bush. Under the national electoral system, which prescribes that voting is by states—not by individual voters—it became apparent by early morning of Thursday, November 9th, that the vote of Florida, with its twenty-five electoral votes, would decide who would be our next president.

Because of confusion in the counting, and in the format of some of the printed ballots,[158] there was uncertainty in determining what Florida vote would officially be recognized. The question was thus presented as to how to solve uncertainty in a presidential election. Our Constitution has clear language on the subject in its Twelfth Amendment:

> The President of the Senate shall, in the presence of the Senate and House of Representatives, open all the certificates [from the states] and the votes shall then be counted;—The person having the greatest number of votes for President, shall be the President, if such number be a majority of the whole number of Electors appointed; and if no person have such majority, then

---

158. See Annex hereof for a description of the vitriolic public debate over the format of the ballot used in Palm Beach County—the "butterfly ballot"—which, according to most who have examined the facts, caused thousands of voters to mistakenly vote for Reform Party candidate Patrick Buchanan when they intended to vote for Al Gore, thus costing the Democratic candidate the election.

from the persons having the highest numbers *not ex-ceeding three on the list* of those voted for as President, the House of Representatives shall choose immediately, by ballot, the President [emphasis added].

It is most obvious that our forefathers wanted the House of Representatives, elected by the voters of this country, to have great discretion in selecting our president whenever there was a close election. That body is most clearly given the power to even select the candidate with the third highest number of votes! And, there is absolutely nothing in our Constitution that suggests that the U.S. Supreme Court is to usurp from a supposedly equal branch of our government the right and duty to determine a close presidential election. The intent is so very, very clear. This important decision was to be made by persons elected by popular vote. Not by persons appointed by politicians. And the Constitution is the document which each of our Supreme Court justices have taken a solemn oath to uphold—is it not?

Prior to its getting involved in the election of 2000, the Fraternity's only interference in this presidential election process, *in the entire history of this country*, had been limited to when state legislatures themselves had provided that certain contests could be filed in a court, in the limited circumstances prescribed by these state, not federal, laws. And there is no comparable federal law.

We need to realize, in appreciating the enormity of this action taken by our power-hungry Supreme Court, that there were no national laws giving the Nine Semi-Gods such authority nor anything in our history to suggest that they had such power. Though there had been a number of very close presidential elections in the past, *there had never in our history been a judge, or judges, deciding who had been elected our president.*

Historically, whenever there had been such close votes in presidential elections, and if the states themselves did not solve the problem, the contest had been decided by Congress. This procedure was thought to be in obvious compliance with the

Constitution's above-quoted mandate that: "The President of the Senate shall, in the presence of the Senate and the House of Representatives, open all the certificates and the votes shall then be counted."[159] A "count" has always included the decision of what to count as being included in whatever is being counted, and what not to include in that count whatever does not meet the particular criteria. What else does one do when one is "counting" something?

And, always, since the beginning of our system, the mechanical "counting" has initially been done by local citizens serving on election boards, using their discretion to determine the voter's intent and sufficiency of meeting technical requirements. This historic process is exactly what the decisions of the Supreme Court of Florida would have accomplished—had not the Almighty Nine (which in this case was the Almighty Five) usurped power.[160]

Our historic tradition of how our president is selected when vote-counting is ambiguous was discarded in the year 2000, as the country witnessed the extent to which the Fraternity had increased its power.

The first and, in retrospect, the determinative interference by the Mighty Court occurred on November 24th, 2000, midafter-

---

159. One previous presidential election that rivaled, or perhaps surpassed, the closeness of this Bush/Gore contest was the election of 1876, a contest between Republican Rutherford B. Hayes and Democrat Samuel J. Tilden. To resolve a dispute over what had occurred at the November 1876 election, the House and Senate passed a joint resolution creating an Electoral Commission of fifteen members to make the decision.

160. On November 21, 2000, the Florida Supreme Court, in its unanimous decision of *Palm Beach County Canvassing Bd. v. Harris*, 772 So. 2d 1220, set aside Secretary of State Harris' refusal to accept late tallies and ordered her to accept amended returns filed by 5 *p.m.* on Sunday, November 26th. This relief was rendered after a careful analysis of Florida's election code. It is implicit in this decision that the election boards of Florida should continue to manually count ballots in the disputed counties.

noon, when the All-Powerful granted—*per curiam*[161]—a writ of certiorari as to the order of the Supreme Court of Florida.

Traditionally when a higher court grants such a writ, it is construed as an order holding in abeyance the order or judgment as to which the writ is issued. Thus, this writ put the order of Florida's Supreme Court—requiring the hand-counting of ballots—in limbo. And this gave the Secretary of State of Florida (an openly avowed Bush adherent) the opportunity to stop all further manual counting.[162] Thus, this action of the All-Powerful blocked for all time a manual recount of the votes in Florida—as it undoubtedly was intended by the Five to do.[163]

Interestingly, in its order depriving the Florida courts of jurisdiction, the *only* things that the Court stated that it was going to look at were just two possibilities of the Florida Supreme Court's order being in error:

> [W]hether the decision of the Florida Supreme Court, by effectively changing the State's elector appointment procedures after election day, violated the Due Process

---

161. Meaning simply that the author of the opinion is anonymous and not, as many lawyers suppose, that all of the judges sitting on the case joined in the decision made.

162. At 7:30 P.M. on Sunday, November 26th, Katherine Harris appeared at a public ceremony called by her in the cabinet room of the State Capitol in Tallahassee and declared that George Bush was the winner of Florida's twenty-five electoral votes by a margin of 537 votes (out of more than 6.5 million votes cast in Florida for president).

163. The election board in Miami-Dade County had commenced a manual recount, had found 168 additional votes for Gore, but abandoned its efforts without completing the recount. See *New York Times* of November 28th, at p. A-21, and see *Gore v. Harris,* 772 So. 2d 1243 at 1262 (Dec. 8, 2000). The 168 votes are part of the votes ordered by the Florida Court to be included for Gore, which order was wiped out by the December 12th order of the five Republican-appointed justices. Similarly, a recount in Dade County was abandoned and its partial tally never included in the final results. See *Gore v. Harris,* id. at 1260.

Clause or 3 U.S.C. § 5, and whether the decision of that court changed the manner in which the State's electors are to be selected, in violation of the legislature's power to designate the manner for selection under Art. II, § 1, cl.. 2 of the United States Constitution.[164]

This was it! This is what was to be checked—theoretically by a court that could be fair to all concerned. There was no mention of the Equal Protection Clause of our Constitution in this order by which it assumed jurisdiction—in this order that halted the counting of ballots by the election boards of Florida. But amazingly, the Equal Protection Clause was to emerge when these two *expressed* reasons for assuming jurisdiction could not be verbalized by the Great Court into semilucid language to support an order to block manual counting of the votes—even with the help of its law clerks, the brightest young lawyers in the land.

The Great Court's attack on the counting of ballots in Florida took specific form at 11:45 A.M. on Saturday, December 4th, when the Great Court "vacated" the order of the Florida Court because it was "unclear" as to the *reason* for that court's order.[165]

Being "unclear" in itself is not a common reason for a higher court to special-writ a lower court as the Exalted Court was doing here. It is common for a higher court to give deference to a lower court's ruling, and, if there is ambiguity, the higher court will presume, if there is a *possible* valid reason for the action taken below, that this *was* the reason for the action taken.[166] Were it not for

---

164. The quote is from the opening paragraph of the per curiam decision of the Great Court rendered on December 4.

165. 531 U.S. 70, 121 S. Ct. 471 (Dec. 4, 2000). In this order, the Great Court makes clear that it was taking upon itself this unprecedented authority because It was "unclear as to the extent to which the Florida Supreme Court saw the Florida Constitution as circumscribing the legislature's [Florida's] authority under Art. II, § 1, cl. 2.[of the U.S. Constitution] [and unclear]…as to the consideration the Florida Supreme Court accorded to 3 U.S.C. § 5 [the "safe harbor" statute]. 121 S. Ct. 471 at 475. There is nothing in this decision even hinting that the Equal Protection Clause has anything to do with the problem before the Court.

this respect, there would be a great deal more reversals of judicial decisions in this land.

Here, if there were *no* possible valid reason for the lower court's order, then this was the time, forthwith, to overrule the Florida Court—that is, assuming this matter was something that the Great Court had any business interfering in at all, which, historically, it did not.

Contrariwise, if there were a valid reason for the Florida court's decision, among obvious possibilities, it should have been left alone. But this, of course, is not what the All-Powerful Ones did.

So the Florida Supreme Court, in obeisance to the order from Above, set about further explaining its already explained order. It responded promptly, stating its reasons in a twenty-nine-page, four-to-three decision,[167] rendered on December 8th.

This decision would have brought Gore—by the specific calls that the Florida Supreme Court had made—within 154 votes of Bush's total in Florida, and the order left much to be done in the way of counting of the "undervote."[168] What the outcome would have been if the Florida Supreme Court order had not been countermanded by order from the World's Most Powerful Five will never be known. Retrospective speculation suggests we would be served by a different president.[169]

The Great Court's final coup de grâce of the already mortally wounded movement to hand-count ballots in Florida was then delivered on December 12th. This five-to-four per curiam deci-

---

166. This legal axiom is found at 5 Corpus Juris Secundum, Appeal and Error, Sec. 714.

167. *Gore v. Harris,* 772 So2d 1243 (Dec. 8, 2000).

168. The Florida Court's nullified order would have required a hand-count of "undervotes" (ballots as to which there had been no vote for president recorded by voting machines)—which "undervote" had principally occurred in the counties using punch card voting machines.

169. Postmortem studies by leading newspapers came to inconclusive results. An Associated Press release of May 11, 2001, reported that a study made by *USA*

sion (from which Justices Stevens, Breyer, Ginsburg, and Souter dissented vigorously) stopped the election boards of Florida from hand-counting ballots, that is, from doing that which Florida law, as interpreted by its own Supreme Court, required them to do.

Amazingly, the only reason that the Great Court (per its controlling five Republican appointees) gives for this final reversal of the Florida Supreme Court is *the Fourteenth Amendment's "equal protection" clause!* Neither of the two constitutional clauses it had used to assume power over Florida's elective process is even mentioned in the dispositive decision! According to the five-judge per curiam decision that selected our president, the fact that different standards in the recounting of the ballots *might* be used in the Florida counties in which the count of the "under-votes" was to take place, and because there wasn't *sufficient time* to devise uniform standards, was justification for nullifying the order of Florida's highest court![170]

Thus, after delaying the Florida voting process as they had done, the Five had the audacity to base their final decision on the *lack of time* to set up standards to determine the legality of the votes cast—not enough time, that is, as they determined the time to be in order to meet a newly discovered "safe harbor" deadline that had not, ever before in the history of this country, terminated the counting of votes.[171]

Today and the *Miami Herald* of Florida's 170,000 uncounted [the "undervote"] presidential ballots determined that: "…George W. Bush would have narrowly won a hand recount under the strictest standards for judging votes, while Al Gore would have won under the most liberal." This article further reports that *USA Today* "…concluded that Al Gore probably lost 15,000 to 25,000 votes—enough to decisively have won Florida and the White House—through mistakes made by Democratic voters that legally disqualified their ballots [the so-called "overvotes"]. The papers found that Gore's name was marked on overvotes far more often that Bush's name …." This is the interesting speculation discussed in our Annex, infra.

170. 121 S.Ct. 525, at 532 (Dec. 12, 2000).

171. An historical example of the tolerance for the time necessary to make such a decision is the procedure that resolved the dispute arising from the November 5,

Justice Breyer's dissent points out it has always been Congress that has determined presidential election contests, some just as close as the one presented by the 2000 election, and that a time deadline has never before been accepted as determining the selection of our national leader.

Bottom line: what a poor way to select the president of a country!

The "per curiam" rendered by the Five, if actually followed as a precedent in the elections around this land, would do incredible mischief. Anyone who has ever served on an election board knows that there are close questions presented—situations in which good judgment and fairness is the standard in the counting of votes. When different voting devices and methods are being used in various locations in this country, sometimes differing from precinct to precinct, there are an infinite number of variations used by election boards of this country in determining the validity of a vote. There is much less possibility of getting uniformity in these decisions than there is in getting uniformity in the judicial decisions of the appellate courts of this land, which notoriously (at least to lawyers) vary from state to state. Diversity in these judicial decisions—of which every law student is made aware in first year of law school—has *never* been conceived to be an equal protection problem.

If uniformity in the decisions of the election boards of this country in a contested election is mandated by the "equal protection" language in the U.S. Constitution—as this perverse decision, determining the identity of our president—holds, then there

---

1876, election. The congressional act appointing a commission to decide this close election was signed by President Grant on January 20, 1877—a time interval after the election of 76 days, considerably longer than the 35-day time interval between the 2000 election and the dispatch of the Bush/Gore dispute by our Intrepid Court. The congressional commission of 1877 was itself so evenly split that it did not reach its decision giving President Hayes the nod until 4 A.M. on March 2, 1877, two days before the term of President Grant expired.

is hardly an election in this land that could not be challenged and taken over by the judiciary. A frightening thought!

The standard of the Supreme Court of Florida set forth in its order sending the count back to election boards—thus rejected by the Five—was as reasonable as the system itself: "…the vote shall be counted as a 'legal' vote if there is 'clear indication of the intent of the voter.' " The quoted language was taken by the Florida Court from the controlling Florida statute.[172] This Florida approach is what election boards throughout this land have been doing since the beginning of the Republic.

Another fatal flaw in the reasoning of this unusual decision—and now we get technical for the benefit of members of the Fraternity who may be reading this, with rebuttal arguments boiling in their minds—is the lack of standing of George W. Bush to even raise an equal protection attack. We need to go back to the reason for the adoption of the Fourteenth Amendment, where the Equal Protection Clause is injected into our Constitution, to understand the impropriety of what the Five did.

The Fourteenth Amendment was adopted after the Civil War to guarantee that the newly freed slaves would be given treatment equal to that afforded all others in our society. Accordingly, equal protection relief as accorded by our courts has always been premised on a showing of unequal treatment that is detrimental to the rights of a class to which the litigant seeking the judicial remedy belongs—in other words, a showing of prejudicial treatment of a person belonging to a class of persons being discriminated against.[173]

In order to have standing to take advantage of this amendment, Bush would have needed to show that the differences in

---

172. § 101.5614(5), Fla. Stat. (2000).

173. See *Akins v. Texas*, 325 U.S. 398, at 403–404 (1945); *Oyler v. Boles*, 368 U.S. 448, at 456 (1962); *Washington v. Davis*, 426 U.S. 229, at 240 (1976); *Wright v. Rockefeller*, 376 U.S. 52, at 56 (1964); *Yick Wo v. Hopkins*, 18 U.S. 356, at 373 (1886).

voting standards to which he was objecting were intended to discriminate against a class to which he belonged. The record here—in some ten different court actions—is completely devoid of any such evidence. All that had been ordered by the Florida courts was a manual counting of ballots by bipartisan boards, with no order directed at Bush votes, and with no showing that any election board was doing anything to favor one candidate over the other.

The bottom line is that the Bush team knew they were ahead with what had been tabulated as the machine count, and they were absolutely desperate for some theory, just *any* theory, to stop a count by responsible human beings, because such a count might not come out to the desired result.[174]

With such weakness in the reasoning of this judicial decision, it is understandable that none of the Five Great Ones who made it were willing to put their name on this per curiam decision. So we really don't know who authored it.

In addition to this perversion of voter intent, the *New York Times* analysis purports to have detected a racial difference in the allocation of voting machines, the votes of which were the ones

---

174. An interesting analysis of the accuracy of voting machines came out at the trial before Judge N. Sanders Sauls of the Circuit Court of Florida, where the Gore team was seeking an order for manual recounts. This was on Sunday, December 3rd, 2000 (yes, court was being conducted on Sunday). Bush counsel had placed on the stand a John Ahmann, a mechanical engineer, to testify as to the accuracy of the voting machines used in Florida's election. On cross-examination, Ahmann was handed a copy of the patent application for the very voting machines that had been used in critical Miami-Dade County. In this application, Ahmann had stated that this design could produce unreadable votes by leaving chads hanging on the ballot "…which can cause serious errors…" and that there had been occasions when voting machines could not read properly punched ballots and that would show different numbers when a recount took place, and that in "very close elections" a hand count was "necessary." See *New York Times*, December 5, 2000, p. A-16. So, Mr. Ahmann's testimony explains the multitude of uncounted votes in Miami-Dade County; they were voting machine errors that a hand-count would have tabulated.

eliminated. The November 29th, 2000, issue of this paper, on
p. A-19 carried this:

> RACIAL PATTERN IN DEMOGRAPHICS OF ERROR-
> PRONE BALLOTS ...the majority of the state's black
> voters, Vice President Al Gore's most reliable voters,
> stalwart supporters, cast their ballots on punch cards
> that were more prone to voter error and miscounts.
>   Across the state, nearly 4 percent of the type of
> punch-card ballots most widely used in Florida were
> thrown out because the machines read them as blank
> or invalid. By contrast, the more modern, optical scan-
> ning systems rejected far fewer votes—only about 1.4
> percent of those cast.

*   *   *

> Had all people cast ballots that could be counted along
> the same lines as their neighbors, Mr. Gore would have
> gained nearly 7,000 votes.

But analyses like this did not stop the Great Court from re-
storing the decision of Katherine Harris, the Republican secretary
of state of Florida, to the effect that her candidate had carried the
state by 537 votes (2,912,700 for Bush and 2,912,253 for Gore).

So we have a presidential election determined by a conglom-
eration of voting machines, with uncorrected proclivities of error,
which were programmed by unidentified persons who, as far as
we know, were not under any oath of office. Upon this ugly and
fragile foundation has been placed the imprimatur of the Great
Court, and that is all that it takes to give finality, for this is our
national Religion, and this is the most beneficial aspect of this
religion—its finality.

While the situation in Florida can be debated to the end of
time, it remains crystal clear that Al Gore received, nationwide,
approximately 337,576 more votes than his opponent, even after

taking into account the full margin of 537 Bush votes certified by Secretary of State Harris, *and* that George W. Bush is now our President, *and* our anointed leader to whom we owe allegiance while he is functioning under the mantle of his office.

All religions have some basic virtue, and this acceptance of the Rule of Law is the shining quality of our governmental system that serves us so well. This is our Faith, developed over the centuries, and it's far better than an armed revolution—any day—or at least, almost any day.

Our High Court has now definitely established itself as all-powerful, in the most powerful of all nations, and that power is being exercised by lawyers, all true members of the Fraternity, who have never, with few exceptions, sat on a trial bench so as to have observed firsthand the problems that beset our society.

So is the power of the Fraternity! But, shouldn't we be looking for a wiser way to restructure a system that can reach such an unfair result?

EPILOGUE

A Few Suggestions for the Future

Considering all of the destruction that went on, it is amazing how wonderful life has been, and *still is*, as I close this Thing down. Looking back, I credit myself for having contributed just an infinitesimal amount to our great legal system.

When I refer to "our great legal system," it is with both a sense of respect and one of impending doom. The system is grandiose in its conception—that we are a government of laws and not one of dispensation of autocratic mandates. The downside is that this once great system has been massaged by the Fraternity into something quite different from what was intended—*one that derives power from claiming to have come from our Forefathers*, but which in fact is a system that has been restructured, almost beyond recognition, by the Fraternity, for the benefit of the Fraternity.

Part of the restructuring has been to make it more complex—having the inevitable effect of making the services of the Fraternity more necessary. The complexity is driven by the awesome power that the Fraternity achieves from making rules so abstruse that only the specially educated—the Fraternity—can deal with them. From something that Daddy, an Irish immigrant with a fifth-grade education, could master, our system has accumulated so much religious intricacy that twelve years of precollege education, plus four years of college prelaw education, and then three years of law college prepare only the most intelligent and gifted, carefully selected as such, to be apprentice-priests, though admittedly well-paid apprentice-priests.

There was no need for lawyers at the inception of this system, when local juries dispensed justice. But now one needs, not just a lawyer, but a *specialist*-lawyer, to be paid by the minute if one wants to win his or her due. The Fraternity has sold this country on its gamey contests—on these battles of wits—in which the best lawyer wins—to determine what is right and wrong. And what a diabolically clever way to do it—by selling this system as an integral part of our religion—as coming from a sacred Constitution!

The result is pageantry, with brilliant lawyers needed to make the right moves at the right times—so that juries will not learn about facts that sensible people would think should at least be considered before the rendering of judgment—and then to hypnotize juries with their well-practiced powers of persuasion.

The pageantry is the only thing that makes it tolerable—public support for it is reminiscent of the Romans who loved to watch the gladiators kill each other in the Colosseum of Rome.

The most deleterious aspect of this centuries-evolved justice system is its constant movement toward keeping more and more evidence from juries. Much of this hiding of facts is occurring in the criminal law field, but it has also infected the civil law system. Here are a few examples pulled from press releases:

From an Associated Press release of September 9, 1999:

> JUDGE FREES BOY ACCUSED IN MICHIGAN SCHOOL PLOT A judge ruled a statement a 13-year-old boy made to police about an alleged school massacre plot could not be used as evidence, so prosecutors dropped

the charges and let him go home yesterday.

Jonathan _____,[175] 13, was one of four boys
who prosecutors said plotted to steal firearms, seize the
school office and call an assembly in the gym where
they would massacre students and teachers.

Judge James P. Adair ruled that the statement could
not be used as evidence because police *did not first advise the boy of his right against self-incrimination.*

This young man would have received very different treatment
had not the juvenile courts of this country been closed down by
the *Gault* decision. Counseling of the child and his family and
some degree of monitoring is so obviously in the public interest as
to this lad. Comparing this modern scene in Judge Adair's court,
supra, with what occurred in the juvenile courts of this country
before Justice Fortas's despicable decision will lead any sensible
person, with the facts not censored by the Holy Nine, to conclude
that the Fraternity has created a very sick situation, out of which
school massacres may result.

May 21, 1998. Front page, *Arizona Daily Star* (Tucson, Arizona's morning newspaper):

CHARGES DROPPED AGAINST ALLEGED 'MIDTOWN
INTRUDER' All criminal charges have been dismissed
against the man Tucson police suspected was the 'Midtown Intruder,' who terrorized women in 1995.

*   *   *

Authorities say blood and DNA samples link Thornton
to the April 27, 1995, sexual assaults. But court rulings held the evidence was inadmissible at trial because
Thornton's June, 1995, arrest lacked probable cause.

The Midtown Intruder' broke into 10 homes be-

---

175. Again, we withhold names, because of our training as a juvenile judge.

tween April and June 1995, raping one woman and touching nine others on their feet and legs.

This "Midtown Intruder" case, of course, is *Mapp v. Ohio* at work again. In the case of this particular raper-toucher, the exclusionary rule has been enlarged by the "fruit of the poisonous tree" concoction of the Holy Nine—i.e., the blood test, which was the result of the "improper" arrest, is to be kept from the knowledge of all juries.

Justifying a reexamination of these inane exclusionary rules (which have multiplied like breeding rodents—to keep juries from knowing what has really happened) is the development in this country of the most generous tort system the world has ever known for the retribution of police browbeating and the like, whenever and wherever it may exist. There are many, many competent and eager lawyers to take such cases, and generous juries to factor them.

Here are a few examples of jury awards in police brutality cases:

> In 1992, a jury warded Ricardo Perez $443,000 [PV04 $567,608] for personal injuries because New York police stomped on his foot, breaking three bones; in addition Mr. Perez was awarded $122,000 [PV04 $146,182] for malicious prosecution and $68,000 [PV04 $87,140] for false arrest.[176]

And then there are these:

> **LOS ANGELES COUNTY SETTLED A POLICE BRUTALITY CASE FOR $1.75 MILLION**[177] [The verdict touted here amounts to $2.3 million in '04 dollars.]

---

176. *New York Law Journal,* May 11, 1992, P. 2, Col. 6.

177. *New York Law Journal,* April 15, 1991, p. 6, col. 1.

And in March 1995, a plaintiff Levine, beaten by an arresting officer after being stopped for a traffic violation in the Bronx, settled his civil action for $1 million ($1,168,400 in 2004 dollars).[178]

And then there is this one, of July 13, 2001:

> **$8.75 MILLION SETTLEMENT OVER POLICE BRUTAL-ITY,** New York—A Haitian immigrant, Abner Louima, tortured in a New York police station bathroom, said Thursday he hopes his $8.75 million settlement sends a message.[179]

And this one, of October 9, 2003: "$17 million dollar judgment rendered in the case of *Campos v. City of New York* for police brutality."[180]

And before we leave this effort, let's take a look at what the abominable *Bruton* decision has been doing. This abortion, mandated by the Nine, takes on poignant significance when criminal charges are brought against two or more persons charged with a a single offense, i.e., murder or whatever, and, because of *Bruton*, they must be tried separately.

Such separation presents many opportunities for the Fraternity to serve its clients in the way of plea bargaining and coerced testimony. Here is an example:

A May 27, 1999, headline in the local Tucson press reads: COURT PLEA BARGAIN ENDS TRIAL OF MAN ACCUSED OF KILLING GIRL, and introduces the story of an Antonio Wilbert who has abruptly entered a guilty plea in the midst of his trial:

> Wilbert, 21, pleaded guilty to second-degree murder *and agreed to testify against* friend Kim Proud, 19, whose

---

178. *New York Law Journal,* March 30, 1995, P. 4, Col. 4.

179. From Internet, <*http://www.cnn.com/2001/Law/07//12/louima.settlement/*>

180. *American Lawyer Media,* December 29, 2003.

first-degree murder trial starts in October. Wilbert faces 16 to 22 years in prison when he is sentenced *after her trial....* Proud maintains her innocence and has no interest in entering a guilty plea, Bloom [Kim's attorney] said" [Emphasis added].

The above scenario presents the sickening possibility that Kim *is* innocent (can prosecutors, who, after all, are only human, occasionally make a mistake?), and that Wilbert has been induced to testify against her to avoid a death penalty. Could there be any greater coercion? And has it been suggested to Wilbert, in order to make this "deal," that—when he finally comes up for sentence—the prosecuting attorney, when speaking to the judge finally imposing sentence on Wilbert, will comment upon the quality of Wilbert's testimony at Kim's trial? You're damn right, this will occur!

Every daily paper contains information with the same sickening message as the Wilbert and Kim story. How much fresher the air was in pre-*Bruton* adult courts, when defendants who had jointly acted were jointly tried in the same courtroom, before the same fact finders, and the truth was much, much easier to ascertain and with much, much less involvement by the Fraternity.

Let us look at our criminal justice system as a whole. Any fair appraisal will declare that it runs on coercion.

Whenever you read in your daily newspaper about a Mr. Somebody pleading guilty (and remember that over 90 percent of criminal charges in this country are now disposed of with a guilty plea) and being sentenced to, say, "two to four years" for "assault," or something conveniently generic, you may read on and find that this Mr. Somebody had been first charged with, say, rape, kidnaping, or aggravated assault, and that this Mr. Somebody *could* have been sentenced to forty years or more in prison, if convicted of the coercive charges brought against him.

So, when these Mr. Somebodies enter their pleas, are they motivated, more or less—depending upon their constitutional makeup—by fear? Are they *all* really guilty?

And yet no one dares—no member of the Fraternity, certainly—to suggest that any of the thousands upon thousands of guilty pleas that end almost all criminal prosecutions in this country are the result of the coercive tactics of prosecutors. With such successes, will not prosecutors become more and more abusive in their overcharging?

Most of you accept this "overcharging/copping-of-plea" system as being acceptable justice, because you have been brainwashed to believe that this is the way that it has to be. But I am here to testify that it was not always so, that justice was dispensed well in this country until the Fraternity took over, and that this old system, based on truth, could return if the stranglehold of the Fraternity upon our judicial system can be broken.

The justice that Daddy participated in didn't need religious dogma to sell it, but it had a great deal of common sense to make it just. Absurdities such as the above, and the many stupidities that happen every day in the courts of this country, simply would not happen under judges like Judge Kelly, who regarded themselves as judges, not lawyers.

The only defense of this perverse system postulated today is that there is no way to go back to a system in which juries ascertained what really had happened, because the many protocols inserted into the system by the Great Court makes it impossible. This conclusion has been reluctantly reached by an experienced trial judge, the late Hon. Harold J. Rothwax of the New York Supreme Court.[181] Any realistic look at the numbers will convince anyone that this impossibility—under the present idiotic system that has been mandated by the Nine Gods—is actually upon us.

What has happened is that this Fraternity-structured system

---

181. See *Guilty: The Collapse of Criminal Justice*, by Judge Harold Rothwax (Warner Books). In a reasoned analysis, Judge Rothwax concludes that the judicial decisions have painted our legal system into a corner, and it has no realistic solution for the horrible problem it has created except more and more plea-bargaining. At p. 234.

has become so burdened with these "sacred" procedures that it does not have the capacity—there are not enough judges, staff, and courthouses despite the geometric increase in their numbers—to provide a factual trial for the legitimate disputes between our citizens. The controlling rules have been so complexed by the Fraternity that this is so.

And, ominously, all of this nonsense—the exclusion of evidence from juries, the blatant plea-bargaining in our criminal courts, the ever-increasing panoply of civil actions—in which the controlling facts and the outcome are selected by artificial rules mandated from on High (after skilled objections by members of the Fraternity) is not abating, but is increasing. And, as this occurs, the earnings of the Fraternity are increasing magnificently.

Salary statistics compiled by the National Association of Law Placement indicate that the starting, newly graduated lawyer's average salary has increased from $65,000 in 1998 to $85,000 in 2000, an increase of 31 percent in these three years. For comparison, the national average teacher's salary has risen from $39,347 in 1998 to $43,398 in August 2001, an increase of 10 percent, in a period of three years. Of course, these are beginning averages, and the more experienced of the Fraternity earn much more, leaving teachers' salaries minuscule by comparison. Salaries of more than a million dollars a year for partners in large law firms are not uncommon.[182]

But let's see if we can improve here, just a bit, upon the ominous, hopeless picture just painted. After all, Judge Rothwax's pessimistic assessment did not factor in the suggestions being made that you are now reading.

---

182. *American Lawyer's Media* reports that the four most gainful law firms in this country in 2002 were: 1) Skadden, Arps with income of $1.31 billion, giving $802,696 as an average for each of its 1,632 lawyers; 2) Latham & Wakins with intake of $906 million—$650,394 for each of its 1,393 lawyers; 3) Sidney Austin Brown & Wood with income of $83 million, $603,485 for each of its 1,377 lawyers, and 4) Jones Day, with an intake of $908 million—$534,746 for each of its 1,698 lawyers. Many other firms are not far behind. And see Caplan, *Skadden—Power, Money, and the Rise of a Legal Empire,* (New York: Farrar, Straus, & Giroux, 1993), pp. 318–321.

Elimination of the exclusionary rules—blindfolds upon the juries of this land—would alone do wonders to increase the efficiency of our judicial system. It would eliminate the double trials that take place in both criminal and civil cases, while judges listen, sometimes for days on end, to evidence and arguments on motions to exclude evidence from juries.[183] The bottom line is that if we would take out of our trial system the artificial blockages to determining truth which the Fraternity has been inserting into our systems, the pursuit of justice would be much, much less time-consuming and infinitely more accurate—but also infinitely less lucrative for the Fraternity.

And, if this desperately needed reform doesn't happen, this last will be the reason!

And then there is much court congestion that would not be there if the Great Court, with its very limited trial experience, would just leave more matters to state trial judges. As an example, I call your attention to a recent decision of the All-Knowing Nine, mandating from their marbled Olympus in Washington, that the Court of Appeals of Arizona (my old court) must "further consider" (and presumably reverse and set aside) a trial judge's decision that had granted two grandparents visitation rights with their two minor granddaughters. The Arizona trial judge, who had listened to the evidence pertaining to this particular family and who was reversed by this decision from on High, acted under an Arizona statute expressly permitting an order for grandparents' visitation whenever the trial judge determined it to be in the "best interests" of the child.[184]

The "best interests of the child" was the standard that I had

---

183. For example, in the second Miranda trial, most of an eight-day jury trial was devoted to court hearings, in the absence of the jury, to rule upon problems presented by exclusionary rules.

184. A.R.S. § 25–409. The Mighty Court's order that would have blocked my old court from granting visiting rights to grandparents is the case of *Dodge v. Granville,* found at 121 S.Ct. 2584, 69 USLW 3806 (June 29, 2001), holding that our Arizona court has violated the Great Court's decision of *Troxel v. Granville,* 530 U.S. 57, 120, S.Ct 2054, at 2064 (2000).

used as a juvenile court judge in deciding hundreds of child custody cases, but that standard is no longer sufficient, thanks to the mandate of the Nine, whose experience does not include much in the way of dealing with the problems of neglected children. Our Founding Fathers would turn over in their graves in disgust if they knew they were being attributed with writing the words that bring about results such as the above. Perhaps, if even one of these All Powerful Nine had ever served as a juvenile court judge, and viewed up close the problems that beset some families in our culture, the Great Court would be coming to better solutions. Problems such as this should be left to judges such as Judge Kelly, who are much, much closer to these problems than these members of the Fraternity who chose a president.

My instinctive repulsion goes absolutely nowhere. The religious worship that has been carefully cultivated for this system by its Priests is such an awesome power that decisions such as this will be accepted as Gospel by every child welfare worker in the land.

One has to know that a power as awesome as this may become the Achilles' heel of the survival of our culture. Yes, we should think of survival. Only a few civilizations have prospered as long as this one.

But, caution! If we are to move away from this potentially fatal favoritism that the Fraternity has achieved for itself, it will require delicate tailoring because the present system is still working—and, in some respects, well. But, change course we must, for we are on the "edge of chaos," as an objective observer of this system has concluded.[185]

Changing course does not necessarily mean throwing away a precious baby with the bathwater. There is great good in parts of our system—proven by our standard of living and freedom from tyranny, oppression, and discrimination. But the legal system that achieved this is simply not the same legal system that we have

---

185. Quoting from Mary Ann Glendon's *A Nation Under Lawyers*, (New York: Farrar, Straus & Giroux, 1995), p. 285.

today, as it has been massaged to the benefit of the few—the Fraternity.

Changes as fundamental as now needed should be achieved in increments, keeping always to the twin objectives of providing a judicial system that will effectively reveal the truth and that will discourage forces that are anti-social, i.e., discourage burglary, rape, murder, etc. And it is in this category of the "anti-social" that the dominance of our society by the Fraternity should be placed.

This means that every opportunity should be taken to sever the Fraternity into its two constituent parts—lawyers and judges—so as to deprecate the awesome strength that it obtains by having the bench and the bar as one fraternal organization. This separation should take place in as many ways as possible and whenever possible.

Anytime that we have an opportunity to bring the selection of judges back to an informed electorate and away from selection by fellow lawyers, we should do so. Judges should be selected by vote in geographic areas where they are *known*. This probably means that only one judge should be chosen at any one election. In this way, voters can have knowledge of the integrity, or lack thereof, of candidates, their experience and qualifications, and their comparative understanding of the problems of their fellow citizens. For the long haul, this would be much better than the present system of selection by the Fraternity, to suit its purposes.

One remedy would be to bring the courthouses out to the voting districts, out of the crowded central business core, so that much inefficiency in travel and parking for those *not* in the Fraternity—the jurors, the witnesses, and the parties—can be eliminated, and a move back toward the "neighborhood jury" can be achieved, such as those that Daddy practiced before.

Let the lawyers travel to where the people are in litigation and let burglars be tried in the precincts where they practiced their profession.

So much of our law of today is being mandated from Above

in the judicial hierarchy, so, we must move in the direction of promoting more trial judges to the appellate level. Lawyers who have made themselves politically acceptable by making campaign donations or voting the right way in legislatures, or serving as campaign managers for governors—as lowlifes like yours truly did—should not have the inside track in becoming a judge.

And then, experience at viewing justice dispensed firsthand, from the trial bench should be regarded as an indispensable qualification for appointment to an appellate court, if the public good is the test. By striving for appellate judges who have had trial-judge experience, we will cut down on the atrocious impracticalities being imposed on our system from Above. Few judges who have actually presided at trials will endorse the madnesses of *Miranda*, *Bruton*, or *Alford*. A judge who has sat as a juvenile court judge under the pre-*Gault* system would never vote to destroy these courts, which were so very effective in handling violations of law by children.

Even the underlying qualifications for these two disparate jobs—that of the bench and of the bar—should be different. Most successful legal systems of the world separate the professions of judging and advocating more than we do. In this country, perhaps we could even achieve the separation of these two professions in their education. There is no need for a judge to take all of the law school courses that lawyers are required to take before they are allowed to take the bar examination and to go out to sell their talents to the public. Most of these law school courses have nothing to do with being a good judge. Lawyers can educate judges, if the case involves some intricate presentation of law, *and* there would be much less intricacy in our law if we took lawmaking out of the control of the Fraternity.

An example to give us hope is found in England, from whence we adopted—to pervert it—our legal system. England suffers far less from a proliferation of litigation and high-dollar verdicts. There, lawyers are divided into two professions—solicitors and barristers, and, they, in turn, by Inns of Court, and the like. Thus, those who hold themselves out as having special knowledge of the law do not coalesce into one Fraternity. And, without the awesome strength of a Fraternity, English jury trials in tort cases have become the exception rather than the rule.

By reason of England's freedom from a Most Sacred Constitution, its legislative bodies and judges have been able to limit civil jury trials to a mere handful of special cases: libel, slander, malicious prosecution, false imprisonment, seduction, and breaches-of-promise-to-marry.[186] And, and even in such actions, the granting of a jury trial is discretionary with the trial judge and should be denied when the court "…is of the opinion that the trial requires any prolonged examination of documents or accounts or any scientific or local examination which cannot be conveniently made with a jury…"[187]

What an abominable system for the Fraternity, depriving them of lucrative work!

Another approach, not requiring the constitutional amendment that would be essential for an adoption of England's curtailing of jury trials, would to open up law colleges to a good many more, so that law graduates are not just the selected few of our college graduates. This, of course, is inconsistent with my portrayal of the growth in the number of lawyers in this country, which has been phenomenal since Daddy's day. But sometimes one has to fight fire with fire, and my prediction is that, if we open up our law schools to more, the fees of lawyers will go down and the ordinary citizen will receive much, much better service.

Learning the essences of our legal system should not be restricted to just the few who have excelled in the strenuous prelaw requisites now demanded, but should be imparted to far, far more of our people. The more there are of our citizens who understand the system, the better it will work for the commonwealth, and the less the Fraternity will be able to insist on charging for its knowl-

---

186. See Smith, Bailey & Gunn, *The Modern English Legal System,* particularly chapter 3-B (Sweet & Maxwell, 2002), hereinafter "Smith, Bailey & Gunn."

187. Smith, Bailey & Gunn, chapter 15-C, and especially fn83.

edge of that system.

More important than the formalistic education of our law schools, now reserved to the very few, is the need on the bench for intelligent, sincere, public-minded people, who are willing to listen intently and patiently to the problems of those before them, and to base their decisions on the true facts, as they, or a jury, impartially determine them to be. The revelation of the truth under our present system depends far too much on the skill of the particular members of the Fraternity advocating before the court.

Furthermore, a judge should *not* be permitted to resign his/her post to forthwith become a lawyer—as yours truly did. There are obvious things wrong with this game of musical chairs played between bench and bar.

Clients *do* come to ex-judges—to this I can testify—with the thought that they are getting an "inside track" in the judicial machinery. In no other legal system of any successful government in this World is it so easy, and so lucrative—so very lucrative—to pass from the bar to the bench, and then to return to the glorious earnings of the Fraternity.

In the so-called "civil law" countries (meaning—simplified—the German, Spanish, and French language countries), the bench and bar are much more separated than here.[188] The same is true in Japan.[189]

Even in England, from whence we get our tradition of selecting practicing barristers to be judges, appellate judges are almost invariably selected from experienced trial judges[190] instead of

---

188. See J. Merryman, *The Civil Law Tradition*, (Stanford University Press, 1985), pp.108–109, and *Comparative Criminal Justice as a Guide to American Law Reform: How Do the French Do It, How Can We Find Out, and Why Should We Care?* 78 California Law Review, May 1990, p. 539; and *Comparative Legal Traditions* by M.A. Glendon, M.W. Gordon, and C. Osakwe, (West Publishing Co., 1994), p. 158–159.

189. See E. Blankenburg, *Courts, Law and Politics in Comparative Perspective*, (Yale University Press, 1996), p. 321.

190. Glendon, *Comparative Legal Traditions*, p. 157.

picking lawyers for political reasons as we do in this country.

Judges simply should not be put in the position of making law that will make money for themselves after they go back to the lawyer side of their profession. Perhaps, just perhaps, after, say, two years off of the bench, an ex-judge might be permitted to practice law for gain.

An attribute of the present system that we must preserve and safeguard is the integrity of the bench. At the heart of this integrity is that our judges are held up to esteem, and, they, with hardly any exceptions, live up to the esteem paid to them. Esteem is part of their remuneration and is a key to what success our legal system has had in the past. The worst damage done by the recent frustration of our electoral system by the Five-Who-Chose-Our-President may be loss of esteem of the High Court—as some savants have predicted.

But esteem alone is not enough. We must always provide adequate remuneration to our judges—something that is sadly lacking in many countries of the world—particularly in the civil law countries. We need the very best of talent on the bench to cope with the Fraternity. Only skilled and talented jurists will be able to work us out of the morass of legalism into which the Fraternity has taken us.

An essential and primordial goal should be to restore the pursuit of truth as the preeminent goal of our courts rather than judging the respective skills of trial lawyers. The present, universally accepted concept that only lawyers/judges are to know the true facts of a case—of which the jury may be kept in ignorance—should be totally and permanently dismantled. Jurors, when they are the fact finders, should know what there is to know about the case and be able to make full affirmative inquiry of what happened so as to perform their sworn responsibility with as much knowledge as possible.[191]

Juries, for instance, should hear what gave rise to a confession of guilt in a criminal case—and then should be given law that would

---

191. A law review article advocating against the blindfolding of juries is *The Jury's Role in Administering Justice in the U.S.; of Mushrooms and Nullifiers: Rules of Evidence and the American Jury*, 21 St. Louis U. Pub. L, Rev., 65 (2002).

permit them to disregard whatever they determine to be coerced. But let's abandon, for the sake of Truth and our Culture, the asininity of having two trials to determine such things—i.e., *first* a judge-only trial to "sanitize" the evidence, *and then* a second trial, to a jury, to find out only what the intricate rules of the Fraternity permit.

Let us relegate to the curious past the concept that only the Fraternity is entitled to know what our police officers are doing. If there is improper conduct on the part of the police, let us forthwith expose it to the examination of the jury box. The very fact that juries would be permitted to know about whatever sleazy police conduct that may be occurring will help immeasurably in keeping police from overstepping.

When the police luck onto incriminating evidence without the proper search warrant, let's use common sense, for the sake of us all, and not engage in the ridiculous program of disciplining police officers by letting criminals go free. After all, the Fraternity has brought in other adequate remedies for any such nasty police overreaching—such as million-dollar verdicts for those wrongfully treated—from which the Fraternity will continue to take its percentages. If police trespass, they should be held to respond in civil cases, with punitive damages allowed when appropriate. But let's stop letting police errors give immunity to hardened criminals.

Some changes in the jury system itself would be highly desirable—and we are now treading into an area that the Fraternity wants us to believe is absolutely sacrosanct. Judge Rothwax, to whose expose of the inadequacy of our court system we have referred, has suggested that we should drop the insistence on unanimous verdicts in criminal cases—as England has done—and should permit guilty verdicts in criminal cases with one dissenting vote.[192]

This would most certainly be a step in the right direction—to

---

192. Rothwax, supra. The English rule may be even more tolerant. Professor William T. Pizzi, who teaches comparative law at the University of Colorado School of Law, in his *Trials Without Truth*, (New York University Press, 1999), asserts that convictions are had under English law with two dissenting votes "...after at least two hours of deliberation." id. at p. 109.

thus eliminate the veto power of any one irrational juror, and, in the process, increase the difficulty of organized crime to jury tamper. This proposed change will, of course, be condemned as pure sacrilege by every member of the Fraternity specializing in criminal practice, because it will make it more difficult to free their clients, and might require a constitutional amendment to thus slightly change the "sacred" right of jury trial.

An example of Judge Rothwax's concern might be the prosecution of Arizona's governor for making false statements to financial institutions and for wire fraud. In this case, after jury deliberations had commenced, the jury sent out notes to the judge complaining about the conduct of one particular juror. A final note to the trial judge from this long-deliberating jury stated:

> We have earnestly attempted to follow your last directive to continue with our deliberations. However, the majority of the jurors sincerely feel that the juror in question cannot properly participate in the discussion with us. Reasons: Inability to maintain a focus on the subject of discussion. Inability to recall topics under discussion. Refusal to discuss views with other jurors. All information must be repeated two to three times to be understood, discussed, or voted on. Immediately following a vote, the juror cannot tell us what was voted. We question the ability to comprehend and focus on the information discussed.

This nonfunctioning juror was thereupon excused by the court, and Arizona's governor Fife Symington was thereupon convicted by the remaining eleven jurors. But this affront to the Fraternity was, two years later, overturned on appeal as violating the right to be tried by the full, twelve-person jury.[193] As of this writing, Governor Symington has not been retried.

This situation of one irrational juror does not by any means hap-

---

193. *U.S. v. Symington*, 195 F.3rd 1080 (1999).

pen only when governors are being tried. On several occasions in trials, I have experienced similar obstinance/individuality on the part of a single juror, causing a mistrial at considerable public expense.

Let's look at another recommendation made by Judge Rothwax—to the effect that we cut down on the number of peremptory juror challenges exercised by trial counsel in the jury-selection process. These peremptory strikes are the treasured prerogative of trial lawyers—the right to eliminate a prospective juror for no cause whatsoever—at jury-selection time. Judge Rothwax's proposal would curtail to some extent the power of clever lawyers to control trial results.

To this judge's wise proposal, I would add one more, and this is a real biggie for the Fraternity to swallow: Let's take away from plaintiffs' lawyers the right to make both the opening and the final argument to the jury in civil cases (and this coming from a plaintiffs' lawyer!) This final argument is an awesome tool for plaintiffs' lawyers and is the straw, or, with the skilled and practiced plaintiffs' lawyer, a crowbar, that determines the outcome of jury trials in the tort cases of this country.

If a rebuttal argument is necessary to fully deal with the facts in a particular case, then let there be a surrebuttal argument, as in all standard debate practice. There is no good reason that one side of the debate should always be favored with the first and last argument at this most critical moment in the dispensing of justice—no good reason, that is, except to benefit the Brethren, in the fees of both plaintiff and defense lawyers.

The argument made to justify this extreme advantage is that it is the plaintiff who has the "burden of proof." This is, of course, a stock instruction to every jury but, after all the evidence is in, judges usually further define this burden as being nothing more than "tipping the scales of justice" one way or the other. If this "burden" is a factor at this point in the trial, it is minuscule compared to the advantage of the first and last argument, delivered by a professional persuader of juries, schooled in their profession by the best of teachers.

In a criminal case, in which there are vivid instructions as to the necessity for proof "beyond a reasonable doubt," there is much more reason to favor the prosecution with a first and last argument.

In suggesting reforms, we are all faced with an insidious aspect of this Fraternity-generated revolution—the changes it has made in our jury system. The Fraternity has sold this country on the concept that jurors should be selected at random, after the more endowed—physicians, public officials, lawyers (yes, this profession, too, has more than its share of brains)—and similars have been excused from this onerous duty by judges recognizing various statutory exemptions. The effect is to turn trial courts into playing fields for clever lawyers.

The juries of Grandfather's time were much more immune to the tricks of the Brethren. Picked by the Board of Supervisors as responsible citizens, they were proud of helping to dispense justice and much less gullible to the persuasions of trial lawyers.

In this facet of the evolution of our culture, the religion is not all lawyer-generated, but has deeper roots. There have been inexorable forces moving our mass thinking in the direction of egalitarianism since the birth of our nation. Hence, enthusiasts for reform of our legal system should step gingerly in this area of changing the make-up of our juries. Tampering with the concept of the "cross-sectional" jury can stir up primordial opposition that might very well cause the sudden death of any reform movement.

But, if we must leave this one alone because of the obvious politics, then let's look at bringing judges back to the role that they had in an earlier stage in the development of our trial system—when they took much more of a lead in the determining of truth by asking witnesses questions and by commenting upon the evidence to the jury.[194] This, of course, again is a proposal that the

---

194. See *Structural and Functional Aspects of the Jury: Comparative Analysis and Proposals for Reform*, 48 Ala. L. Rev. 441 (1997) at p. 40, where this analysis quotes the eminent Dean Wigmore:: "This departure ['The abandonment of the practice of authorizing judges to freely comment upon evidence and to express an opinion concerning the credibility of witnesses...'] has done more than any other one thing to impair the general efficiency of the jury trial as an instrument of justice."

Fraternity will resist and ridicule, for the alchemy of the skilled lawyer has much less worth when judges are permitted to lend their experience and training to jury intelligence.

A recent[195] jury verdict here in Arizona, for the tidy sum of $8 million, illustrates a point. It was against the YMCA, because a seven-year-old girl had drowned in its swimming pool. After a reduction in the amount of the verdict was denied by the trial judge, the plaintiffs' lawyer, Richard Grand, is quoted in the press to the effect that in his forty-four years of practice, he has brought in—as a plaintiffs' lawyer—over one hundred in-excess-of-a-million-dollar verdicts, and no trial judge ever reduced any one of them.

Intrigued with the possibility that I might have reduced a verdict for this lawyer in my judging days, I called Grand and was informed by him that he did not remember my reducing any of his verdicts. In the cordial conversation that followed, Grand confessed that, though he is recognized nationally as a leader in plaintiffs' verdicts, he is often outdone, dollarwise, by lawyers on the East Coast, where jury verdicts usually come in higher than out here in the West.

As I was putting the phone down, it crossed my mind that the $8 million judgment that had prompted our conversation is perhaps not appropriate as compensation for the loss of a daughter—losses of such kind, in most minds, are not valued in dollars.

If this YMCA has been paying substantial sums of money to have liability insurance, the loss will add to the premiums that all YMCAs in this country will have to raise from their donors to stay in existence, and, because of this verdict, premiums for liability insurance will continue to rise so as to make appropriate corporate profits for insurance companies. And, if our local YMCA does not have insurance coverage for this verdict, it will turn over its building and assets to the highest bidder, and close.

This is where the Fraternity savors in taking us.

---

195. *Arizona Daily Star*, November 22, 2002.

A published study indicates that, of the billions now spent by industry in defending against product claims, perhaps only one-sixth goes to the injured—the rest to the liability system.[196] Thanks to the Fraternity's ministrations, liability insurance now costs five times, and more, as much as it did when I first started practicing, and this despite the fact that the insurance industry has benefited from a tremendous increase in the volume of its business. Household liability insurance, which now is a substantial part of that volume, was unheard of when yours truly first joined the Fraternity. It simply was not considered appropriate, because such intrahousehold lawsuits were so rare.

More intimidating, there are various impressive analyses that indicate that our liability system is punishing and suppressing the industrial innovations of this country—that which has given us preemptive status in the world.[197] Companies do not innovate because of fear of retribution.

Litigation has become a major industry in this country, with both the Fraternity and the insurance industry profiting from what has happened. In short range, the marvelous revolutions in liability law imposed upon our economy by the Fraternity, and the skilled inducement of high-dollar jury verdicts by focused members of the Fraternity, have hurt the insurance industry on one side of the ledger sheet, but nevertheless, the more the risk, the higher the premium, and the more buying by worried insurance clients. So, the bottom line is that the only ones hurt by the Fraternity's takeover is everybody else besides the liability insurance industry and the Fraternity itself.

So, are you tired of this old man's counselings? Well, stay aboard for just a wee bit, for the tirade is almost over. And you and I may have both wasted our time, for these recommendations buck an

---

196. See *The Liability Maze,* edited by Peter W. Huber and Robert E. Litan (Brookings Institution, 1991), at p. 500.

197. See ibid., particularly chapter 9 entitled "The Chilling Effect of Product Liability on New Drug Development."

awesome force, fostered and defended vigorously by the well-entrenched Fraternity. The chance of any one recommendation seeing life is slim. But the stakes are high—at issue is survival itself. So, I lay these thoughts, gathered from a lifelong immersion in our legal system, before you, and pray that they achieve life here and there.

In closing, I again refer to *Gault*, the Fortas decision that destroyed our juvenile court system. Lawyers, with their tricks, should simply not be dealing with the problems of our youngest ones. I can assure the reader that nothing good has come from the destruction of our juvenile court system—nothing good, that is, other than for the Fraternity. Lower the age of "juveniles," if you feel that the old juvenile courts were not sufficiently punitive for your taste. But restore the honest pursuit of truth to this dealing with the problems of our young ones—whether the cutoff age for this truthseeking be 14, 16, or 18 years of age.

Bring trained social workers back to solve these problems, and bring parents back to their proper role when their children transgress upon the rules. But, above all else, *get lawyers, and their bargaining, out of these most delicate family problems.*

The foregoing series of suggestions—a congealment of a lifetime of intimate involvement with our legal system—should not be implemented too rapidly, because revolutions breed confusion, and our way of life depends upon an orderly course of events. We must build on the past—not destroy it—for it has served us well.

But, there can be a beginning, and for the sake of my offspring, and yours, I am hoping that there will be movements here and there, *and whenever and wherever possible*, in the direction of reducing the power of the Fraternity.

We've come to a final word: If you have offspring contemplating a career, encourage them, please, to be a lawyer, for it is the noblest of all professions, but not—no, no, no—not like the ones who are managing the law firms of today, but one like Daddy.

ANNEX

The Fraternity Selects Our President

One of the closest presidential elections in the history of the United States appears to have been determined by the design of a voting machine ballot, used only in one county of this entire country—Palm Beach County, Florida. Here is the photo of that peculiar voting machine with the ballot in place.[A1]

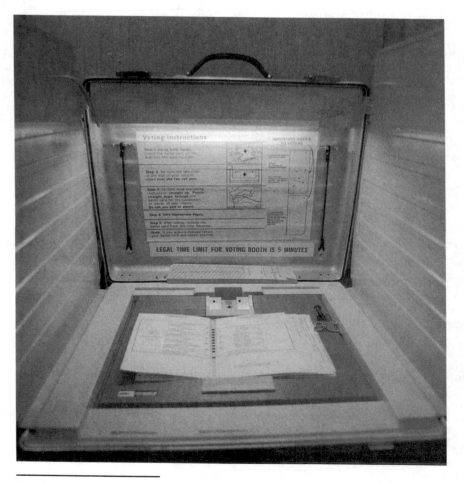

A1. Provided by the *Palm Beach Post*.

The critical pages for the presidential vote looked like this:

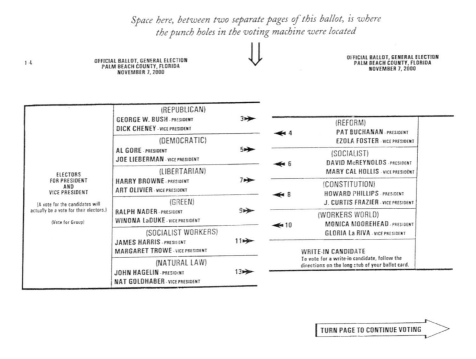

Space here, between two separate pages of this ballot, is where the punch holes in the voting machine were located

With this mechanical set-up it is little wonder that a good number of voters made mistakes in punching holes! In this election, declared by the Fraternity to have been won by George W. Bush by a margin of 537 votes, there were 19,120 (!) ballots in this one Florida county alone that were not counted.

It came about in this way: Florida law, similar to the law of other states, is to the effect that if a voter inserts the stylus in two holes which have been programmed by the voting machine for two different candidates for the same office, when only one can be elected, neither hole is counted as a "vote"—both of such holes are totally ignored. Such disqualified votes are called "overvotes."

The possibility of causing an "overvote" by the use of the "butterfly ballot" you see pictured above can be assigned to at least four of its unique features: (1) all people are accustomed to reading books, which open up to opposing pages, with a division of attention at the center of the book, and *not* to read from the *opposing* pages of the book at the same time, as required by this unique ballot; (2) all previous ballots to which these voters had been exposed have had a sequential listing of candidates, with the designated place to mark an affirmative vote being, sequentially, to the right of the name of the candidate, *and* with such designated places being in the *same order*, sequentially, as the names of the candidates on that page (*not so in the case of this specially tailored ballot—look again, above*); (3) minor variations in the printing of tens of thousands of ballots, and in the mechanics of the holding of the ballot itself in the voting machine (causing movement of the printed material in relation to the stylus punch holes); and (4) psychological factors, arising from the strangeness of the environment and the apparent pressures of time and space in the voting booth.

The problems seen by Democrats with this butterfly ballot are not totally sour-grapes-*after*-election complaints. Consternation with the layout of this ballot surfaced *before* the counting of the votes. The *New York Times* reported:

> ...by mid-morning [of election day], hundreds of voters swamped the phones of local officials, complaining that they had mis-read the ballot. But their frantic and angry calls elicited little help from electoral officials whom they described as overwhelmed by the flood of complaints.[A2]

The evidence is cumulative that these complaints were justified and that the misreading of, or the total failure to read, ballots miscarried this election.

The key to unraveling how this happened is to look at the vote recorded for candidate Buchanan. Any fair analysis of the garbled-up situation in Florida indicates that a substantial number of voters in Palm Beach County—enough of them to change to result of this close election—mistakenly gave Buchanan their vote when they intended to vote for Gore.

Let us look at that evidence.

Mr. Buchanan was officially credited with a total of 3,704 votes in Palm Beach County—the most, by far, that he scored in any county in

---

A2. From November 13, 2000, *Times*, p. A-1.

Florida. These 3,704 votes were 20 percent of Buchanan's *total* vote in the entire State of Florida. His second-best showing was 1,012 votes in Pinellas County, which was the site of his campaign's headquarters in the state of Florida. Buchanan received only 561 votes in Miami-Dade and only 789 in Broward County, both of which have considerably higher populations than Palm Beach County.

So why this anomaly of 3,704 votes in Palm Beach County?

The answer simply has be the peculiar ballot used in this one county, inducing voters to mistakenly place a mark in the wrong place for what they intended.

Palm Beach threw out 4.1 percent of its ballots (approximately every twenty-fifth vote!) because voters had punched a "hole" that were attributed by the particular voting machine to more than one candidate. This percentage grossly surpasses the norm found nationwide in more than thirty years of use of punch-card voting machines—historically less than 1 percent have been so disqualified.

A postmortem study by the *Palm Beach Post* determined that in Palm Beach County there were 5,330 ballots that were invalidated ("overvotes") by punching both for Gore *and* for Reform Party candidate Pat Buchanan. Another 2,908 votes were disqualified because the ballot was punched for Gore along with Socialist David McReynolds. Another 1,631 were punched for both Bush *and* Buchanan. The two Gore combinations, minus the Bush-Buchanan votes, add up to 6,607 votes intended for Gore—that were lost.

If a normal ballot had been used in Palm Beach, Gore would have won this election handily. But this, of course, did not happen. What did happen was that Florida's Republican secretary of state, an avid supporter of George W. Bush, determined that her candidate—Bush—had won her state, and the presidency, by a majority of 537.

And thus was our leader selected.

But, whatever the bollixment that may have occurred in Florida, it does not appear to have been a devious Republican plot, but just a matter of accident—just a "brilliant" idea for a new form of ballot that messed up. Palm Beach's unique ballot was devised by a Theresa LePore, an experienced election supervisor and a *registered Democrat*. It was her misdesign that provided the opening for a Republican-appointed Supreme Court to have its way.

This butterfly ballot problem was not something that a court could retroactively correct without ordering a re-vote in Palm Beach County. This a court refused to do,[A3] and for what appears to be excellent reason. It is a stretch of the mind to conceptualize our political system being tested in this one county in Florida, in a specially called election, to determine the presidency of the United States. It is frightening to think of what might occur. One can even speculate that the horror of buying votes, as has occurred in our political history, would have returned to plague us.

Yours truly finds himself philosophizing that perhaps those voters who were sufficiently intelligent and careful to figure out the "butterfly" ballot would ordinarily be better endowed with intelligence to make this important decision for our country. But, perish the thought, for this is my Grandpa speaking from the grave, advocating the old way of selecting juries and today, that is not only heresy, but heresy of the totally unacceptable kind.

A3. Judge Labarga of the Palm Beach County Circuit Court rejected the revote remedy that was sought by dozens of petitioning voters, pointing out in his denial order that the federal Constitution stated clearly that the presidential election must be held on the same day throughout the United States. See *N.Y. Times*, November 21, 2000, at pp. A-1 and A-22.

INDEX

Page numbers in *italics* refer to illustrations.